Hit The Ground Running
THE FIRST YEARS OF YOUR ACTING CAREER

The Smart Actor's Guide

Written by
CAROLYNE BARRY

CAROLYNE BARRY CREATIVE enterprises

Hit the Ground Running
The First Years of Your Acting Career
The Smart Actor's Guide

Written by: Carolyne Barry

Published by: Carolynebarry.com
www.hitthegroundrunningbook.com

Copyright © 2009

For general information on our other products and services, please contact our website: www.carolynebarry.com

ISBN-13: 978-0-9822360-0-0

ISBN-10: 0-9822360-0-X

Printed in the United States of America

First Edition

ACKNOWLEDGEMENTS

It took many years, jobs, experiences and people to gather the information and insights that Hit the Ground Running offers. There have been wonderful experiences and too many that were ultra challenging, but from everything and everyone I have learned what works and what doesn't, whom to listen to and whom to just smile and nod at, and what's real and what I want to be real but isn't. This book is my legacy – an accumulation of almost everything I know and teach about being an actor.

I acknowledge

- Peter Leftcourt for giving me the wonderful title,
- Carl Nakamura for designing my inspired book cover,
- Marybeth Short and Lorraine Uranga for making sure I was grammatically correct.
- Jonathan Levit for his creative interior layout,
- And all those who will be helping me get Hit the Ground Running to the actors who are looking to find a guide for their acting careers.

I am very grateful for the valuable input from my contributing writers:

- Ray Bengston, Terry Berland, Michael Donovan, David Grapes, Abby Girvin, Lauri Johnson, Leslie Jordan, Todd Justice, Hugh Leon, Amy Lyndon, Anthony Meindl, Alicia Ruskin, David Sweeney, Bernard Telsey and Kevin E. West.

It is with great pride that I thank

- all the industry professionals with whom I have worked and my teachers who have taught me about the craft, business and humanity of being an actress, a casting director, a teacher, a director, a writer and a creator.

And on a personal note, I honor

- my best friends Lauri Johnson and Terry Hanauer, my many friends, ex-husband, mother, father, Shelly and Rob Light, my assistant Tracie Burton and my students for encouraging me to write Hit the Ground Running and inspiring me to make it a beneficial contribution.

- my therapists, life coaches and four dogs, who have trained me to be the best person I can be and to keep working at it.

As your career benefits from what you learn in these pages, I hope you take a moment, once in a while, to acknowledge my mentors, along with those who will be yours.

Finally, I acknowledge <u>you</u> for being intelligent and investing in *Hit the Ground Running* to lead you on your trip down the road to becoming a professional working actor.

TABLE OF CONTENTS

THE ROAD TO YOUR ACTING CAREER

Welcome. My name is Carolyne Barry and I am your guide for your investigation or pursuit of an acting career. As you embark on this exciting voyage, if you feel lost, overwhelmed, confused or afraid of making the wrong choices, or maybe even are questioning if acting is really for you, know that you are not alone. Most everyone has questions, doubts and concerns as they look down this road. I understand all too well and that is why I wrote *Hit the Ground Running, -for you*. This *Guide for the Smart Actor* will answer your questions, help you navigate the unknown and comprehensively lead you through the quagmire of misinformation.

The first few years are the most crucial time for the new actor. In order to have a chance at a career you must know

- how to start
- where to get the most beneficial information
- the best type of training for you and the best place to train
- where to live
- whom to listen to
- what to do first, next and at each juncture
- the costs
- how long it will take
- when and how to start finding work
- if you have what it takes to be an actor
- …and a lot more information that you don't even know you need to know.

As you begin your journey, you will probably encounter many people who have good intentions and maybe some understanding of the process. They will offer information they have heard about or experienced. It is crucial to understand that many of these helpful people may not have the input needed to best serve you. When I interview potential students for my workshops, I find that most have received poor direction. They have wasted valuable time and money and have developed bad habits, thereby making the training process more difficult. Bad advice is expensive and can increase the time needed before starting your career.

If you do your research, there is no need to be unduly concerned. There are many who have traveled the road, weathered the storms, experienced the pitfalls and succeeded. These are the professionals whose opinions you should seek out. They may not always agree but they have credible input for you to consider. It is often troublesome to locate <u>valid</u> sources but they are out there. So get motivated – find them. The necessary information can come in the form of books, lectures, interviews on PBS and Bravo, biographies on the A&E Channel, magazine articles, websites, podcasts and/or blogs. Often friends and family might know someone who knows a well-informed person working in the business. Whom you choose to listen to can be the biggest influence on whether you will be successful. It can create a world of opportunities or send you down a long and costly path that takes you nowhere you planned to go. Choose wisely whose advice you will follow. Be sure that the information I offer, which I truly believe is solid (but not absolute), feels right for you. My input may not be the only prevailing point of view or work for you 100 percent of the time so, if you agree with 80 percent of what you read, then implement that. For the 20 percent that you may question, get validation and/or other educated points of view.

Reading this book is going to be a significant part of your research. You probably chose this book because it looked as if my contributing writers and I would be qualified to give you the information you seek. Listed here are my credits, which should give you an idea of my background and the validity of the information I offer. Over the course of my career, I have

- acted in approximately 400 national commercials and 100 television shows and films

- co-owned and managed the largest casting and training facility in the United States for six years

- been among the top commercial audition teachers in Los Angeles since 1982

- voted 2009 Favorite Commercial Workshop in Los Angeles by the readers of Backstage West

- managed the most successful sole-proprietor acting workshop programs in Los Angeles since 1991

- taught and/or supervised the training for more than 20,000 actors

- been a recurring guest teacher at universities, numerous Los Angeles Talent Agencies, L.A. Casting, The Actor's Network and The SAG Conservatory at AFI

- have cast hundreds of commercials and infomercials since 1986

- co-owned and was the president of the Caliber Creative Advertising Agency for five years,

- directed and helped write a successful off-Broadway play
- been featured as a teaching authority in The Hollywood Reporter, The Los Angeles Reader, The Examiner, and Backstage West as well as on CNN, KHJ, KTTV, and numerous other TV and radio talk shows throughout the country
- was a contributing writer for Backstage West's "Commercial Break" column from 2006-2007
- created Lights, Camera, Kids, a DVD program helping kids start their careers (currently in distribution)
- co-created the CD program, Getting The Job, to help actors do their best auditions (currently in distribution).

Even though these accomplishments may be impressive, what I am about to tell you in the following pages is only <u>my opinion</u>. It is knowledgeable input, but just my opinions based on my experience and research as well as the experiences of others I have worked with. Traditionally, one or two authors presenting one opinion write most "how-to" books. Yet it is my firm belief that there is no one way to be successful in any career. That is why this book also offers the opinions of successful, highly respected agents, managers, casting directors, actors and other industry professionals. Many will agree with some or all of what I have written. Others will disagree and offer different options. I believe that the combined input of what I know and the views of these contributing writers can and will be an invaluable source of empowering information for you, the next generation of professional actors. Take from these pages the information that works for you and apply it to your career and life. Never forget that you are the driver so get the best directions to take you where you want to go.

It is my privilege to share my ideas, experience and opinions as well as those of my contributing writers. I thank you for your trust. I truly believe that what you glean from these pages will be an empowering influence. One day, you may be in the position to offer your experienced opinions to help a new actor. I'd like to believe that what you have learned here will be at the heart of the information you impart to others.

THE TRIP

Why do you want to be an actor? Have you seriously asked yourself this question? Do you honestly know the answer? Is your intention to star in movies, television, commercials or theatre? I suggest you take the time to contemplate whether this quest is

- an investigation (of the possibilities of a career, hobby or self-growth experience)
- a hobby
- a career to which you are ready to dedicate yourself or
- an improvement of your craft and a desire to grow as an actor.

CRAFT: *A profession requiring skill and training or experience or specialized knowledge.* I define it as: *the knowledge and development of the techniques that are essential to creating authentic, multi-dimensional characters and performances and the ability to apply them.*

INVESTIGATION

For new actors, this trip <u>must start</u> with an investigation, even when they are positive that they want acting to be a career. I believe that the investigation period takes between three months and a year. This time is spent in professional training and becoming educated about the entertainment business. The main purpose is to make a decision on what <u>you</u> want.

Depending on time and money, you can jump into the investigation or casually move through it. You can take two or three classes a week, read lots of information, watch classes, study plays and movies, join actors groups, and so on – or take just one class. In order to call this a true investigation, you must take at least one professional (not college) acting class. (In Chapter Four, I will discuss acting classes.) The more you do to educate yourself during this phase, the surer you can be at the end of it about how you want to proceed.

After this period, you might decide not to continue. This, for many, is the right choice. With a committed investigation, you should never be disappointed with yourself that you didn't give acting a shot. And, if you selected good people to train with, your time was well spent because your life will be greatly enhanced by the experience. You should have more confidence and freedom;

you will have met interesting, creative people; have had a lot of fun; and acquired an understanding of what motivates you and others as well as a rich appreciation for good actors. You will still be a big winner if this voyage turns out to be just an investigation. (You can always come back at a later time and give it another go.) Plus, I consider professional acting training an inexpensive form of therapy.

> *Acting workshops can break through fears, make you feel more confident and enable you to face and discover many feelings. But they are not a substitute for therapy if you need it. Your acting coach is not your therapist.* **TERRY BERLAND,** Commercial Casting Director & Author of *Breaking into Commercials*

Many people take acting and/or improv classes for reasons other than becoming an actor. They do it to have fun, overcome fears, explore and/or expand their creativity or to learn about themselves.

HOBBY

After your investigation period, you may realize that developing your skills and being an actor works better as a hobby. You enjoy acting and want to pursue it as a creative outlet, but you don't want to make it a career. So take classes when it's convenient. Submit yourself for acting jobs. Audition and work in projects, local theatre and films that you find through your contacts and listings in entertainment trade papers and online casting websites. You may even find a small agency to represent you if (and it is a big "if") they are willing to work around your priorities.

> *Most worthwhile agents will not take on a client to indulge a hobby.* **HUGH LEON,** Commercial Agent @ Coast to Coast Agency

For those pursuing acting as a hobby, most of the information in the following chapters will apply but in moderation. You will train and work in your spare time because you enjoy it and it feeds your creative appetite. If you change your mind and decide to make it a career, it will have been time well spent.

> *I don't believe anyone can be a satisfied, successful actor competing with professionals on a part-time basis. Acting is as rigorous in its own way as dance or music, but no one would think of pursuing a career as a violinist or a ballerina without years and years of training and serious financial investment in the best equipment. Yet I have sat in meetings with actors who have no money for headshots, no proper audition wardrobe, no savings put away toward the day they must join the union, no training in the market they hope to work in, etc. If it's a hobby, stay where you are, keep your day job, do community theatre and do not confuse the pleasure you get from acting with the commitment to forging*

a professional career. **ALICIA RUSKIN,** Commercial Agent & Partner, KSA
Talent Agency

CAREER

If, after the investigation, you choose to dedicate yourself to an acting <u>career</u>, your life as you know it will change. Much of your time and money will be spent on training, marketing, research, and the pursuit of your career. Your circle of friends will expand to include a rather eclectic group of creative and entertainment industry people. Your life experiences and personal growth will speed up. For some, it means moving to an entertainment business area. You will learn that acting is not only an occupation. It's a way of life. You have to be willing to work possibly for years before you make any real money. It's got to be a passion or it will be a burden.

> *There are some who do become successful quickly. It doesn't always take years. You may get lucky but do the work and commit so you are prepared either way.* **MICHAEL DONOVAN,** Casting Director Commercial, Film and Theatre

I believe that the most memorable and empowering time in an actor's career is the first two or three years. It is my responsibility in this book to give you the guidance necessary to make it a rewarding time.

YOUR CHOICE

After you complete your designated investigation period, decide whether to make acting a hobby or career or to investigate another profession. Once you make the choice, don't flounder or waste time that you could be using to further your acting career or pursue another one.

> *Know that your choices can and do change. You may first want to experience yourself as an actor as an opportunity to express yourself creatively. Then, as you begin to grow and become more confident in your understanding of the work, you may decide you want to take the next step and begin to pursue options as career choices. Or conversely, you may love the creative side of the art but after time, become bored or impatient with the "business" side and decide that acting may be more of a hobby for you. You don't have to make the choices your parents or your agent or your friends are telling you to make. Trust your choices. They will lead you to where you need to go.* **ANTHONY MEINDL,** Acting Teacher, Los Angeles

You will have a stronger chance of making this an enriching journey when you are clear on your purpose and commit to whichever path you choose.

ABILITY, TALENT, OR GIFT

I use three determinants when evaluating an actor's creative aptitude:

ABILITY: *The quality of being able to do something. A natural or acquired skill.*

For me, ability means that an actor, at best, can do an adequate-to-good interpretation with scripted material and/or performance in an audition or improvisation situation.

TALENT: *A marked innate, exceptional ability for artistic accomplishment. Natural endowment or ability of a superior quality.*

I believe a talented actor has unique, intelligent and strong instinctive interpretations of characters and dialogue fairly consistently when rehearsing or performing in scenes, monologues and/or improvisations.

GIFT: *A talent, endowment or aptitude*

For me, gifted actors are more instinctively endowed talented actors. Their choices are uniquely creative and their acting work is intuitive and freed up nearly <u>all</u> of the time. They are originals, the embodiment of artistic energy and inspiration. When you see gifted actors in movies, on TV or in plays, you can't take your eyes off them. Everything they say and do is compelling.

Understanding which of these determinants best describes your acting aptitude might help you make choices in the pursuit of your development and career. Training is vital in the development of an ability or talent but can't make you a gifted actor if you are not one. In all sports or artistic endeavors there are the standouts, like Tiger Woods, Kobe Bryant, Robin Williams, Meryl Streep, Johnnie Depp, Josh Groban, Angelina Jolie, Venus Williams, Stephen Sondheim, Andy Warhol, Steven Spielberg, etc. They are recognized as gifted and even possessing genius. There are others in every field that are talented and have their moments to shine as well as many more who have ability and are vital to each sport or artistic arena.

... AND YOU ARE?

It is assumed that talent is a prerequisite for any actor. Yet there are different degrees of talent and it is subjective. How do you know if you're talented or gifted? Most truly believe they have the "it." Assuming that you do doesn't make it so. We can recognize talent or the lack of it in someone else. Can you be objective and honestly assess yourself? It is difficult for most. After six months to a year of training with professional teachers and some audition and work experience, the evaluation process will reveal if acting is an ability, a talent or your gift. It requires a truthful, personal evaluation to discern which best describes you as an actor. Don't be self-deprecating or blissfully self-approving. And realize that you're still learning and don't allow your expectation to do consistent, brilliant work early on influence your decision. Be objective. Ask for an assessment from teachers, directors and friends whom you respect and who know your work but don't rely totally on their opinions. Listen to your inner voice that knows the truth.

If you are objective enough to discover that you are not a major talent, it does not preclude you from being a working actor if you really want to be. The purpose of having this insight is to help you to make the right choices for your training and your acting career or to motivate you to change paths and find one that will better utilize your talents. Early in my career, I realized that I was a talented actress, but I wasn't gifted. I was pretty good and worked a lot but I was never going to be a Meryl Streep. I have a big ego and I wanted to be the best. I found that teaching, creating and directing were my gifts. I never gave up acting (it became my hobby) but I chose to follow a different path that honored and developed my gifts. Investigate, be honest with yourself and make choices that work for you.

Those with talent or a gift have an advantage because, bottom line, they are better actors, which makes their journey often more purposeful and satisfying. However, having a talent or a gift doesn't guarantee success or that you are ever going to get work: much more is needed. There are a lot of talented and truly gifted actors who don't train, who are not motivated, have no confidence, passion or resilience and/or make bad choices and thus do not succeed. I also know many actors who have ability but no real talent who do work and even succeed. They love acting, believe in themselves, create their niche, make smart business and marketing choices and work hard to develop their craft and promote their careers.

RELATED CREATIVE PURSUITS

Many actors have additional talents and/or also want to pursue other creative avenues in the entertainment business, like singing, dancing, modeling, writing and directing. Do you want to be an actor/singer? Actor/dancer? Actor/model? Actor/writer? Actor/singer/dancer/model? Actor/director/editor? Actor/director/singer/dancer/model? Actor/singer/dancer?

Having choices is great but also overwhelming. The time and finances necessary to excel and build a career in each of these mediums is a major commitment. So, unless you are independently wealthy or have a high-paying job with lots of time flexibility, I suggest you pick your primary talent and devote at least 70 percent if not all of your available time to the pursuit of that craft. If you have a secondary creative endeavor, then you could pursue it with 30 percent of whatever available time you have. Be careful. Developing several talents, especially when getting established, can dissipate your focus and can cause you to lose momentum. I strongly suggest you choose your primary one and pursue it with all the time, effort and money you have. After you've established yourself, you can start the work to develop and pursue your second talent.

 EXCEPTION: If you are an experienced and proficient dancer, model, singer or writer who makes an income doing it but wants to pursue acting, I suggest you work at it like it is your day job. Also, with these jobs, you could make contacts that can help you in your acting career. For example, you might sign with a dance agent who may also represent commercial actors. Commit to your performer or creative day job talent while engaging in "The Plan" (which is spelled out in Chapter Five).

COMMITMENT

Some figure that they could be the exception or that they will get lucky and not have to go the route that has worked for many others. Honestly, there are always exceptions to what you will read here or what you learn from other credible sources. But I strongly suggest you put the odds in your favor. Training to be an actor and pursuing a career is a process that takes much more time, money, energy and courage than you would first imagine. It is a major commitment.

> *There is a definite distinction between "wanting" and "committing." "Want" lives in ideas, dreams, fantasy and imagination – you can "want" lots of things and never HAVE them. Implicit and required for "commitment" is ACTION. When one is committed, action is a natural behavior, which leads to results consistent with one's commitment. So ask yourself: "Do I WANT this?" or "Am I COMMITTED to having it?" – big difference! We have results in life consistent with what we are COMMITTED to, not with what we "want."* **LAURI JOHNSON,** Entertainment Industry Life Coach

Your decision-making process will eventually be challenged even further with the numerous acting arenas you can choose to pursue: film, television, soaps, sitcoms, episodics, theatre, industrials, commercials, infomercials, music videos or some combination of these. Choices, choices, choices. Investigate and make smart ones for you and your career.

PERSONAL TOOLS

TOOLS: *The equipment or elements needed to manufacture or create things*

Every profession has "tools." I believe business "tools" fall into two categories, physical and nonphysical. Both are necessary to be successful. They can be tangible objects that you create with as well as mind-sets that guide creativity, choices and business decisions. For example, a tangible tool is a hammer, and an intangible tool is the knowledge of how to use that hammer. For an actor, photos are tangible marketing tools. The professionalism of how they are marketed and the ambition to submit them are examples of intangible personal tools. Theatrical productions are showcasing vehicles and the discipline, confidence and talent to be a standout are personal tools. Here, I will address the primary intangible "personal tools" necessary for the actor (as well as most businesspeople). Often they can be more potent than the tangible ones.

PASSION - *The object of somebody's intense interest or enthusiasm*

I often refer to acting as more of an addiction than a career. While rehearsing, doing scenes for class, performing in a play, auditioning or working on TV and film sets, many actors enjoy a "high" when they find the connection to the material and/or the character. This connection and creative expression is exhilarating and most actors want to experience it as often as possible. It's exciting when they get callbacks and bookings and when they see themselves on TV and in films. These "highs" are just some of the reasons why actors are passionate about being an actor. Without passion, this career has little meaning.

CALLBACK: *After the initial audition, the decision-makers select which actors they are interested in and invite them to return for a second (and sometimes a third) audition. There can be a few actors called back or many. The producer, director, writer and sometimes the stars of the television or film project are usually present for the callback. In commercials it is usual for the director, ad agency execs and maybe the product client to be present.*

BOOKING/BOOK: *The term designates that an actor is going to be hired for a specific job.*

Enjoy what you're doing. If you don't enjoy it, then you need to find something else to do. **DAVID SWEENEY,** Los Angeles Talent Manager

SELF-ESTEEM - *To value oneself highly*

This profession is riddled with obstacles and emotionally challenging times that can take a major toll on how actors feel about themselves. No matter what frustrating experiences happen in your quest to succeed and get approval and acceptance, you must never stop valuing yourself. Even if others treat you badly or situations don't turn out the way you want, don't let it affect how you feel about yourself. Never forget, you are unique and special. If you start to devalue yourself, talk to a professional or someone you trust who can help you. Without self-esteem, you have nothing to contribute.

DISCIPLINE - *Mental self-control used in directing or changing behavior or when training for something*

Without discipline, it is almost impossible to accomplish all that is required to be a professional anything. The demands of acting training, career preparation, marketing, auditioning, working, your personal life and financing everything are challenging but doable if you stay focused and true to your goals. Staying on-course in this business requires serious discipline. You either have it or you must develop it. If you can't or won't, then you should consider another line of work where it is not as important.

COURAGE - *The quality of being brave, gutsy, daring*

My favorite definition of courage is "*to be terrified and do it anyway.*" I like this definition because it dispels the assumption that heroes have no anxieties or fears. I believe that courage is about the willingness to take full-out action no matter what you feel and it is something you develop not always something you have. Most actors have some degree of courage or they wouldn't make an attempt at this career. Many pursue acting against the objections of family, friends and business associates. Courage also helps an actor's talent to flourish. It allows them to take chances with characters and creative choices, which makes their work distinctive and multi-layered.

CONFIDENCE - *Self-assurance or a belief or in your ability to succeed*

Most businesses produce and/or sell a product. In the acting business, actors are the product and they must believe in their talents and themselves or there is nothing to sell. Confidence is an essential "personal tool" for everyone. For many actors, confidence is innate. For others, it may be cultivated by family support or life experience. If you must nurture your confidence, I would like you to contemplate a theory that I believe to be very helpful:

- Experience creates confidence.
- Confidence produces freedom.
- Freedom generates courage.
- Courage frees up you and your talent.

Experience - *Active participation in events or activities leading to the accumulation of knowledge or skill*

The more you do anything, the more experienced and skillful you become. So the more you properly study, rehearse, audition and work, the better actor you are going to be.

Confidence: Actors gain confidence when they have successes or "wins": when they get auditions, secure representation, receive good feedback or reviews, get callbacks and book jobs, etc. Unfortunately, these successes are dependent on the acceptance of others. If measured by these successes, confidence is mercurial, and a shortage of achievements can undermine it.

> *So much that occurs in this business is NOT personal. Don't let booking a job or not getting a callback define you. Stop trying to figure out what you think they want. They don't always know. Just keep moving forward and don't let credits, or time, or age or whom you know or what agency you are with define you.*
> **ANTHONY MEINDL,** Los Angeles, Acting Teacher

Confidence in your talent is powerful and depends mainly on your willingness to be supportive of yourself. With this kind of confidence, you are not dependent on anyone else to feel successful. You must acknowledge yourself when you know that you have done your creative best, whether or not you get the job or the positive feedback you desired.

> *A working actor must have a very strong stand on him/herself. It amazes me when I will ask a client, "Are you a good actor?" and I get responses like "I'm not sure" and "I don't know" and "I think I'm okay." And some of these comments come from more seasoned actors! If my stand for them is stronger than theirs, that's not good! Take a strong stand for yourself. Declare that you are a good actor and then LIVE into that statement till it becomes a reality!*
> **LAURI JOHNSON,** Entertainment Industry Life Coach

 WARNING: Vanity, arrogance or egotism is not confidence. They are usually facades for someone who lacks authentic confidence. If you are honest with yourself, you know the difference.

Freedom - *A state in which one is able to act and live as he or she chooses without being subject to any undue restraints or restrictions*

When "confident" is who you are and no longer what you are working to be, you begin to experience creative freedom. When you are feeling confident about what you do, there is no need to worry or be concerned about how you do. You are "out of your head" and "in the moment" and thus are freed up.

OUT OF YOUR HEAD: *Being so focused and involved in the scene that the thoughts and feelings an actor is having are totally instinctive and relative only to what is being performed. Actors are not thinking about how or what they are doing. It's as if the performance is coming through them, not from them.*

When you start focusing on creating "freedom," it might occur a few moments at a time. Then you will experience it for extended periods of time. It is an incredible feeling that opens the door to your talent.

BUILDING CONFIDENCE

Confidence can and should be cultivated. Don't depend on booking jobs to sustain and build it. Be proactive. Here are a few suggestions that have helped many actors:

- Train with great acting teachers. Learning the craft from professionals for a consistent period of time gives you the security that you know what you are doing. The more you study, the more secure you feel then the more confident you become. Specific information on how to find and choose good teachers as well as how long to train with each one will be presented in Chapter Four.

 WARNING: If you stay in classes too long (more than two years) without pursuing work, you could become comfortable there and afraid of auditioning, which will undermine confidence.

- Take improvisation workshops. I truly believe that improvisation workshops taught by gifted teachers during your first few years do much to build confidence.

- Be prepared. Whether putting up scenes in your classes, auditioning for work, or doing an acting job, always be prepared. If you aren't (especially when first starting), the probability of your doing well sharply decreases. Each time you fall short of what you believe you are capable of, your confidence level drops.

- Acknowledge yourself for your successes and don't emotionally beat yourself up when you feel you've done less than your best. Constant self-criticism is undermining to self-esteem and confidence. Many are quick to find fault with what they did or should have done. They feel being self-deprecating is the only way to work harder. I truly believe this kind of thinking is neurotic, indulgent and

16

self-destructive. Whenever you fall short or perform actions that are beneath who you are, take a hard, honest look at your deeds (without self-deprecation) and make adjustments.

- Learn from mistakes. During these first few years, you will make mistakes. Most people, if objective, learn more from their failures than their successes. (If you have problems being objective about your mistakes, then I suggest you learn how to become objective.) Mistakes are a big part of any development. In fact, the more you fail, get frustrated, work through problems and learn from these times in safe places, the less afraid you are to make mistakes. Classes and rehearsals are a safe place to experiment with characters, physicality, techniques, interpretations, emotional choices, degrees of commitment, etc. Experimenting is a process of trial and error. When you go through this process often and have the experience of benefiting from mistakes, you could learn that they are not horrible, humiliating experiences and you can start to have fun with your mistakes, and thus become fearless. I will go into detail on this theory in the "Mistakes Are Gifts" section in Chapter Fourteen.

- Train yourself to trust your instincts and quickly adjust without stress when anything goes awry during a rehearsal, an audition or a performance. Make it an enjoyable challenge for yourself. Knowing that you can handle whatever happens is a great confidence builder.

- Audition for jobs you don't want so you can practice auditioning with less pressure and thus probably do well, which builds confidence. Then when auditioning for the jobs you do want, you will feel more secure and do better. More about this in Chapter Ten.

- Record yourself. When preparing (at home) for an audition or rehearsing a scene for class, record your <u>last</u> rehearsal. Since actors don't see what they do at auditions and in classes, most tend to be critical or doubt themselves. Your work is usually better than you think. Seeing that it is good or knowing the adjustments that are needed will give you some certainty. If you can be objective about yourself and your work, recording it <u>once</u> can boost confidence. If you are a hypercritical person and not objective, then please don't record yourself.

 WARNING: Don't rehearse in front of a mirror. When you watch yourself while you are rehearsing, you are "in your head" judging your work. If you are judging yourself, it is impossible to be connected and motivated.

IN YOUR HEAD: As it relates to acting, *being totally conscious of how and what you are doing while you are in a scene, scenario or monologue. This is the opposite of being "connected."*

- Avoid negative, jealous, angry or bitter people. Fill your world with supportive and positive friends, fellow actors, family members, teachers and representatives. Your spouse or partner must be totally on board with your being an actor: otherwise the relationship or the career won't stand a chance. If family or friends are not supportive, do not talk to them about your career. They just don't understand the business or your passion. It's not personal. It just doesn't make sense to them. Don't expect them to be supportive, and you won't be disappointed.

- Be supportive of friends, family and acquaintances when their spirits need boosting. When you encourage others to bounce back from disappointments, failures or frustrations, you remind yourself of the importance of confidence and the empowering mind-sets you need to stay focused on.

- Have a full life: engage in social activities, working out, sports, hobbies, projects, travel, relationships, volunteering, etc. The pleasure you experience when participating fully in your life feeds confidence.

- Stay out of debt. If you are depending on acting work to pay your bills or get you out of debt, you are creating pressure for yourself at every audition. When you have a well-paying survival job and have a minimum amount of financial pressures, it is feasible that you will have more freedom at your auditions. In Chapter Six, financial information and suggestions will be presented to assist you.

RESILIENCE - *The ability to recover quickly from setbacks*

An acting career is riddled with highs and lows, wins and losses, and successes and failures. You will love the good times and will probably be sad, frustrated, angry and/or disappointed during the rocky periods. It is all part of the voyage. The occasions when everything falls into place and you feel like a winner and unstoppable are easy to accept. However, a lot of positive self talk is required in order to recover from those times when you feel defeated or think that you will never be a working actor.

> **TIP** You have goals to lead and focus you, not to run your life. So don't be upset or feel like a failure if you don't achieve your goals on schedule. They are just guidelines and can be readjusted as you go along.

Actors are some of the most sensitive and emotional people. This is what attracts most of them to this art form and usually why they can excel at it. It is also why they take so much to heart and can be so tough on themselves. The ability to bounce back emotionally from disappointments is a very important character determinant. There are major hurdles and difficulties in the pursuit to be a professional anything. It is that way for most everyone, not just you – even though it often feels as if you are the only one who is experiencing defeats and frustrations. Accept that there will be challenging and emotional periods. These problematic times will be gifts because you will learn a lot and what you learn about yourself helps make you a better actor and person. You <u>must</u> become skilled at dealing with the disappointments, working through your feelings and then jumping back in the game as soon as possible.

 Don't obsess on the problems. Focus on the solutions.

Watch how much time you require to "recover." Is it a day? A week? You want to get it down to about a minute. For bigger disappointments, set a time limit for yourself to recover. If you lost a big role that you were to close to getting, give yourself permission to "wallow" for a week. You can determine your recovery time. You are NOT a victim here – remember, you CHOSE this business, and not getting a job is just a part of the process. Leave auditions with only this question – "Did I succeed in doing everything I wanted to do?" If the answer is yes, Bravo! Now release it. If the answer is no, this is the time to look at what was missing…like an examination…not to beat yourself to a pulp and become a victim. Learn and put in the corrections for next time. There are far bigger things to upset us than not getting an acting job! Really!! **LAURI JOHNSON,** Entertainment Industry Life Coach

AMBITION - *An earnest desire for some type of achievement or distinction, as power, honor, fame, or wealth, and the willingness to strive for its attainment*

In order to be successful at anything you must be hungry to accomplish your goals. The entertainment business is tough and competitive. You can't just want success. You must be resolute and determined. You must invest the time, effort and money needed to build a career <u>but</u> not at the expense of diminishing the quality of your life. Without ambition you can't fuel all the personal tools presented here. With healthy ambition you have fuel.

 Here is some simplistic life advice that I love to convey to my students about how to approach anything you are hungry to accomplish: Play to win and never to "not lose." In an attempt to protect ourselves, we can, play it safe and justify being cautious. Commit to your ambition and play to win.

PROFESSIONALISM - *The competence, skill or character expected of a member of a highly trained profession. The standing, practice, or methods of a professional, as distinguished from an amateur*

Many actors don't realize that acting is a business, - an illogical, unpredictable, and sometimes unreasonable business. This venture, like any other, requires training, marketing, financing, networking, strategy, partnerships, etc. Most people just see the end result of the actor on the movie or TV screen or in the theatre. They don't see all that it took to get him/her there. When most new actors are hit with the realistic business side of being an actor, they are unprepared. Be a great actor <u>and</u> a powerhouse businessperson. If you are not good in this arena, learn to be. In the upcoming chapters you will garner the essential information to help you become the professional you need to be. Also, talk to working actors, agents and casting directors about professionalism and study the work ethics of accomplished businesspeople.

> *As an actor you are your own business. You are the CEO, VP of Finance, Personnel, Housekeeping/Maintenance, Marketing Development AND you are also the PRODUCT! The only time you are only the product is when you are actually AUDITIONING or ACTING. You are one of the other positions when you are not. You need to know when to wear which hat. Taking responsibility for the fact that this is a BUSINESS will give you a leg up on other actors. One of the biggest complaints I hear from agents, casting directors and managers… "I wish he/she understood that this is a BUSINESS."* **LAURI JOHNSON**, Entertainment Industry Life Coach

TENACITY AND PATIENCE

TENACITY: *Sticking firmly to any decision, plan, or opinion without changing or doubting it*

PATIENCE: *The ability to endure waiting or delay without becoming upset or to persevere calmly when faced with difficulties*

Success comes quickly for some but for the greater majority success is an arduous voyage. If you want instant results and are ready to quit with the first disappointments, this is definitely not the career for you. It takes true character, a love of the craft, tenacity and patience to persevere during the times when things are not going as planned.

> *I had an actor move to LA from NYC after some commercial work and nice theatre credits. He signed with me and started auditioning the same day… 97 auditions later he had booked his first job, a guest star on a major TV show. He often coached for auditions, spending on average $60 dollars per audition. He told me that after he received his first television check he hadn't even broken even…and that first job took nearly a year to book.*
> **TODD JUSTICE**, Talent Representative @ Marshak/Zachary

I tell actors about my survival guide, -the three P's: Patience, Passion and Persistence. If you practice all three (and have real talent) then I truly believe you will make it as an actor.
DAVID SWEENEY, Los Angeles Talent Manager

I once read that one job in 30 auditions is a good booking rate! That means that 29 out of 30 times you were turned down. Do not take it personally! This business is brutal. A person training to be a nurse knows that the work is out there waiting. When the training is complete a nurse gets to be a nurse. A person training to be an actor knows that the work is out there waiting. But there are no guarantees that an actor will get to work. **LESLIE JORDAN,**
Emmy-Award-Winning Actor

HEALTH - *Overall physical condition; soundness of body or mind; freedom from disease or ailment*

Mental and physical health provides the clarity and stamina needed in any business. We usually don't pay much attention to our health until we aren't well. Actors are expected to give 110 percent and are frequently overwhelmed, which causes stress that can lead to mind and body issues. Being sick costs time and money. The actor's face, body and physicality are also the product: health affects how you look. Take care of yourself. <u>Be proactive with your health</u>. Tend to your energy, strength, emotional stability, mental clarity, and physical fitness. All the other personal foundation tools work better and your acting potential is maximized when you are healthy.

....

Confidence and courage, passion, self-esteem, discipline, resilience, professionalism, ambition, tenacity, patience and health are crucial personal tools for an acting career. It is difficult to develop your craft, empower yourself, do great work and be a successful actor without them. It is easy to lose focus on these tools because they are intangible. You can't see them. They are within you. Most people don't pay much attention until one or more of these mind-sets/tools break down or cause problems. So check in with yourself frequently to see how you are doing in all of these areas.

TRAINING

To excel in the craft of acting normally requires substantial training. I subscribe to a deliberate plan of committed professional training for the actor who wants to do exceptional work as well as have a real chance at a career. There are many new actors who refer to themselves as "naturals" and think that they don't need training and that classes would damage their talent. Yet you would train and educate yourself to be a doctor, lawyer, architect, accountant, yoga teacher, cartoonist, editor or any other type of professional. The better the training, the better you will be. Many don't truly understand that being an actor is a profession. Don't be one of them. Those with abilities and talent with little or no instruction might get some acting jobs but those with training have a much better chance of having a career.

Training doesn't necessarily mean professional acting classes, though I believe they are the best settings to learn the craft. Many get professional instruction from the major universities known for their acting programs or highly respected regional theatre companies. Then there are actors fortunate enough to get their training on film sets either because they started young, were physically specific for a role, had heavyweight contacts or were incredibly lucky. Bottom line, for the great majority, the craft of acting requires instruction and time to develop. Respect your profession and train.

ACADEMIC TRAINING

Many aspiring actors study theatre in college and feel they are ready to pursue an acting career when they graduate. Although I believe that colleges and universities offer tremendous educational programs, 90 percent of them don't provide the sustained emotional foundation training needed for professional film, TV and theatre actors.

EMOTIONAL FOUNDATION TRAINING: *Acting instruction that focuses on motivating the dialogue, character and action primarily with instinct and emotional connection*

The majority of (but not all) theatre professors teach an academic approach to acting.

While private and studio coaching is a powerful tool, it cannot substitute for the public performance opportunities that academic institutions provide. It is one thing to work on a scene from Shakespeare in class with a master acting teacher and quite another experience to perform that scene under the direction of a capable director in front of a large audience. A strong academic education also provides new actors with vocal and dialect work, on-camera training, period movement and dance, an understanding of design and, last but not least, the cognitive skills that they will need to research and work on the roles that they will perform. It is a wonderful opportunity to do one-stop shopping.

DAVID GRAPES, Professor & Director of the School of Theatre Arts & Dance, University of Northern Colorado

In all fairness to these institutions, it would be very difficult in the academic setting (and there are notable exceptions) to have the students do the emotional, visceral and experiential, one-on-one, investigation and techniques taught in professional workshops and in some regional theatres.

The vast majority of 17-22 year olds who have an interest in the dramatic arts as a career are not prepared psychologically, socially or spiritually to move to a huge urban center and face the rejection and hardships that go with that decision. The function of a quality academic training program is not to provide vocational training. Our goal is to educate the whole person. We want to make each of our students a better actor but we want to make them better human beings as well. They need an academic environment that will nurture their spirit and hone their skills as they prepare for the transition to a professional environment.

DAVID GRAPES, Professor & Director of the School of Theatre Arts & Dance, University of Northern Colorado

My university taught me a great reverence for the craft of acting but absolutely NOTHING about how to earn a living at it. You MUST work with professionals who have their "thumbs on the pulse." You don't usually find that in theatre programs at colleges.

LESLIE JORDAN, Emmy-Award-Winning Actor

When actors with Fine Arts degrees in acting seek placement in my workshops, I direct most (but not all) to start in the beginning classes. Since the majority of university/college students are not taught emotional foundation work, they often will "act as if" they have the connection when performing in academic scenes and productions – which often develops bad habits. These bad habits must be dismantled before the actor can learn an effective, professional technique for TV, film and theatre work.

If you are getting an acting degree at a college or a university and want to augment your training, I strongly recommend that you take a professional acting class in your area and/or during summer vacations go to a major market and take several workshops. (Be sure to do your research and select wisely.) Then incorporate the information and training you received into your scenes and productions at your academic institution. Getting professional training off campus should provide an actor with the best of both worlds – the emotional foundation work with the academic training and performance opportunities.

PROFESSIONAL WORKSHOPS FOR ACTORS

Comprehensive professional training is your acting education. You won't get a degree, but then again a degree has never gotten anyone an acting job.

> *One of the best things an actor can do after he has finished his academic training is to work with a good master acting teacher and coach.* **DAVID GRAPES,** Professor & Director of the School of Theatre Arts & Dance, University of Northern Colorado

FORMS OF TRAINING

I strongly advocate the traditional approach for developing your craft – an extended, sustained and comprehensive training period in <u>professional</u> workshops. These are the main training workshops for actors:

- Acting/Scene-Study
- Improvisation
- Commercial Audition Technique
- Cold-Reading/Theatrical Audition Technique
- Speech, Accent, Diction and Dialect
- Specialty Workshops
    - Soaps
    - Sitcom
    - Comedy
    - Theatre
    - Shakespeare
    - Stand-Up Comedy
    - Voice-Over
    - Character-Voices

- Hosting
- Private Coaching
  - Training
  - Audition
  - Career

Each has its time, place and value, which I will cover in THE PLAN in Chapter Five.

Acting/Scene-Study: I strongly encourage you to start your training with acting/scene-study.

> *It is imperative to have acting training. Acting is a craft. I am sure that there are some people who with a lot of dumb luck have risen up through the ranks with little or no training, but the majority of really good actors that I have worked with all have trained and continue to train.* **LESLIE JORDAN,** Emmy-Award-Winning Actor

In professional scene-study workshops, actors will do monologues and scenes from plays and movies and do connecting exercises. The instructors focus primarily on character development, script analysis, emotional connection, commitment to instinct and often voice and body work.

CONNECTION / CONNECTING: *When the actor, without thinking about dialogue, choices or direction, is immersed in and linked to the authentic energy and core feelings of the character he/she is portraying.*

There are numerous acting techniques and methods. The more popular ones in the United Stares are Meisner, Strasberg, Adler and Hagen techniques. Most teachers have their own version of the established approaches. Some combine styles and others create their own technique. Investigate to see which one feels like a fit for you – the way you process and create. Then audit the teachers who specialize in that approach until you find the one with whom you connect. Finding, auditing and selecting teachers will be covered later in this chapter.

AUDIT: As it relates to acting classes: *to be a non-participating observer. Auditors watch and are not allowed to ask question or give comments. Often the teacher or class assistant will answer questions at the break or at the end of class.*

> *If an actor does not have talent then I believe it can't be taught. Assuming the actor has raw talent, then a great acting teacher can refine and enhance the natural gift. The best training is experience – learning how to break down scripts, creating a character, and finding one's voice.* **DAVID SWEENEY,** Los Angeles Talent Manager

Improvisation: In my opinion, there is no better workshop than improvisation (with a good teacher) to help actors learn to trust their instincts as well as assist in developing creativity, freedom and confidence. These workshops utilize games and exercises initially created by Viola Spolin. It might be helpful to read her book, *Improvisation for the Theatre*. Most instructors teach their own approach to "Spolin" or have created games and exercises to add to the established repertoire. Actors should do this work for at least six to nine months.

> *There is nothing better for the beginning actor than improv classes. It gets the student up, thinking and moving in front of people. These classes taught me to move organically, be silly and think on my feet as well as to try new things without a net and not be afraid to fall on my face or make an ass of myself! Improv classes are invaluable.* **LESLIE JORDAN,** Emmy-Award-Winning Actor

Scene study and improvisation, especially when taken concurrently in two separate workshops and for an extended period of time, will create a strong foundation for the new actor.

Commercial Audition Technique: Many new actors think that taking a commercial-audition workshop is where they should begin their training. They have heard that doing commercials is the best way to get started. That is ridiculous. I personally would like to track down the people who are giving out this advice and make them stop. Obviously, I can't stop those misinformed people but I do fervently try to dispel that propaganda. After an actor has done acting and improvisation training for a minimum of six to nine months and then takes a commercial-audition workshop, it is reasonable for him or her to start auditioning for TV commercials. In most cases, the well-trained actor (with a good commercial "look") has a better chance of booking work than the total novice. Commercial types and "looks" are covered in Chapter Seven, "Packaging Your Product."

Commercial-audition-technique workshops primarily focus on preparing actors to audition well and book TV commercials. They are on-camera and utilize commercial scripts and scenarios. The methods and techniques vary with every teacher. Commercial casting directors and successful commercial actors teach most of these workshops. In major markets, there are a lot to choose from.

Being a commercial-audition-technique teacher as well as a casting director and actress, I have rather strong opinions on what makes a good teacher and a valuable workshop. I fervently believe that good commercial-acting technique is good acting and that this specialty workshop should do the following: teach commercial acting techniques and specific on-camera auditioning tips; encourage creativity; clean up habits that disempower performances;

give constructive feedback on the personal "issues" that could hinder actors from doing their best auditions; help distinguish each actor as a unique personality; work on activating authentic connections to audition material; get the actor on-camera enough times so he/she is comfortable being recorded at auditions; build confidence; and give feedback on wardrobe, hair and make-up to help actors to create or define their "look." (Detailed information regarding creating your "look" is covered in Chapter Seven.) If the timing is right in your development and you choose an acting-oriented teacher, the commercial-technique class can be an asset to your acting training and theatrical auditioning.

THEATRICAL: *refers to film and all television roles and productions*

 One of the big challenges of auditioning for all types of acting work is finding a connection to start the piece. Since commercials are short, you will get a lot of practice quickly finding starting connections.

Theatrical Audition Workshops/Cold-Reading:

COLD-READING: *The term used to describe scripted auditions for TV and film productions.*

After training for eighteen months or so, it is time to take a theatrical audition technique class, also referred to as a cold-reading workshop. (I don't really know why they call it cold-reading. Most times you have hours, if not days, to prepare.) These workshops provide actors with audition training for TV dramas, comedies, sitcoms and soaps as well as films and sometimes theatre. The instructors impart techniques that assist actors to quickly investigate audition material, make strong personal and creative choices, facilitate emotional character connection, commit to instincts and sustain effective readings for the full length of the material (which can be one line or many pages), plus understand and learn how to navigate the audition process.

> *A great teacher should give you the necessary skills to become self-sufficient. You should never need coaching on an audition if you know what you are doing. If you're taking a class and still don't know how to approach a script, then you're in the wrong class.*
> **AMY LYNDON,** TV & Film Audition/Booking Coach

For many, being a formidable, well-trained actor and taking one cold-reading workshop does not guarantee that you will be a <u>consistently</u> strong "auditioner." Auditioning skills (like a muscle) need to be worked regularly to stay in shape and get even stronger to keep actors competitive.

> *No matter how good you are as an actor, if you cannot cold-read you probably will not work. The reality of this business is that*

actors who are really good at standing in front of casting people and producers and giving an exciting cold-read will work more even if they are not as accomplished as some of the other actors. Then, once again, the actor who can cold-read must also be able to deliver on the set. That is where ACTING TRAINING comes in! **LESLIE JORDAN,** Emmy-Award-Winning Actor

Voice/Diction/Accent/Dialects: A good speaking voice without diction problems or accents is a major asset for most actors. If you question this, the next time you watch TV or a film, close your eyes and listen to all of the characters. Most of the voices you hear are clear, resonant and free of accents except maybe for the character actors. If you have a voice, accent or diction issue, consider taking private lessons or classes to work on it during the first year of your acting training. You want to have every advantage. Another actor may just get the job instead of you because he or she has no accent, better diction or his or her voice is more authoritative, pleasant, interesting, sexy, confident or warm.

EXCEPTION: If you have a distinctive vocal quality or a character voice and it works for your physicality, essence and personality, it could be beneficial for the majority of roles for which you will be auditioning. Voices and accents that are not considered common can work when they fit the actor's look or personality. Determine if your voice needs work or you are blessed with a unique voice that is suited to you.

I used to worry about my Tennessee accent. I come from a theatre background so I have had plenty of diction and elocution classes. When I first got to LA, a casting director suggested that since I worked mainly in commercials, I should lose my accent. I tried everything imaginable. I found that the only way to truly lose an accent is walk around talking without the accent in one's day to day life. I felt like such a fake so I gave up. I am sure I have lost jobs because I have a Southern accent, but since I am such a character anyway, I have worked steadily. The argument can be made both ways regarding whether to keep or lose an accent, but for me just being myself, accent and all, has helped as opposed to hurt my career. **LESLIE JORDAN,** Emmy-Award-Winning Actor

For actors who have a good ear for dialects and can play specific character parts, it is smart to learn the dialects of the characters you could play; e.g., if you are blonde and fair, you might want to learn a Swedish or German dialect. If you are an olive-skinned brunette with brown eyes and have a strong-looking face, you might learn an Italian, Hispanic or urban-street dialect. The more dialects and accents you can believably do for roles you can physically portray, the more audition opportunities you could have.

Often teachers who instruct these subjects will say that they are able to cover all four areas. I believe that each one is a specialty and that it is more beneficial to work with a teacher who is an expert in either correcting speech, diction or accents or one who teaches dialects. Granted, there may be a few who specialize in speech and diction or dialects and accents or three of the four, but check around and make sure that you find the very best instructor for your specific issue.

Specialty Workshops: I refer to specialty workshops as classes that focus specifically on one of the acting mediums such as daytime soap operas, sitcoms, Shakespeare, hosting, comedy, theatre, voice-over, character-voice, etc. Each requires good acting skills and the knowledge of the unique styles of the individual mediums.

> HOSTS: *The people who present and/or interview guests or contestants on radio and TV programs and game shows or pitch products in corporate films and "infomercials" (30-minute TV sales programs).*

If you want to target any of these specific mediums or want to be a more versatile actor, I recommend you take the specialty workshop(s) that interests you. Unlike acting, improv or cold-reading, a six-, eight- or twelve-week workshop for any or all of them will provide the necessary information and practice needed to delineate the variations in acting styles and performance techniques. If you choose to focus on any of these specialty mediums then, of course, spend more time training for it.

- Soap, sitcom and hosting classes are usually, but not always, done on-camera and offer playback of recorded work.
- Theatre, Shakespeare and comedy workshops are held in theatres, clubs or classrooms and cameras are not normally utilized.
- Voice-over or character-voice classes are held in recording studios.
- Most teachers who instruct these specialty workshops are or have been actors, stand-up comics, acting teachers, directors or casting directors.

You won't have to look too far in the major entertainment industry cities to find teachers who specialize in each of these specialties.

Private Training: If you choose to do private coaching, I suggest that it be done in conjunction with, not instead of, your acting class and only be utilized for a short time as an intervention if you are stuck or have hit a plateau in your development. Acting training is a process and the necessary information is best absorbed from watching and listening to the other students in a class as well as doing the work. It is easier to understand and learn when observing others being challenged, having breakthroughs and processing the teacher's input, especially when first starting.

Audition Coaching: Many actors utilize private coaching when they want to prepare for a specific role or audition. The value is subjective. Most times you won't need to hire one, but when you are auditioning for larger, important roles or ones that need special direction, private coaches can give you an edge. It also helps actors to feel more confident. Coaches usually charge from $50 to $150 an hour. Some use video, but most do not.

> *Make sure the coach is not directing you! If they haven't seen the show or don't know the style and tone, do not take their advice. Their job is to know what's out there, the styles and who is doing what.* **AMY LYNDON,** TV & Film Audition/Booking Coach

> *With the competition as fierce as it is in today's marketplace, most of my actors coach for their auditions. It helps them look beyond what's on the page and give the best possible performance! Often a good coach can pull a better performance out of the actor!*
> **TODD JUSTICE,** Talent Representative @ Marshak/Zachary

Career Coaching: A qualified life/career coach can be extremely helpful when an actor is at a crossroads in his/her career or life, confused, frustrated and/or looking for personal direction. The good ones who deal with the entertainment industry have experience and expertise in the craft and the business as well as with personal issues. Their guidance can help actors make choices that save time and money. They give personal direction, build confidence and help with stress and anxieties. I often recommend career coaches for students who have issues that don't require therapy. The sessions are usually one-on-one and cost from $75 to $250 per visit. There are also seminars and workshop programs taught by career coaches with numerous people participating. They range in price from $25 to $500 for a day or an evening. The fees for the programs with a series format will depend on the number of participants, sessions and hours and the status of the group leader or career coach.

Whether or not to get career coaching is a personal choice. If you feel you have a handle on personal issues and career choices or have industry contacts who will help guide you, then you may not need one. If you feel you would benefit from a coach, then find yourself the most qualified one that you can afford.

> *I also suggest working with hypnotherapists. They often can boost confidence, help actors overcome stage fright, fix speech impediments and build self-esteem.* **ABBY GIRVIN,** Owner of DDO Agency

FINDING TEACHERS

No matter what kind of workshop you choose, the instructor is the key to attaining effective and empowering training. Just because a teacher has a great reputation, is geographically desirable, is inexpensive and/or some of your friends love him or her, that doesn't mean he or she is the right fit for you.

Most successful teachers are or were actors, casting directors or directors and have experience in the industry. In the major markets, there are hundreds of teachers to choose from. I would venture to guess that only twenty percent of them are worth your commitment and money, so research is crucial. In local markets, you don't have many from which to choose. If you can't find a teacher(s) that you are excited to study with in your vicinity, it would be worth the drive to a bigger city to work with a great one.

SUGGESTIONS FOR FINDING YOUR TEACHER:

- Ask working actors and industry professionals
- Find out who the teachers were for the actors you admire
- Check the trade papers
- Read books and articles written by teachers
- Research teachers' websites and online actors' organizations
- Audit several teachers

Working Actors and Industry Professionals: Get teacher recommendations from industry professionals and successful actors. These people are involved in the business and have already done some of the research for you. Don't take the first recommendation. Ask as many people as you can. When you hear the same names several times, those are the teachers you should check out.

> *Find out about the teacher's track record. Do they have students who are actively working in the industry, on a series or in feature films or commercials?* **AMY LYNDON,** TV & Film Audition/Booking Coach

Actors You Admire: Find out who trained the actors whose work you respect and admire. Often if you go online and hunt around for information on your favorite actors you should be able to find out the names of those they credit as their primary teachers.

Trade Papers: Many teachers and workshop programs advertise in entertainment industry trade papers. But large advertisements (as well as small ones) are not an indication of the teacher's quality. Check out some of these teachers, especially if they are names you have heard from other actors or industry pros. Also, know that many prominent teachers hardly ever advertise in the trade papers, yet often there are articles about them.

Books and Articles: Many teachers have written books and/or articles or articles have been written about them. Read the material and see if what they profess feels like a fit for you. If you do a name search on the Internet, you will find articles on most professional teachers.

Websites and Online Actors' Organizations: Go online and do a search for acting teachers in your area or where you plan to move. The more established ones have websites where you can learn about their approach, background, costs, policies, etc. Also, there are online actors' organizations that help inform and support the acting community. Some organizations you need to join and pay a fee and others are a free service. Go into their chat rooms or to their bulletin boards and ask general questions or request information regarding specific teachers. You will get various, if not conflicting, opinions. Sort out the comments then check out the recommendations that appeal to you.

CHOOSING TEACHERS

AUDIT

Okay, you have done your research and have the list of potential teachers you are considering. Next, call and arrange to audit their classes. If they do interviews, meet with the teachers or their coordinators for an evaluation. That one-on-one time will give you a chance to see if you will be compatible. Even if you are sold on a teacher in your meeting, still audit his or her class before signing up. Meet with and audit several teachers. Most, except for improvisation teachers, allow potential students to check out their classes without a fee. It is my belief that you should not study with an acting or technique teacher whom you have not been able to observe.

> *I always suggest that actors audit 5-10 different instructors. Finding the right teacher may take time but will save you hundreds of dollars. Why find out a week or two into the class that you don't like the instructor or agree with his or her style of teaching? If there is an instructor you've heard is really great, but he or she won't let you audit a class, MOVE ON. Would you buy clothing without trying it on to make sure it fits?* **TODD JUSTICE,** Talent Representative @ Marshak/Zachary

> *Many acting teachers don't allow auditors. The auditor, the unfamiliar person, changes the energy and disturbs the trust and flow built through weeks of people working together. I myself would not appreciate someone who is not a member of the class copiously taking notes.* **TERRY BERLAND,** Commercial CD & Author

Picking an acting teacher is like dating. Check around until you find the one you connect with. Then STICK WITH THAT ONE. Committing is the only way to make progress. That's why it is important to AUDIT. Any acting teacher worth their salt would want you to sit in on a class or two to see if their approach works for you. **LESLIE JORDAN,** Emmy-Award-Winning Actor

FACTORS TO CONSIDER

When you audit, do you know what to look for and the factors to evaluate? Most actors want only to like the teacher and feel comfortable with him/her. Yes, that is important but there is much more to consider. I suggest you ask about and contemplate the following factors:

- teacher's approach and style
- the teacher for <u>your</u> class
- compatibility
- number of students in the class
- how often you will work in class
- class policies
- cost
- class level(s)
- video and playback

Teacher's Approach and Style: Ask yourself these questions in order to determine if the teacher(s) you are considering is a fit for you:

- Does their style or approach make sense and appeal to you?
- Is there a technique that the students understand and can apply or is he/she just teaching tricks or giving direction that produces flashy, instant performances?
- After he/she works with actors doing exercises, monologues and/or scenes, do you see an improvement in their work?
- Does the teacher utilize the class time well: starting punctually, allotting time and giving attention equally to all the students, dealing directly with what is needed and not going off on ego trips or telling too many stories of their accomplishments or bad experiences?
- Is the teacher constructive and supportive as he/she critiques and directs students?

Make sure the teacher does not allow feedback from his or her students. Sometimes a student's critique can be extremely damaging and inappropriate. **AMY LYNDON,** TV & Film Audition/ Booking Coach

Your Teacher: Many experienced "celebrity" teachers have associate instructors who teach their intro and intermediate levels. Most studios will have you audit the "name" teacher and probably the more advanced class that he/she teaches because it's the most impressive presentation for the potential student. I strongly suggest that if you like their teaching method that you

- ask to audit the class of the teacher you will be studying with then evaluate that one. If this second audit is denied, move on to the next teacher on your list

- enroll for the minimum time if you want to be part of that school, and if you don't like the associate teacher, then quit and study with your second choice

- find out how long you will need to work with the associate teacher before you get into the "celebrity" teacher's class. It might or might not be worth the wait.

Compatibility: Determine whether

- you feel comfortable with the manner in which the teacher deals with the students

- he/she feels like someone you can emotionally and intellectually trust to train you for an extended period of time.

SUGGESTION: When you audit, on a break and away from the group, talk one-on-one to a few students to get their feedback about the teacher. Ask how long they have studied there and what they like and don't like about the teacher, class and students.

When you find a teacher who inspires and challenges you to move into emotional territory that may make you uncomfortable – STAY. Don't say it's time to go check out another class. Stay with a teacher you trust so that together you can move past blocks that are keeping you from being fully expressed in your work – and your life. The best acting comes from studying with someone over a long period of time so that you can overcome the habits that keep you from going deeper in the work. If you keep changing classes every year (or less) once your stuff starts to come up, you will never lay the foundation required to reach the places you need to get to in your work. The teacher/student relationship is one of the most profound you could ever develop. You wouldn't bail on your lover just because you are going through a rough patch in your communication. Similarly, you must stick it out with someone you trust to take you to places you are probably unconsciously terrified to go. If the teacher isn't challenging you and taking you to new heights, then yes, move on. When you have found your creative and spiritual home – stay there. It will be one of the most rewarding, maddening, challenging, honest and gratifying relationships you will probably ever experience.

ANTHONY MEINDL, Los Angeles, Acting Teacher

Size of Classes and How Often You Will Work: Ask about the maximum number of students enrolled in the class. Class sizes vary greatly, from six to sixty students. Some teachers don't have it in the literature and may not give you a straight answer, so insist they tell you. I recommend

- acting teachers who take no more than twenty-five students in a class
- improvisation teachers who take no more than twenty
- on-camera commercial teachers who take no more than fifteen
- cold-reading teachers with no more than twenty-four.
- Ask how often you will work in class. This is important to know because
  - in acting classes, eight to ten scenes will be put up in a four- to five-hour session. That usually means sixteen to twenty students will work during each class. With more participants, there is a good chance you will only put your work up in class once, twice or maybe three times a month depending on the number of students.
  - in improvisation workshops, two to five exercises and/or games are taught each session. Most times the teacher can get eighteen to twenty students working two to five times depending on the complexity of the exercises or games.
  - on-camera commercial teachers usually will have their actors work once, twice or three times during a three or four-hour session depending on the number of students
  - cold-reading/audition technique teachers (with sixteen to twenty-four actors in a class) pair up the students and have each twosome work once each night
  - in on-camera cold-reading/audition technique workshops, with twenty students, participants work individually on-camera once a class for ten to twenty minutes.

Know that with the celebrity teachers, there are more students in class; thus each actor works less often or for a shorter period of time. I believe that actors commit and learn more when they are in a scene study, cold-reading, or an on-camera audition technique class where each student does at least one monologue, scene, cold-reading and/or an exercise every session. In improv and on-camera commercial workshops, students benefit more when they can work several times each session.

Sessions and Number of Hours: The majority of teachers offer a once-a-week format and each session runs three to five hours. There are instructors who prefer a twice-a-week format and their sessions will run two to four hours. Your schedule, teacher preference and/or commitment will dictate which is the better choice for you.

Class Policies: Teacher/workshop policies are worth finding out in advance. Ask what the teacher's or school's policies are in regard to arriving late, leaving early, missing classes, student responsibilities, refunds, payment and bounced checks. A policy that I would suggest you also ask about when considering scene-study classes: What happens if your scene partner has to miss class? Does that mean that even though you are prepared, paid and present, you will just watch? (For the acting classes in my workshop program, the teacher allows for a student to do a monologue or a cold-reading if his or her partner is absent.) If consistent participation is important, find out about the policy that covers this.

I believe when reasonable policies are enforced, professionalism is high. Most actors never check out the teacher's policies then get upset when they discover that what they assumed was the case, wasn't. There are no right or wrong policies. It's what feels right for you. Knowing them before you start acknowledges that you choose to agree and respect them._

Cost: The teacher or the school determines the cost of a class. Fees are usually based on the instructor's reputation, whether the class meets once or twice a week, the number of hours per session, location and number of students. The more experienced or celebrated the teacher, the higher the fee. At this time, in major markets, classes can range from $100 to $300 per four-class session. For those whose fees are at the lower end of the scale, I suggest you check out the teacher and his/her teaching ability, reputation and experience. Remember the adage, "you get what you pay for." There are always exceptions. You could find the next great "guru" teacher at the beginning of his/her career, or you could waste money and time. If you consider working with a teacher on the upper end of the fee scale, make sure he/she is worth it to you and your career. Just because someone is more expensive and his or her name might look great on your resume doesn't mean he/she is the best one for you.

Find out:

- Do you pay for one or more months at a time?
- If you pay for several months, is there a discount?
  - You only want to do this when you have trained with the teacher for a few months and know that this is the right class for you.
- Do you need to pay for a second month in advance? (For scene-study classes)
- When is the deposit due and cashed?
- Is the deposit deducted from the total?
- What is the cancellation or refund policy?
- Is there a payment plan or is the full amount due when you start?
- Will they accept credit cards?
- Are there additional fees or expenses?

I suggest that you factor value and time into the cost. Don't get put off by a class that may be more expensive before you figure out if it is really the better value. For example, if you are considering two classes and the teachers are on a par, figure out:

WHICH IS THE BETTER VALUE?	
CLASS #1	CLASS #2
Costs $300	Costs $400
5 sessions	8 sessions
15 students	12 students
Runs 3 hours a night	Runs 4 hours a night

The first class costs $60 a night, has more students and has fewer hours, so you have less time to work. The second one is $50 a night, has fewer students, more hours and more sessions, so you have more time to learn.

Class Levels: Most established teachers have three or four training levels for their workshops: beginning, intermediate, advanced and/or professional. Some only have one or two. Inquire how many are offered. Also, ask about the type and amount of training and experience that is expected from the actors in each level. I suggest that you study with teachers who offer a few levels.

New actors should initially take workshops with other beginners because

- the primary techniques focused on in the intro classes build and reinforce the necessary basic acting foundation
- everyone in the class needs the same fundamental information so most every question reaps answers that will benefit all the students
- there is less chance of students becoming insecure and frustrated and maybe even quitting because they feel inadequate compared to the more experienced actors
- new actors will be less likely to develop bad habits by trying to replicate the work (before they have the foundation) of the more advanced actors in the class.

Conversely, more experienced and professional actors should be in workshops with their peers because

- the information and direction will be on a higher level
    - Since most of the students will have already learned the basics, the focus of intermediate and advanced levels is usually more about developing a deeper connection, dealing with individual issues, nurturing creative interpretations and honing subtleties
- experienced actors will be inspired when their peers do brilliant work
- students will be challenged when working with their partners
- the teacher can focus on both actors' work, as opposed to "talking down" to the level of the less-trained partner.
    - Often when an experienced actor works with a novice, the teacher will spend more time critiquing the one who needs the most help. In an intermediate or advanced class, when peers are being critiqued, both actors will get the same level of direction.

Videotape and Playback: The use of camera and videotape playback is something you may also want to factor in to your decision-making process for specific classes. I am an advocate of recording and playing back class work for commercial workshops, audition workshops, soap- and sitcom-technique classes, workshops taught by directors and occasionally in acting classes.

Some scene-study teachers utilize a camera in every session. Most don't. I do not believe a camera should be used in every session of a scene-study workshop. When doing "process" work, it is important to know how it feels, not the way it looks. I believe that when actors start focusing on what their scenes and monologues look like too early, their work will become superficial. I advocate that if scenes or monologues are to be videotaped, it should be done when they are complete (once every four weeks or so) and not during the process. Then actors can objectively see what worked and what they should focus on in their next assignment.

You now understand the different forms of acting training and what is needed. You are armed with the information and criteria of how to find and select your teachers. Go forward confidently and train. Develop your craft and create the acting foundation necessary for your career.

THE PLAN

Do you understand all an acting career entails: the time, money, training, dedication, energy, lifestyle adjustments, personal and business challenges? It is vital to know as much as possible before embarking on this journey. Too many people approach an acting career with no strategy or idea of what is necessary. Most try to get acting work way before they are ready, jump from teacher to teacher, make bad business decisions and/or are financially unprepared. Don't be one of them. This is a business. When preparing to be a doctor, dentist, lawyer, accountant, contractor, teacher or most any type of professional, there is a strategy: schools to attend, financing, entry-level work, business plans, etc. Professions have established paths to be traveled and one can usually determine what is required – the costs and courses of action. Yet most people approach becoming an actor as if it were an improvisation. From my years of being an actress, teacher, casting director, director and producer, I have seen thousands of actors come and then go because they didn't have a plan. I strongly believe that having a well-thought-out plan that actors commit to is crucial for a successful career.

> *Amen. I tell actors this all the time.* **HUGH LEON,** Commercial Agent
> @ Coast to Coast Agency

The plan that I am about to outline is what I propose to new actors as well as those who were actors ten years ago (or more) and folks who have had bad training or have done the kinds of acting work that has created habits that are not conducive to film and TV work or professional theatre productions. This plan should help you avoid many pitfalls of the first few years. It is based on my career, the experience of thousands of actors I know or have trained and successful actors whom I have researched. It is not the only strategy, but it is the one I strongly believe makes the most sense and have seen work for the great majority of those who have followed it.

> *This PLAN suggests an often-followed routine in which to proceed when making long-term acting goals for one's self or when stuck at a career roadblock. I cannot begin to count the number of working actors I have met who lament about how much easier their careers would have started had there been a plan given to them to follow.* **BERNARD TELSEY,** New York Theatre and Film Casting Director

THE PLAN

WHERE TO START

If you do not live in New York, Los Angeles or Chicago, seriously think about moving to one of these cities. These are the major entertainment markets in the United States. Many consider San Francisco, Seattle, Detroit, Dallas/Houston, Miami/Orlando and Las Vegas strong secondary entertainment markets. In Canada, the major markets would be Toronto, Vancouver and Montreal. The major entertainment centers offer the best overall training and the most career opportunities and work. Bottom line: If you want to be a professional working actor in film and TV and/or high-end theatre productions, you will need to move to a major or secondary market area either at the beginning or no later than by the end of the first year of this three-year plan.

> *It may be smart to establish yourself in your city and move to a major entertainment city after you've accomplished as much as you can in the smaller market.* **HUGH LEON,** Commercial Agent @ Coast to Coast Agency

> *While you are training, find the closest smaller city where there is a SAG branch and go there. Work to get cast in whatever movies film there and if possible get your SAG card or SAG eligibility. Then move to a major market. Having your SAG card already when you arrive in a major market puts you far ahead of those who are trying to get one. Theatrical agents are far more interested in SAG members since their earning power is greater than non-union actors.* **LAURI JOHNSON,** Entertainment Industry Life Coach

FIRST SIX MONTHS

- Take acting and improvisation classes
- Audit classes
- Additional preparation
- Rehearse a lot
- Develop skills and sports abilities
- Make as much money as possible

Acting Classes: First and most importantly, start with an acting teacher whom you want to train with for at least a year. How to research and select the right teacher is covered in Chapter Four. Your acting/scene-study training is the foundation of your craft. The sooner you find the right teacher and commit to the process, the sooner you can start learning the techniques and tools needed to be a well-trained actor.

Acting classes are essential and extremely important. They teach actors to react to other actors, which in my humble opinion is what real acting is about. I recently worked with an actor who has won every award imaginable and is supposed to be at the top of his craft. His performance was so planned he never even looked at me or reacted to what I gave him. I realized that this man's entire career must have been made in the editing bay. No matter what line reading I gave him, he responded with the line reading he had planned. It was disconcerting and in my opinion selfish. In scene-study classes actors learn to react and that is what creates exciting performances. **LESLIE JORDAN,** Emmy-Award-Winning Actor

Improvisation Classes: At the same time you start an acting class, enroll with an improvisation teacher whom you plan to train with for at least six months. I believe improv in conjunction with an acting class helps to speed up the training process, stimulates creativity, lays the foundation for auditioning and promotes commitment, spontaneity and freedom. I am a major advocate of the benefits of improvisation training.

Audit: When permitted, audit other workshops that your acting instructor teaches as often as your schedule allows. When objectively watching actors perform their work and listening to the instruction, it is often easier to see how the teacher's process works, which helps you better understand and trust his/her technique and commit to it. This can speed up your progress.

Additional Preparation: A great way to get more from your acting class is to rehearse as much as you can with your partner. The more you rehearse, the more you can investigate the scene and experiment with ways to tap into your emotions as well as find richer interpretations thus, the more you can grow as an actor. I also recommend that you always work on monologues and possibly an additional scene with a second partner (other than the one who was assigned to you). In most acting classes, you are only allowed to put up one piece of work at a time. If prepared, you can let the teacher know that you have a monologue or a second scene that you would like to put up if there is time, or if your assigned partner is absent. As a teacher, when I see that an actor is hungry to learn, I give him more time and attention.

With improv classes, normally there are no outside-the-class practice sessions, but you can get together with people from the class and practice the games and techniques. Also go to improv shows with fellow students then afterward discuss what worked and what didn't.

*An actor must approach his or her career like an Olympic athlete.
The more you practice the necessary skills, the more you will book.*

With a high level of discipline and concentration on the work, you will see results. **AMY LYNDON,** TV & Film Audition/Booking Coach

If you can invest more in your training, ask your acting teacher if there are books, articles, DVDs, or CDs they would suggest. Get what is recommended and read, listen to and watch it. If you have questions about the information you obtain from these products, ask your instructor for clarification at an appropriate time. This type of exchange (if not done too often) lets him/her know the level of your commitment and could create a better teacher/student relationship.

Skills and Sports Abilities: If you have special skills or talents or excel at any sport, continue to do, play and/or develop them. The more activities you do well and talents you possess, the more job opportunities are available. Many commercials and lots of theatrical roles require specific abilities. Dancing, horseback riding, tennis, skiing, landscaping, cooking, skydiving, rock climbing, languages, dialects, stamp or coin collecting, yoga, mosaics, Pilates, weight training, running, painting – whatever it is you enjoy, pursue it in your free time. Although I place this instruction in this period of The Plan, I encourage you to continue with it. Besides potentially having value in your career, these activities help you to have a fuller life, which enhances your well-being and helps you to be a healthier actor.

> *You have a better shot at getting in the door for auditions when you have special skills (especially for commercials). Languages and dialects can also help separate you from the masses.*
> **AMY LYNDON,** TV & Film Audition/Booking Coach

Money: Get a survival job or jobs where you can earn enough money for your living and acting expenses as well as enough to put into savings. Business and marketing expenses, especially during the second and third years, will get pricey, and it is important to start saving sooner than later. I will detail these expenses in Chapter Six.

After the initial training period when actors start looking for acting jobs, many are not prepared for the costs involved with the business aspects: union membership, shooting and reproducing photos, subscribing to casting websites, joining networking groups, participating in activities and showcases, or being able to support themselves when taking time off from their survival jobs to do a film for which they earn very little or nothing. If you have not saved for these expenses, your momentum will be interrupted. Actors caught in a financial bind oftentimes stop training so they can pay the business and marketing costs. This action can prevent them from taking their craft to the next level. Some continue to study and forego their marketing, which prevents them from taking advantage of work opportunities. With either scenario, careers can take a downward spiral or never get started. So it is vital to your training and career to be financially prepared.

Time Required and Scheduling

The time needed to undertake what I have outlined in this first period can range from twelve to twenty-five hours a week. Depending on your commitment, availability and finances, you could be working on your training for the minimum or maximum amount of time. The more time you can put in during this stage as well as the rest of the phases I am about to outline, the stronger your acting foundation will be. It is not a guarantee that you will become a better actor than someone who isn't as committed, but if I were a betting person, I would put my money on you progressing faster unless you have major issues.

During the first year, most who follow my plan won't be going out on many acting auditions so there is no need to keep your days free. I recommend getting a 9-to-5 job or weekend work (depending on the job) because that is where you can usually earn the optimal income. Keep most weeknights free for classes, auditing and rehearsing – becoming a well-trained actor. If you join a daytime acting workshop then you can do nighttime work. There are many well-paying night jobs. (I suggest a large number of actor-friendly jobs in Chapter Six.) Create a schedule that serves both your talent development and your ability to earn a good income.

SIXTH THROUGH THE NINTH MONTH

- Continue training
- Take an improv class or a commercial workshop (depending on your progress and intentions)
- Rehearse often
- If needed, work on your speech, diction or accent
- Saturate yourself with craft and business information
- Make and save money

Training: I would suggest that along with the acting class you have been taking, you either continue with the next level of your improv class or take an on-camera commercial workshop.

Commercial Audition Training: Whether to take a commercial class at this point depends on how your acting training is going. Before doing any on-camera workshop, you should have the beginning of a solid acting foundation. It is important to know how it feels to be connected to the role, character, dialogue and your emotions and to have the freedom to commit to your instincts before you start to focus on how your work looks. If you are feeling confident and freed up and are doing consistent work then it should be okay. To be sure, discuss whether you are ready with your acting teacher. If you choose to do a commercial workshop, continue with your acting class as well and when you're finished with the commercial class go back to improv.

Unfortunately, many commercial-audition classes focus primarily on the performance of audition tips and tricks that can put you "in your head" and undermine the foundation work you have been developing. So choose this teacher carefully. How to select teachers and the criteria for what is a good commercial-audition workshop are covered in Chapter Four.

Rehearsal: Rehearsing the scenes and monologues for your acting class with your partner and on your own, as often as possible, will help you progress faster. To speed up your development in your commercial workshop and your film and TV audition class, I suggest you buy, rent or borrow a video camera. Practice with copy from magazines or TV commercials and theatrical monologues and scenes. After you have thoroughly prepared and rehearsed, record yourself <u>once</u> then view your work to make sure it is on target.

Speech, Accent and Diction Classes: If your voice or speech needs work, find a teacher, learn your lessons and practice, practice, practice. It is the only way to create a speaking voice that will be your ally. Be objective. Or ask people you respect if your speech or voice could use some attention. If there is an issue, the sooner you fix it the sooner there may be one less reason for someone not to hire you.

Information: Audit acting classes. Watch well-acted theatrical productions, TV programs and films. Read books, blogs and articles. Listen to CDs and podcasts and watch TV programs about actors and the craft. When you watch and hear professionals speak and work, you learn more about the creative process and you are inspired to do your best. It is even beneficial to watch bad actors and get clear on what it is that is missing in their work. Learn from everyone. When you get insights and new information, apply them right away to your scenes, monologues and auditions. There is a lot to learn.

Also, go to workshops and seminars that teach the business of acting. (Doing business preparation now will prepare you for your second year). Be voracious but be selective with the information you choose to utilize. This is a very creative and exciting developmental period. Keep feeding yourself with artistic and business insights.

Money For Year Two: Continue to work a job or change to one that makes you enough money to pay for your living expenses and classes as well as enough to save for when you start marketing.

Time Required

What I have proposed in this time frame for your development will take from fifteen to thirty hours a week. The amount of time needed has increased and your commitment should be escalating. You are cultivating your acting foundation and preparing for the business.

LAST THREE MONTHS OF THE FIRST YEAR

- Continue taking acting classes
- Rehearse often
- Take a commercial class (if you took an improv class in the last three-month period)
- Go into the next level of improv (if you did the commercial class in the last three months)
- Take professional pictures
- Create first resume
- Secure a commercial print agent
- Submit for parts in student and graduate films, Webisodes, music videos and theatre
- Work to become SAG-eligible
- Do "extra" work (in order to get the vouchers needed to become SAG-eligible)
- Work backstage or do a small part or ensemble work in a theatrical production
- Re-examine your intention

Ongoing Training and Rehearsals: A staple of this two-year plan continues to be working hard at your acting training – doing as much rehearsal as you can to prepare for class, participation in classes and rehearsing additional material. If you are still getting value from your acting teacher, I suggest that you stay put. You have invested nine months and this teacher knows you – your strengths and your weaknesses. It would be more beneficial to continue your training with him/or her than to find another acting teacher and start over with the "getting-to-know-you" process. Too many new actors change teachers too soon and therefore a solid foundation is delayed or never achieved. If you believe that the teacher is not serving you any longer, do your research, audit classes and choose one who will. Don't quit your current workshop (unless there are problems) until you find one you want to join. Register to start and then quit the old one. It is not a good idea at this point in your training to take breaks.

I believe that this might also be an ideal time to join a reputable theatre company to further develop yourself as an actor. If you are serious about becoming a quality actor, doing theatre raises the bar. **MICHAEL DONOVAN,** Casting Director, Commercial, Film and Theatre

Improvisation/Commercial Training: If you took the on-camera commercial workshop in the last three-month period, now take the next level of improvisation training with your instructor or if you want, find another one. Changing improvisation teachers after six months, unlike with acting teachers, can be helpful in developing your freedom and creativity. After all, the craft of improvisation is designed to teach actors to be adaptable and to be comfortable with being uncomfortable. If you remained in your improv workshop during the last three months, I suggest that now you do an on-camera commercial-audition class.

 SUGGESTION: If you have discovered that you have a gift for improvisation, you might want to continue with your improv training or join or create a group and start performing. Those who are gifted improvisers should develop this talent, which can be beneficial to your craft, is a great showcase, and can separate you from the pack.

Professional Pictures: If you have done the commercial class, you will probably be ready now to select a professional photographer and shoot your first set of pictures (also referred to as headshots). In the commercial workshop, you should have gotten experience and confidence working in front of a camera as well as learned about your type and the wardrobe, hair, makeup, etc., that suit you. These insights and information will be great preparation for your photo shoot. Everything regarding shooting your headshots is covered in Chapter Eight.

Watch a lot of TV and film! Figure out what shows you should be on and dress at the photo session as if you're on the show. Pick up entertainment magazines and look at the popular styles.
AMY LYNDON, TV & Film Audition/Booking Coach

First Resume: It's time to create your first resume. Although you probably don't have impressive acting credits yet, you can still put together a professional-looking resume to submit for acting work and commercial representation. You will find the information needed to create your first resume in Chapter Nine.

Submissions: Once you have your headshots and have created your resume, you will have the tools to submit yourself for entry-level acting work (while you continue with your training).

In the major entertainment cities and many of the secondary markets, there are online casting websites where actors can join and find out about "castings" for films, TV shows, theatre, "Webisodes," music videos, and university/college student and graduate films. (I will cover these casting websites in several of the upcoming chapters.)

For those investigating and pursuing acting as a hobby, college/university student films provide experience auditioning and working on a set and are fun. Most of them are mainly short films using a voice-over to comment on people acting, whereas in the majority of graduate films the actors have dialogue. Graduate films are the better way to get experience with scripted or improvised dialogue scenes, and they often provide good footage for your demo reel (covered in Chapter Thirteen). If you are committed to acting as a career, submit mainly for graduate films. They are considered a stronger barometer of your abilities than footage where you are not speaking.

> *When first starting out, student and graduate films are good experience. When working on the set be aware of everything, including how the production flows, support crews and lingo.*
> **TERRY BERLAND,** Commercial CD & Author

Print Representation: If there are commercial print agents in your city or within driving distance and you have an accommodating job plus the interest and time to pursue this type of work, seek representation for print ads.

PRINT ADS: *Photographic advertisements appearing in magazines, and on websites and billboards.*

There are two categories of print work.

- Fashion: High-end or trendy model types are primarily hired for print ads that advertise hair products, perfume, makeup, high-end automobiles, lingerie/underwear and other luxury products.

- Commercial: Non-model people of every type and age are those mainly featured in print ads for most other kinds of products.

Print auditions are good opportunities to practice interviewing, auditioning, and working in front of the camera, as well as to meet casting directors (who often cast TV commercials and films). Once in a great while, a print job can turn into a print ad campaign or a TV commercial.

SAG/AFTRA Eligibility:

SCREEN ACTOR'S GUILD and AMERICAN FEDERATION OF TELEVISION AND RADIO ARTISTS, often referred to as SAG and AFTRA: *These are the unions actors join (when qualified) to be eligible to work in the majority of commercials, television shows and motion pictures. Unions provide their members with a full range of benefits plus on-set and financial protection.*

To become SAG-eligible, actors must either book a union job, join a sister union and do one principal job in that union's jurisdiction, or get the necessary vouchers by doing background work (also referred to as being an "extra") in union commercials, films and TV shows. For complete information about Screen Actors Guild, check their website: *www.sag.org.* To join AFTRA, you just have to pay a membership fee. To learn about the American Federation of Television and Radio Artists, go to *www.aftra.org.* Union membership is covered in Chapter Thirteen.

 Actors are technically not allowed to audition for union jobs if they are not members of SAG or AFTRA. Often the actor or his agent can find a way to justify his submission. For example, if the actor has a unique skill or is a distinct type that is being requested, he/she can be given an audition.

Background/Extra Work: To register to do extra work, contact an extras casting service. This work is an option only if you live in a major or secondary entertainment market and have a flexible 9-to-5 job. If not, you need to wait until you can either move or change jobs.

I-9: *A form that is filled out and filed with the government to verify employment eligibility. For more information and to acquire the form go to: www.uscis.gov/files/form/I-9.pdf.*

EARNING VOUCHERS: When working as an extra on a union production, if an actor is in the right place at the right time with the right look, the director or assistant director might choose to feature him or her, and he/she will receive a SAG voucher (and a bump in pay). Once an actor receives the necessary number of vouchers, he is eligible to become a union member. (At the time this was written, the amount was three.) There is no guarantee that you will earn a voucher when you do background work. It usually takes several jobs, networking with the assistant directors and luck. In order to become SAG-eligible doing background work (by the end of the first year of this plan), start working to get vouchers around this ten-month period.

TIP Once you have received the necessary vouchers, you are SAG-eligible. I suggest that you do not join SAG right away. The SAG-eligible status will get you considered for both non-union and union work. When you start looking for work, you will want to get as many auditions as you can and non-union work will offer more opportunities at this juncture. In many situations the same CDs, producers and directors do non-union and union jobs. If you do good auditions or book non-union jobs for them, they might be inclined to bring you in for union work. Being SAG-eligible gives you more work options. However, when you book your the next union job, you must join.

Theatre: Volunteer to help out in a professional theatre production. Locate a theatre or a company with a great reputation or one whose work you admire. Either become a member or offer your services in whatever capacity is needed and for whatever you feel motivated to do. It will be extremely beneficial to participate in the process of mounting and running a play and be able to watch experienced actors rehearse and perform. You might even be asked to be in the ensemble, do a small role, or be an understudy. Whatever your role, the exposure to and experience of being in a professional theatrical production is invaluable to your development and audition preparation.

Re-Examine Your Intention: As the first year comes to a close, this is a good time to congratulate yourself on your journey. If you have followed The Plan, you have determinedly been studying acting, improv and commercial auditioning; rehearsed a lot; audited classes; learned about the entertainment business; studied actors in plays, movies, TV and commercials; shot your headshots; created your resume; booked and performed in graduate films, "Webisodes," music videos and/or theatre productions; maybe worked as an extra on film and TV sets; signed with a print agent; worked behind the scenes in a theatrical production; and with any luck, secured SAG-eligibility. You have built yourself a solid foundation and accomplished a lot.

It is time to re-examine your intention. Is acting everything you thought it would be? Better? Worse? Do you love the work of being an actor? Are you dedicated or still investigating? Is it going to be a hobby? Are you feeling complete in the investigation and are you choosing now to check out other professions?

> *"I don't believe in timelines. It will be obvious when it's time to quit. Something – family, the survival job or lifestyle – will become more important and it will be time to move on. If your time as an actor was brief that was always going to be and you just didn't know it."* **ALICIA RUSKIN,** Commercial Agent & Partner, KSA Talent Agency

Up until now, whether it was an investigation, hobby or career, The Plan has looked pretty much the same. In this second year, each goal will have variations.

FIRST SIX MONTHS OF SECOND YEAR

- Move to a major film and TV market or a city that has a prominent regional theatre program
- Continue with or change your acting teacher
- Take the next level of a commercial class or a TV and film audition workshop
- Secure a commercial agent and start auditioning
- Work on appropriate dialects and languages
- Subscribe to an acting trade paper(s)
- Build confidence doing "safe" auditions
- Do a TV game show or reality program
- Find a network organization or create one
- Submit yourself for larger roles in graduate films and theatre as well parts in union and non-union films and TV shows

Move (or not): If you are positive that you are dedicated to an acting career or want to step up the investigation, now (if you are not already there) would be the time to move to a major (or at least a secondary) film and TV market. If you are sure that being an actor is a hobby, you are probably okay wherever you live.

> *It is not always conducive to move. Search for the work and excel where you are. Accept the reality and the limitations of where you live. Comfort and lifestyle should also determine if and where you move.* **TERRY BERLAND,** Commercial CD & Author

For those who would like to focus on theatre as a career, a training opportunity and/or showcasing vehicle, you might want to join a regional theatre in your area or move to a city where there is a prominent company. (Audition and see if you are accepted before you move.) If you are not accepted as a company member, you might consider apprenticing with a theatre you aspire to work with. Then in a few months, once the "powers that be" have gotten to know you, audition again. If you do well, you will have a better chance of getting in. Doing professional theatre provides valuable training. Many wonderful actors started in regional theatre and went on to be successful in TV and films. If your passion is to do theatre in a major market, move to New York or

Chicago. Los Angeles is beginning to have more theatre opportunities but is primarily a film and television industry town.

Acting Training: For those contemplating a career or a hobby, continue studying acting. Stay with your original teacher or start with a new one whom you intend to be with for at least six months. The first year was about building your foundation and now is when you start having major breakthroughs with your training. If you can only afford one class at this time, I would strongly suggest staying in your acting class. Your commitment will really be tested during this period so do not slack off on your training, preparation and rehearsals.

Audition Workshop or The Next Level of Commercial Training: Are you really ready to start auditioning? If you start before you are prepared, it can hurt your acting work and you can burn bridges with industry pros who might not consider auditioning you again when you are ready. Ask yourself: if you were a casting director, would you be impressed enough with your work to consider hiring you right now? The analogy question I often ask new actors is "Would you paint and create 'curb appeal' for a house and put it up for sale before you built it?" If you believe you are ready to start auditioning and are leaning toward a career in theatre, film or TV, take a cold-reading/audition workshop along with your scene-study class. For those who want to focus first on TV commercials, I recommend that your second class be the next level of on-camera commercial technique with your original teacher or with a new one who offers new information. I believe, at this point in the training, most are truly ready for a cold-reading/auditioning or a more advanced commercial-audition-technique workshop because they have developed a fairly strong foundation.

> *Unfortunately there are many amazing actors who don't know how to audition or work a room. The casting director is not interested in your process. They're looking for results. It's Hollywood.*
> **AMY LYNDON,** TV & Film Audition/Booking Coach

Those who are still investigating or have decided on acting as a hobby and only wish to do one class can take either the commercial-audition technique or the cold-reading workshop. Whichever one you choose to do first, sign-up for two to four months then do the other for approximately the same period of time. These two classes might help you decide whether to commit to an acting career or do commercial work, move ahead as a hobby, or quit.

Commercial Representation: After completing your second commercial class, submit your picture and resume to commercial agents. Commercial agents are deluged with actors who want representation, and it will depend on your type, age and headshot whether you will get an appointment. I believe that if you have followed The Plan (and have a good "look" for commercials), you are prepared to audition and have a good chance to get representation. For in-depth input on submitting to and interviewing agents, read Chapter Eleven.

I once received a note from an actor who wanted to meet me in order to "pick up some extra cash" in commercials until she found her fortune in film and TV. This actor will probably be relieved soon enough of her delusion, but it irks me that anyone would assume just because a commercial is 30 seconds long and features people seemingly being "themselves" that it takes less effort/stamina/talent/drive to land one. **ALICIA RUSKIN,** Commercial Agent & Partner, KSA Talent Agency

Dialects and Languages: If you are drawn to doing characters, you might consider learning dialects, accents and possibly languages that are appropriate for your physical type. Your ability to play many kinds of characters provides more opportunities.

Trade Papers: Read industry trade papers or their online publications. The major ones in Los Angeles and New York are *Backstage, Variety,* and *Hollywood Reporter.* These publications provide casting notices as well as information about shows and movies in production, insights from pros and knowledge of who the players are at all levels. To better understand the business side of your career it is vital to know what is currently happening in the industry.

Confidence: I believe that the more you do something, the better you get at it and the greater your confidence is in doing it, which only makes you better. To this end, when you first start to audition, I suggest that you submit yourself for one or two roles a week that you don't want in safe, low-profile situations and not for prominent casting directors, directors or producers. This exercise gives actors a safe place to experiment, fail, succeed, and thus learn. With less pressure you can do well at these practice auditions and develop confidence. Then you can usually do stronger auditions when going out for the jobs you do want. I know that this suggestion seems unconventional and it is an unpopular tactic among industry pros but it helps build confidence. In order for this to have value, you must work hard to prepare for these auditions with no intention of taking the job.

I have a HUGE problem with actors who audition for things they have no intention of accepting. This has proved to be a VERY serious problem for me, and has resulted in my being no longer willing to bring those actors in again. It's a COMPLETE waste

of time for my clients and me. Actors should NEVER audition for something as a lark or solely as a learning experience. They leave a HORRIBLE impression that they may never be able to shake.
MICHAEL DONOVAN, Casting Director, Commercial, Film and Theatre

As I said, most industry pros frown on actors using their auditions as an opportunity to practice so I reiterate: Only do it for low-profile productions. Bottom line, the more you audition, the better you get at it. Find a lot more on this tricky subject in the "Entry-Level Audition Experience" section in Chapter Ten.

 WARNING: This exercise is only intended for the initial audition. If you go to a callback and are offered the job then you must take it (unless some part of the job description was withheld or misrepresented). It is not fair or ethical to waste the time of the casting director, producer and director on a callback. They will definitely be upset with you. Don't antagonize industry pros on any level because you never know when or where you will encounter them the next time.

TV Game Shows or Reality Programs: Game and reality TV shows offer numerous benefits. These venues present chances to practice auditioning, interviewing and being on-camera. They also give actors a chance to deal with and get comfortable in pressure situations – all of which builds confidence. If you land a popular reality program, the exposure could give you a vehicle to open a few doors into the industry. Some actors are concerned that this kind of exposure can hurt their credibility as serious actors. I believe that any professional and suitable exposure can only be good as long as it is handled intelligently. Being on one of these shows should provide benefits whereas doing more might prove to have a negative effect on your career.

Network and Marketing: At the end of the first six months of your second year, I strongly suggest you join an actors' networking organization. This is important for actors dedicated to a career. For those thinking of acting as a hobby or who are still investigating, joining a networking organization would be of value but is not a necessity. In Los Angeles, I suggest the Actors' Network (www.actors-network.com). They also offer a beneficial online service that is worth checking into. If there isn't an organization in your area, organize one. It is synergistic to have actors supporting actors and working together to research teachers, photographers, networking opportunities, agents, casting directors, acting work, etc. It is also a lot more productive as well as fun when a group of actors get together regularly to report, strategize, motivate, learn and work together to create their careers. I strongly recommend it.

I would recommend that you start your research, networking and marketing after six months' training instead of waiting. Then by this time you have all your resources lined up and have gotten a consensus of who's good and who's not. **ABBY GIRVIN,** Owner of DDO Agency

Film, Television and Theatre Submissions: Around the eighteenth month of The Plan and after you have completed a cold-reading/audition workshop, start submitting yourself for leads in graduate films, co-star roles in theatre productions and small roles in non-union and/or union films and television shows (depending on whether or not you are a union member). Your work, confidence and auditioning skills should be strong enough at this point to be seen by the professionals doing higher-profile work. The credits and the tape/film from these jobs are vital to building a resume and a reel for the career actor and the hobbyist.

MONTHS SIX THRU NINE OF THE SECOND YEAR

- Continue training
- If interested, do a stand-up workshop, voice-over class or another specialty workshop
- Join a theatre company or do plays
- Audition and work as much as possible
- Work at an "actor friendly" job
- Intern for an agent, casting director, producer or director
- Investigate getting a manager

Training: Continue taking your acting class and doing lots of rehearsal for your scenes and monologues. If you are not challenged enough or it feels like it is time to move on to a new teacher, do so. With all the experience you are getting from auditioning and doing acting jobs, class is more important than ever to your development. Training during this time helps to make sure that you don't develop bad habits in your quest to work. I am a purist. It is my belief that if you want to be a quality actor, it is important to keep studying. Many top working actors (even stars) go back to class between jobs in order to continue honing their craft. They love the process, and I'm hoping you do as well. Countless new actors either stop studying too soon or are inconsistent: therefore, they never build a strong foundation or their acting work does not mature. If you are starting to lose interest in studying, take a look to see if your goals have changed or find a new teacher to inspire you.

If you are not in a play or working consistently in commercials, films and/or TV, I strongly suggest that career actors take a challenging cold-reading class or a more advanced improv workshop as a second class. It is crucial for those who want a career to work on auditioning and performance skills while continuing to develop craft. A good actor is not automatically a good "auditioner" and vice versa. Both talents are dependent upon each other, but each needs to be continually developed, especially during this period.

> *Think of yourself at the free throw line. Practice all your auditioning/booking skills hundreds of times, so when it comes to the last two points in the game to win, it's just another basket you're shooting. Your confidence will be at an all-time high when you feel good about your game.* **AMY LYNDON,** TV & Film Audition/ Booking Coach

Stand-Up Workshop: If you love doing improv and have an affinity for comedy, take a stand-up comedy class. Once you finish the class and when you feel good about your routine, go to the local comedy clubs and perform on their amateur nights. (I believe it takes more courage to do a stand-up routine than any other form of performing.) If you have a gift for comedy and love doing it, go for it. There have been numerous stand-up comics who have had their own sitcoms that were based on their stand-up routines. If you discover that you don't have a knack for it, the experience of learning and doing stand-up will help build confidence and hone your comedy technique.

Voice-Over Workshop: If you have a resonant or unique speaking voice or have the ability to do a multitude of character voices, check into doing a voice-over workshop.

VOICE-OVER (VO): *refers to work of those doing the voices in commercials, films, TV, recordings, and audio books. They narrate the story, pitch or promo the product, are the background voices in programs and films, and are the voices of animated or inanimate characters.*

This work is another avenue to earn income and make contacts as well as to hone your craft. Narrators, spokespeople and animation character and dubbing voices are related skills, but require different training. Pursue the one that calls to you. Once you are trained and feel prepared (which takes a minimum of three months), make a demo reel and submit it to voice-over agents. Many "VO" agents are located within the larger commercial agencies. This pursuit takes time, effort and money to prepare for and get established. If you can manage it along with everything else (or instead of), it could be a way to earn money and discover a whole new career, but understand that it is an extremely competitive field.

> *If you are not specializing in the announcer sound, your personality and acting ability are more important than a smooth,*

pretty voice. Actors who do many different kinds of voices, those who have a "real," non-announcer sound, as well as comedic ability, are marketable for voice-over work. **TERRY BERLAND,** Commercial CD & Author

Specialty Workshops: If you are interested in doing or learning more about soap operas, sitcoms, hosting, or Shakespeare work, take a specialty workshop that focuses on the one(s) that you wish to study. If you feel that you have found a niche, once you have studied the specialty for at least eight weeks, then talk to your teacher and get his or her input on what more you need to do to train for and pursue this medium. If you are not interested in the specialty you studied then either move on to another one that interests you or just stay with your other classes and acting pursuits.

Theatre: At this time (if you haven't already), I suggest you join a theatre company or audition for roles in quality shows. Acting in theatrical productions helps build resumes, furthers craft development, increases contacts and is an industry showcase. Choose companies and productions carefully. You don't want to be in a badly directed production or be the only good actor in a mediocre show.

> *It is very important to do theatre especially in Los Angeles. It tends to legitimize your work. Plenty of actors (especially in LA) can "act from the neck up" but the ones who do stage work seem to get much further in this game.* **LESLIE JORDAN,** Emmy-Award-Winning Actor

Audition and Work: Whether you get auditions from agents, teachers, friends, through online casting websites or on your own, go out for acting work as much as possible. Whether it is for money, for experience, to make contacts, to help friends, or build your resume, be a working actor – audition for everything. The more auditions you do, the greater your chance to work. The more you work, the more contacts you make that can help you get more, bigger and better roles. Don't find reasons not to audition. Instead, create opportunities to audition.

Job Flexibility: It is impossible to continue on this plan (for those pursuing an acting career) unless you have work that has flexible hours. Being a starving actor is unnecessary if you have a "survival job" that supports the demands of your acting career as well as your life. In order to go on auditions and do acting work, it is best when actors have their own businesses or have jobs that give them the ability to take time off, exchange shifts, make up hours or finish work at another time. If you don't have that kind of job, you should contemplate making a change. (Numerous suggestions for actor-friendly jobs are offered in the "Earning" section of Chapter Six.) You have been preparing to be an actor for twenty-one months. Having time to go out on auditions without jeopardizing your income is crucial to your career.

> *Your best auditions will be for jobs that you don't "need" for the money. That "need" walks in the room with you if you are in financial straits. It can be a major problem in your craft. When you are "trying to get the job for money," you are NOT focused on doing your job as an actor…you are focused on handling your desperation. Not a good place to audition from.* **LAURI JOHNSON,** Entertainment Industry Life Coach

Interning:

> INTERN: *An actor who works, usually part time for a limited period, at a low-level assistant, "go-to" job for very little or (most often) no money, for agents, managers or casting directors in order to learn about the industry and gain in-the-field experience.*

If you are living in a major or secondary entertainment market, contact an agent, manager or casting director or maybe a producer or director and volunteer to intern. Interning is a fabulous way to learn how and why actors are selected; what happens before, during and after auditions; what actors can do to help themselves and what they do that is detrimental; and what industry professionals do and how it impacts actors. It is also a great way to make contacts. I suggest staying two to three months. If you want more insights and exposure then volunteer to intern for another industry pro.

> *Our interns are asked to stay for three months and work five to ten hours per week.* **ABBY GIRVIN,** Owner of DDO Agency

Often the industry pro whom you are interning for will ask you to audition or help him or her with auditions. If you are prepared, many times this great learning experience can lead to work. That is why I suggest that you don't intern before you are ready to audition – you may only get one shot with them.

Managers: To have a manager or not have a manager, that is the question. It used to be that actors only got one when they had a career to manage. A manager's primary job was to make career choices and oversee the talent's agent(s). Today, each manager's job description is self-created. The competition is so fierce that many actors need to get one in order to secure an agent. A large number of managers submit actors for acting work (whether they have agents or not) – even though it is not permitted. Some will take on clients who are brand new, with a great look and personality but who have never studied, then they oversee their training and development and help get them representation. The prominent ones only sign actors who are already established and working.

You will need to decide if a manager would be beneficial at the juncture. In Chapter Eleven, I will cover in detail the job descriptions and differences between agents and managers.

....

Here it is already, the last leg of your two-year plan. Those who have been devoted are now strong actors and have accomplished more for their careers than 80 percent of the actors who started at the same time. If you are talented or gifted, prepared for the business and smart, with any luck, all of this hard work (that hopefully you have loved) should start to pay off.

LAST THREE MONTHS OF THE SECOND YEAR

- Continue training
- Do theatrical productions
- Take new pictures
- Build credits and contacts
- Update resume
- Do showcases and audition workshops
- Create a project or showcase for yourself
- Market yourself
- Secure a theatrical agent and start auditioning for roles in film, TV and theatre
- Continue to audition for commercials
- Network and submit yourself for acting work

Training: I am, once again, mentioning the importance of staying in your acting class and doing as much rehearsal as you can for all the same reasons I talked about in the previous periods. Money, work, health or family might be pulling at you for more time and it might look as if you could skip a few months. Trust me, if you take a break now, in a few years when you look back at this juncture, you will probably be able to see how the hiatus took a toll on your development. Stay determined to be the best actor you can be and remain passionate about your commitment.

At this point in The Plan, if you are doing a major role in a theatrical production, then it would be okay to take a break from your acting class or not do a second class or audition workshop during the rehearsal and run of the show. Go right back to your class(es) when the production is finished.

> *Some actors take much longer to develop their craft in an acting class, depending on the individual, the educator, and the city in which they're studying.* **BERNARD TELSEY,** New York Theatre and Film Casting Director

Theatre: To help you grow as an actor, continue to audition for and perform in reputable theatrical productions. Many actors are only interested in these as showcase vehicles. Granted it is a wonderful opportunity more times than not to expose your acting work, but that shouldn't be your primary purpose.

> *I suggest that new actors do theatre because it is a great place to work your acting muscle and get exposure.* **DAVID SWEENEY,** Los Angeles Talent Manager

It is equally important not to work with bad directors and actors who might cause you to develop undesirable habits. With rehearsals and performances, doing a play is usually a two-week to several-month commitment. Make sure your time is well spent. It would not benefit you to work in a situation that doesn't help your development or in productions that may be classified as amateurish. Be selective with the roles and people you choose to work with.

 This might be a good time to check into the ACTORS' EQUITY ASSOCIATION, also referred to as AEA and Equity. Once qualified, this union is for actors who perform in professional theatre productions. It offers benefits, protection and opportunities for doing well-paid theatre roles.

New Photographs: Since you are probably embarking on a wider range of acting roles and have learned more about yourself and the industry since your original photo shoot, I suggest you shoot new photographs now. Also, you may have changed your hairstyle or hair color, lost or gained weight and/or realized your type and the kind of roles that are right for you.

> *You will need new photos every time your look changes. Your look not only changes due to hairstyle but also when there is a change of energy, opening up and letting go of fears and generally feeling more confident. These changes will occur from evolving in your craft.* **TERRY BERLAND,** Commercial CD & Author

At this photo shoot, focus on getting pictures that are aimed at securing film and TV auditions as well as new commercial photos. If your first set of pictures is still working, you can continue to use some of them for a while. But new headshots of the improved you might just get you noticed by an agent or CD whom you had previously submitted to without success.

Credits and Contacts: With any luck you should be booking larger roles in prominent productions. The stronger the credits on your resume and the better the samples of acting work on your reel, the more opportunities you should get for larger roles in high-profile shows and films.

Audition for films headed for the festival circuit. Big careers are made from being noticed in films premiering at the Sundance and Tribeca Film Festivals. **AMY LYNDON,** TV & Film Audition/Booking Coach

Resume: Continually update your resume. You should have it on your computer and whenever you work an acting job or take a class, add it. It is important to keep your resume current. As you work and study, you should replace some old credits with new ones that are more credible, current and/or impressive.

Showcases and Audition Workshops: Look into doing showcases or audition workshops, especially if you are not doing a play. They offer auditioning practice in a pressure situation, exposure for actors and their talent to industry pros, valuable input to help develop craft, and tips to assist in auditioning and the pursuit of a career. (Check out the information regarding "Showcase Workshops" in Chapter Four.) I purposely waited until this point to suggest participating in these kinds of showcases. If you had done them much earlier in your development, you might have been paying to be rejected.

Do NOT present yourself to the industry in any way before you are truly ready. This is crucial and why this section is at the end of your second year. Never get in front of ANY casting director with less than sharp skills. **LAURI JOHNSON,** Entertainment Industry Life Coach

Personal Showcase: To get more experience, to get material for a reel, and/or to showcase themselves, many strongly motivated actors create their own projects, e.g., theatrical productions, shows or features for the Internet, recorded scenes, or short or full-length films. If you and a few talented actor friends can write, produce and/or direct, then you could create your own showcase. It can serve your creativity, teach you a lot and introduce you to other areas of the industry. Read more about this in the "Showcase Yourself" section of Chapter Ten.

Marketing: With all that you have accomplished, you are now ready to seriously market yourself.

- Create a demo reel, postcards, business cards, and your own website
- Get your marketing materials to the appropriate industry pros
- Utilize your contacts to meet or audition for agents, casting directors, directors and producers
- Join or create a group that works to promote actors
- Network. Network. Network – go to industry screenings, parties and seminars

- Volunteer for committees and organizations where you can meet industry professionals

Now that you have something to sell, put yourself and your marketing tools out there. Marketing tools and venues are covered in detail in Chapter Thirteen.

Theatrical Agent: The time has come for you to get a theatrical agent (unless you already have one), whose job it will be to get you auditions for TV, film and theatre roles. This may be a challenge because theatrical agents represent a small number of clients (compared to commercial or print agents). Plus, it is important to find one who understands your uniqueness and talent and is enthusiastic about representing you and creating your career. If you have followed The Plan, e.g., trained, amassed credits and industry fans of your work, built confidence and are more prepared than the vast number of people calling themselves actors, you are ready for a good theatrical agent. Being ready and deserving, however, doesn't guarantee anything. It just gives you more credibility. For many, securing the right theatrical agent requires time, resilience, tenacity and commitment. If you have a manager, part of his or her job is to find you one. If not, research agents and then utilize all of your marketing tools, friends and networking contacts to help get you in to see the agents you have targeted. Make it happen as soon as you can. This important topic is covered in extensive detail in Chapter Eleven.

Work For Your Career: Even with representation, continue to network (unless your representatives don't want you to promote yourself) and submit yourself for all kinds of suitable acting work. Your manager and agents have dozens, if not hundreds, of other clients for whom they are also working. You are more dedicated to your success than they possibly can be. Diligently work for your career. Along with your manager and/or agent(s), you have you working for you. That's a powerful team.

....

"The Plan" can be empowering for creating a successful acting career (or a fulfilling hobby). I realize it may appear overwhelming if not impossible, but it can produce results for you if it is done sequentially, one time period at a time. Many might have to make adjustments to fit this plan into their lives, and at times during this voyage, some may need to stop for a while. If you falter, try your hardest to get back on track as soon as possible so that you don't lose time and momentum.

AFTER THE FIRST TWO YEARS

So here you are after two years of commitment and work. You have successfully created a strong foundation for your craft and your career. Congratulations. You can now confidently call yourself a professional actor and can actively pursue your career.

From years of teaching and producing workshops for actors, I can safely say that 80 percent of those who started with you two years ago are aimlessly going nowhere, have cut back to a hobby or have given up. Many have gone back home. And after the next three years, only 5 percent of those who started at the same time you did will still be pursuing acting careers.

Although lots of other actors have fallen by the wayside, there is still plenty of competition. There are always new actors who have done the necessary work – as well as thousands more who have been working for more years than you, are just as dedicated, and have more experience, credits and contacts. I strongly encourage you not to let up. In order to be unstoppable, you must keep learning, creating, networking, auditioning, rehearsing, working, etc. Here are some reminders of what to do:

- Continue to study and develop as an actor
- Do theatre
- Network. Stay involved with actor groups
- Continue expanding your circle of contacts and supporters
- Audition as much as you can. When appropriate, try to get your own acting work
- Do readings, graduate films, "spec" projects, showcases and audition workshops
- Create acting projects for yourself
- Update your pictures, resume and marketing tools periodically
- Market and promote yourself
- Create empowering relationships with your representation, contacts and supporters

GO FORTH and work in theatre, commercials, soaps, sitcoms, TV and films. Don't ever forget to enjoy the work, the process and the voyage.

I think the guidelines and roadmap Carolyne Barry offers are fantastic... it just shouldn't be accepted as a recipe for guaranteed success. There are no guarantees in any business. Every single actor is different. Determining one's individual strengths and weaknesses is the most important step in knowing when to market one's self, and limiting actors to any sort of routine or timeline might sidetrack that. **BERNARD TELSEY,** New York Theatre and Film Casting

MONEY, MONEY, MONEY

One of the more challenging realities of becoming an actor is that it does get expensive. The cost of classes, pictures, marketing, demo reels, scripts, theatre company dues, showcases, union initiation fees and dues and other professional expenses, adds up big time. While most other professions would probably cost you much more, with most other professions you would have a better chance of earning a steady income – unless you are in the 5 percent who make their living as actors.

> *Actors are entrepreneurs whose business is themselves. When starting a business, time and money are invested sometimes for years before a dime of profit comes out. Amassing savings from one or more money jobs or having someone to bankroll your acting efforts is the first step. Do not expect a return on your investment right away. Assume the worst – that like home renovations, this process of working as an actor will take three times the money and time estimated. If money and security are your ultimate goals in life, there are a multitude of easier and more reliable professions to pursue.* **ALICIA RUSKIN,** Commercial Agent & Partner, KSA Talent Agency

When embarking on most professions, people usually have a good idea of the necessary expenses for education, start-up business costs, marketing and the money needed to finance the first few years. Unfortunately, most new actors don't understand or consider all the costs involved nor do they have a plan to finance their careers and lives. That means major obstacles are in place before even getting started. Some get lucky right away. (It is easier to get lucky when you are prepared, knowledgeable and have a plan.) Some have well-to-do families or influential friends. But the great majority of new actors must "get real" and understand that acting is a business. To start, I strongly suggest that you put together a financial strategy so that you can be economically prepared for most every step of this trip. Outlined in this chapter is most of the information you will need for your financial strategy.

SPENDING

THE COSTS OF BECOMING AN ACTOR

To structure a feasible plan, it is important to first understand the costs involved. Please realize that <u>the following are approximate prices</u> based on typical fees and the year this book was published. Also, understand that I have listed a <u>maximum</u> number of workshops and activities you could be involved in and items you could purchase in each year of your development. Although this is ideal, I realize that most might not be able to do and purchase everything listed: therefore, I will also suggest variables and options.

YEAR ONE

Acting Classes

$225 per month for approx. 11 months.................................$ 2,475
(Most acting teachers take a month off at the end of the year.)

Improv Classes

3 twelve-week workshop sessions, @ $475 each....................$ 1,425

Commercial Workshop

1 eight-week session ....$ 435

Books and Scripts ....$ 195

Photographs

Photo session...$ 450

Photo and Resume Duplication (250 copies)..........................$ 150

Mailings

Includes postage, mailing labels and mailing envelopes ....$ 150

Speech or Diction lessons (if necessary) ....$ 500

Gym Membership or Dance or Yoga classes...............................$ 800
(I believe that taking care of your body is an acting expense.)

Cell Phone and Voice Mail ....$ 1,600

MAXIMUM TOTAL OF FIRST YEAR'S
ACTING-RELATED EXPENSES ....(Approximately) $ 7,880

AVERAGE MONTHLY EXPENSE...$ 657

It really adds up, doesn't it? It is better to know the expenses so that you can organize and be prepared. I was taught, "It is not that you can't really afford what you need: it's that you choose to spend your money elsewhere." And "if you don't have enough, make more." As simplistic as that advice sounds, bottom line, both statements are true. If you want to be an actor, be smart about making, saving and spending money.

FIRST YEAR VARIABLES

Here are items that can be cut, delayed or reduced that will trim down some acting-related expenses in this first year:

No speech and voice lessons (if not necessary) .... Deduct $ 500

Exercise on your own .... Deduct $ 500

Hold off until your 2nd year to get pictures and
resumes and to start marketing yourself................................... Deduct $ 750

Barter services for your acting classes .... Deduct $ 2,000
       (Sometimes a teacher will exchange his or her class
       for a student's being a class assistant or a work-study)

If you are approaching acting as an investigation, you
might not take as many classes... Deduct $1,500
       (If you are doing this as a career or hobby, classes are
       the wrong place to cut back)

YEAR TWO

The heat gets turned up this year for your acting-related expenses.
Remember, the costs listed are approximate.

Acting Classes
      $225 per month for 11 months ....$ 2,475

Improv Classes
      1 twelve-session workshop..$ 475

Cold-Reading Workshops
      Eight-week sessions @ $450 each ....$ 450

Commercial Audition Workshops
      Eight-week sessions @ $450 each ....$ 450

Specialty Workshops (sitcom, soap, Shakespeare, theatre, voice-over)
      2 eight-week sessions @ $450 each .... $ 900

Showcases and One-on-One Casting Director (CD) Workshops
(Starting the last six months of the second year)
      One Showcase
      OR Three Casting Director workshops a month for six months
      OR One Showcase and six CD Workshops...
      Average cost ....$ 540

continued on next page

continued from previous page

Theatre Company Dues

    Initiation Fees are rare.

    Average Yearly Dues ....$ 750

Networking Organization Membership

    Six months (Join in the last 6 months of this 2nd year) .... $ 500

Photographs .... $ 400

Photo and Resume Duplication (Commercial & Theatrical)

    300 copies.. $ 300

    Postcards and Business Cards....................................$ 100

Mailings (Includes postage, mailing labels and mailing envelopes) .... $ 260

Gym Membership or Dance or Yoga Classes............................. $ 500

Audition Wardrobe..$ 475
    (Clothes and props that you buy to wear at auditions)

Online Casting Services

    LA Casting Network (www.lacasting.com)

    Unrepresented Talent:
    Setup Fee-$50 and Monthly Fee - $10 ....$110

    Now Casting (www.nowcasting.com)

    Average cost per year for non-represented actor..........................$120

    Actors Access/Showfax
    (www.showfax.comhttp://www.actorsaccess.com)

    Actors Access Registration ....First 2 photos - FREE

    One-year subscription to Showfax ....$ 68

Graduate Films and Theatrical Productions

(Your personal expenses: e.g., wardrobe, makeup, props, gas, parking)
                             guesstimate..................$375

Union Initiation Fees and Dues

    SAG (Screen Actors Guild) (www.sag.com)

    Initiation Fee
    ($2,211 + basic semi-annual dues of $58) .... $ 2,269

    After joining, a member's dues are based on earnings in
    SAG's jurisdiction during the prior year.

continued on next page

continued from previous page

AFTRA (American Federation of Television & Radio Artists)

Initiation Fee , $1,300 plus initial dues of $60.90
covering the first dues period ....$ 1,360.90

After joining, a member's dues are based on earnings in
AFTRA's jurisdiction during the prior year.

AEA (Actors Equity Association)

Initiation fee $1,100
Basic Dues (per year) .... $ 118

Working Dues 2.25 percent based on earnings in AEA's
jurisdiction during the prior year.

NOTE: Most new actors will only join one, or maybe two of
the unions this year (depending on which arenas he/she books
work in). And once an actor is a member of one, the other
union fees are discounted. So, I approximated the initiation
fees for two of the three unions and factored that amount into
the Year Two maximum total.

MAXIMUM TOTAL OF SECOND YEAR'S
ACTING-RELATED EXPENSES .... (Approximately) $ 11,950
AVERAGE MONTHLY EXPENSE ....$ 995

SECOND YEAR VARIABLES

The marketing expenses and union initiation fees could really kick up the costs
to double in the second year. Most new actors might not need all the listed
elements. To save money, factor in these variables that might be deducted or put
off to the 3rd year:

If you are approaching acting as a hobby you might not take as many classes.
(If you are doing this as a career, remember classes
are the wrong place to cut back.). .... Deduct $ 2,000

Join only one of the three unions.
(Which one will be determined by where you start
to do your professional work, e.g., film, soaps,
sitcoms, commercials, radio or theatre.). ....Deduct $ 2,000
OR

You may choose to stay non-union and decide not
to join any of the unions during this second year.   Deduct $ 4,215

continued on next page

continued from previous page

Join just one of the online casting services.   Deduct $ 263

Hold off until the 3rd year to join the networking organization.   Deduct $ 500

Work out regularly on your own so that you can do without
a gym membership or dance/yoga classes.. Deduct $ 500

FACTORING IN ALL VARIABLES:

SECOND-YEAR
ACTING-RELATED EXPENSES.............................(Approximately) $ 6,472
AVERAGE MONTHLY EXPENSE..$ 540

Doable: I bet this still seems like a lot and many might believe it's not doable. You mustn't be naïve. Acting is a career (for those who choose it). If you save money (either before you start or in your first year), plan ahead, are creative and resourceful then you should be able to handle the expenses.

YEAR THREE

Although this book primarily focuses on the first two years, I believe it would be helpful to know the potential estimated third-year acting expenses so that you will be prepared.

Acting Classes ($250 per month for 11 months)......................................$ 2,750

Cold-Reading Workshop (1 eight-week session) ....$ 450

Specialty Workshop (e.g., sitcom, soap, Shakespeare, theatre)
     1 eight-week session (in one of these mediums).........................$ 450

Showcases and Casting Director Workshops
    Two showcases
    OR three workshops a month for eleven months
    OR one showcase and 12 workshops
    Estimated cost ....$ 1,050

continued on next page

continued from previous page

Theatre Company Dues

     Monthly Dues - $ 50 a month .... $ 600

Union Initiation Fees and Dues...

     The Initiation Fees for the three unions are posted under the 2nd year expenses.

     SAG (Screen Actors Guild)

          Average Dues ....$ 140

          Member's dues are based on earnings in SAG's jurisdiction during the prior year.

     AFTRA (American Federation of Television & Radio Artists)

          Average Dues ....$ 130

          Member's dues are based on earnings in AFTRA's jurisdiction during the prior year.

     AEA (Actors' Equity Association)

          Basic Dues ....$ 118

          Working dues are 2.25 percent and based on earnings in AEA's jurisdiction during the prior year.

Online Directory Casting Services

     LA Casting Network (www.lacasting.com)

          Represented Talent ....FREE

          Unrepresented Talent (yearly fee).......................................$120

     Now Casting (www.nowcasting.com)

          Unrepresented actors (yearly fee) $120

     Actors Access/Showfax (www.showfax.com)

          Actors Access Registration ....FREE

          One-year subscription to Showfax ....$ 68

Photographs ....$ 475

Photo and Resume Duplication (commercial & theatrical)

     300 copies...$ 250

Postcard and Business Cards ....$ 150

Mailings

     Includes postage, mailing labels and mailing envelopes .... $ 260

continued on next page

continued from previous page

Gym Membership or Dance or Yoga Classes .... $ 500

Audition Wardrobe...$ 550

Graduate Films and Theatrical Productions
        (Your personal expenses, e.g., wardrobe,
        makeup, props, gas, parking)   guesstimate.......... $ 300

TOTAL OF THIRD YEAR'S
ACTING-RELATED EXPENSES..............................(Approximately) $ 9,181

AVERAGE MONTHLY EXPENSE.. $ 765

THIRD YEAR VARIABLES

Possible additional expense: If you joined one or more unions in the 2nd year, you may need to join the other one(s) this year. ....Add $1,406-$3,867

The following are more suggestions to save money:

Take only six months of acting classes: .... Deduct $ 1,375

> I suggest (if at all possible) you stay in your acting class unless you are doing a theatrical production, working on a film or if you just need to take a break for a short time to do another project or program that is acting-related.

Take either the Cold-Reading or the Specialty workshops: .... Deduct $ 425

Choose to do half the Showcases and
Casting Director workshops:..Deduct $ 500

Subscribe to only one of the online or printed directory
casting services:..Deduct $ 263

Work out on your own so that you can go without a gym
membership or dance/yoga classes: ....Deduct $ 500

If you are only paying dues to one union: ....Deduct $ 225

Plus, whatever other ways you can find to save money,
e.g., bartering or doing class assistant work.

continued on next page

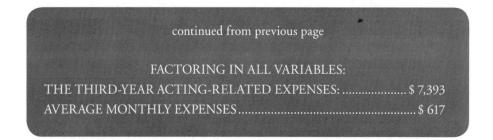

continued from previous page

FACTORING IN ALL VARIABLES:
THE THIRD-YEAR ACTING-RELATED EXPENSES: .... $ 7,393
AVERAGE MONTHLY EXPENSES .... $ 617

The Total: If you do everything that is listed for these first three years, the total would be around $29,000. It sounds like a lot. But if you compared that amount to what it would cost for three years to go a university or trade school to get the necessary education to pursue any career, the $29,000 would look like a deal.

Recommendations: Many actors will invest in their training during the first year and when the time comes for marketing and union expenses in the second year they are not financially prepared and thus often miss work opportunities. Or they might stop training, which will arrest their growth as an actor. Here are suggestions that can help:

- Plan for all of your expenses. Along with the acting expenses, factor into your budget the costs of living: home or apartment, food, phone(s), vitamins, medicines, eating out, insurance, gasoline, car payments, movies, transportation, recreation, phones, Internet and cable access, appearance and health and every other possible expenditure. (These living expenses would be the same with any profession that you pursue.) Once you have a clear financial picture, you will know how much you really need to earn.

TIP Know that everything will cost more than you thought. You can count on it. So factor at least a 15 percent cushion into your best estimate of your basic living expenses.

- Make money. My strongest money advice (especially in the first year) is to work at the best-paying job possible. Many have several jobs in order to support themselves and their careers. It can be overwhelming, but realize it is just part of <u>your</u> game plan. Don't be afraid to take a day job during the first year when you are training. It's not a necessity at this time to keep your days free for auditions. I believe it is very important to focus all your attention on training and making as much money as you can. This way you should have the money to pay for your training, marketing and promotion as well as joining the union(s) in your second year.

You might consider getting an entry-level job in the entertainment business for which you also have an interest. It is an opportunity to make contacts that might help you as an actor, and if you decide not to pursue an acting career, you would have established a foothold in this other field during this time.

- For those who are pursuing an acting career, I recommend that at the beginning of the plan, you open a bank account just for acting-related expenses. A separate account will help you to keep your acting expenditures organized and it is the best way to justify these expenses for tax purposes. Each month, deposit a minimum of $850 (if at all possible). This amount will cover the monthly acting expenditures plus provide savings for your future business expenses.

For those approaching acting as an investigation or a hobby and not taking on all the "Year One Expenses," $350 to $500 is a reasonable amount to deposit monthly into your designated account. This should cover your training and some marketing expenses. It is realistically what you will need to spend to definitively determine if this is a hobby or career and to facilitate continuing after the first year. If you decide that acting is not for you, you will have money saved to start your next investigation.

....

AFTER YEAR THREE

There will continue to be money spent to develop your craft as well as to promote your career. The amount depends on the training, personal development and marketing you choose to do. The good news is your foundation acting expenses will be behind you. Now pursue your career and continue to develop your craft with all of your focus, energy, intelligence and whatever money needs to be spent.

 DISCLAIMER: I truly believe that the money spent on the workshops, activities and products that I have outlined in my three-year plan will give you a better chance of becoming a quality actor as well as creating more opportunities for becoming successful. But spending this money does not guarantee you one job, nor does it mean that you won't succeed if you don't spend it.

SAVING

An important key to having the money for your training and marketing could be how you save on your expenses.

MONEY SAVING TIPS

MANAGE YOUR APARTMENT COMPLEX - The managers of apartment complexes get their apartments for free or at a reduced rate. Often they earn a salary depending on the size of the complex, the responsibilities and the manager's skills. If this interests you, I recommend you find out about apartment manager training classes. Once you're certified, those running the programs sometimes give out a list of apartments that need managers or you can check the want ads.

 Do not take on a building that has more than 24 units. Larger complexes usually require too much time and might make it difficult to do all you need to do for your career. And I suggest that you negotiate with the building owners to pay for all or at least half your cell phone bills. You will be on the phone a lot for this job.

HOUSE SITTING / CARETAKING / NANNY - Three possibilities for a free place to live:

- House-sitting: If you don't have many personal possessions or furniture, taking care of other people's homes while they are out of town could be a great way to get free lodging. Often the homes are comfortable and well-appointed. If there are responsibilities, e.g., taking care of the pets or plants, there might be a stipend. The disadvantage to this living arrangement is that there will be times when you are between assignments and will have no place to live. So house-sitting is best used as a temporary situation to save money.

- Caretaking: Often elderly or disabled people prefer to have someone living with them to help with driving, cooking, shopping, errands, cleaning, etc. If you have references and are licensed though an agency, you usually make a salary as well.

- Nanny: Live-in caretakers of babies or children normally are also provided with meals and a negotiated salary.

SHARE AN APARTMENT OR HOUSE - If you are single, find one or more room-mates who would be compatible to share an apartment or house with. Many find roommates whom they have met in class, at survival jobs or through friends. Some have good luck with services that match up roommates. It is usually best if the person you share with is someone you know fairly well.

 There are often nightmare roommates or those with whom you are not compatible. Unless you know the person well, I suggest that you secure the apartment or house in your name and choose the person with whom you want to share. If you don't know the person, be sure to get references. Create a written agreement stating the conditions under which the roommate can live in your place and get a security deposit. This way, if the living arrangement does not work, you have the right to ask the person to move out. Thus, you are in control of your home.

START YOUR OWN NETWORKING GROUP - Select 10–15 actors who are friends or whom you have worked with in classes or on projects and put together your own networking group. Set up a regular meeting time, for several hours each week or every other week or at the very least once a month. In Chapter Ten, I will lay out tips to help make your group beneficial.

CREATE A COLD-READING PRACTICE GROUP - Organize a few actors to get together on a regular basis. (If you have a networking group, the same people could do cold-reading workouts.) Get TV, film and theatre scripts and practice doing readings. You might even hire an audition teacher or casting director to work with your group for an evening. Unless you can get one to volunteer (which is rare), teachers or CDs will probably charge between $100 and $250 dollars. If you have at least ten to fifteen actors in your group, the fee will be financially feasible for each participant. Then your group could continue to practice what you learned from the guest instructor.

GET A VIDEO CAMERA AND PRACTICE AUDITIONING - If you absolutely cannot afford to take a commercial or an on-camera cold-reading workshop, then, audit several recommended teachers (most let actors audit once), take copious notes, practice integrating the techniques you observed and record your work on-camera. When you watch the playback, you should see what works and what doesn't – then make adjustments. Also, actor friends who take cold-reading classes might be willing to teach you what they have learned. The key elements to get the necessary benefits are instruction, a camera and consistent practice. As soon as you can afford it, take a commercial and an on-camera cold-reading workshop. If you have practiced well and continued with your acting classes, you should be able to skip the introductory level and get into an intermediate or advanced on-camera class, thus saving money. During the workshop and once you have completed it, continue to consistently practice what you have learned. Rehearsing correctly on-camera could speed up the training process and improve your auditions so that you might start getting work sooner.

 WARNING: Being your own teacher for any kind of acting or auditioning technique training is only good for a limited time. You do need the objective feedback of a professional teacher to break bad habits, teach the basics or the next level of the craft and help you to develop faster. If you are not sure that you need a professional class, then you probably do.

While in the learning process, I don't believe actors can teach themselves. They cannot recognize what is and what is not working and why. Actors should go to class, absorb adjustments and evolve. **TERRY BERLAND,** Commercial CD & Author

When purchasing a video camera, know that it doesn't have to be a costly investment. You can buy an inexpensive, basic model with none of "the bells and whistles" or a used one from a reputable company that offers a warranty. Find new and discontinued cameras at excellent prices on websites like overstock.com, nextag.com, dealtime.com, biznet.com, shopzilla.com, amazon.com and pricegrabber.com. Check out the makes and models of the cameras you are interested in on websites that review electronic products, e.g., cnetreviews.com and eopinions.com. You will find that most websites offering product reviews also refer you to sites that sell the products as well as review those online businesses. So if you do your research, you can get a good camera at a great price from a reputable online business. Using this same process, get a tripod suited to your camera. Once your camera arrives bring it to an electronics store and let them help you select the wires and hook-ups necessary to attach it to your computer, video-deck or TV.

FIND A PHOTOGRAPHER TO SHOOT "TEST SHOTS" - Search for new or established "crossover" photographers who want to shoot sample pictures for their portfolios and websites. Or find student photographers looking to shoot assignments for their classes. Most of them are willing to shoot headshots (which they refer to as "test shots") for free. They usually give you an agreed-upon number of prints, but many insist on owning your negatives. Some may charge you a minimal fee for developing the film or printing the pictures, but there should be no charge for the shoot. Get the receipt from their lab to make sure you are being billed correctly. Check with talent managers, agents, universities, other photographers and friends when locating "test shot" photographers.

> **TIP** ▶ Be sure to get a signed statement from the "test shot" photographer stating exactly how they will be using your photos. And if you are asked to sign a release, read it very carefully.

GET INEXPENSIVE 4 X 6 PROOF PRINTS - Instead of getting a proof sheet or 4 x 6 proof prints from your photographer, ask him/her for a CD and take the disc to a store that develops photographs inexpensively such as Costco, Sam's Club or drugstores. Most of these places do 4 x 6 prints at a fraction of the price that a lab would charge. Also, there are online websites, e.g., snapfish.com, where you can download JPEG picture files and have the prints sent to you within a few days for even less. The quality is not as good as the professional labs but plenty good enough to help you narrow down the choices – making it easier to select your headshots. Save even more by paring down your selections and only printing your favorite twenty to forty proof prints instead of all the pictures from the shoot.

MAKE PHOTO DUPLICATIONS FROM THE CD - Since most photographers give the finished prints on a CD, it is no longer necessary to have 8 x 10 photos for touch-up or duplication purposes. Just bring your disc to the photo lab to get your selected photos duplicated. Most labs will do touch-ups when requested or you can bring your CD to a touch-up specialist.

WORK-STUDY OR BE A CLASS ASSISTANT - Most every teacher has a work-study, an assistant or a monitor in his/her class whose job is to take care of the paperwork, monitor the attendance, make phone calls, do data entry and/ or personal jobs for the teacher. In exchange, these students take the class at a discounted price or for free. Once you have found an acting, improv, cold-reading or commercial teacher you love (and possibly have already studied with), talk to him/her about being an assistant. If that position is not available, ask if, in exchange for the class or a discounted rate, you can clean, baby-sit, run errands, etc. If the answer is no and if you continue to study with this teacher, ask again at a later time. Or look around for another teacher you respect who might be willing.

BARTER FOR MEMBERSHIP IN ACTING ORGANIZATIONS OR FOR ACTOR SERVICES - You probably have skills that you might be able to barter for services you need. When dealing with networking organizations, theatre companies, photographers, etc., check to see if they would be willing for you to do designated work in exchange for their fee or a part of it.

GET YOUR HAIR STYLED AND COLORED AT BEAUTY SCHOOLS - Businesses that train beauticians usually have their more advanced students cut and color patrons' hair for free or a minimal fee. They are trained but not experienced. There is normally no reason to be concerned about their inexperience because their instructors are supervising them but I have heard of people who have had problems with their hair color or cut. Play it safe; ask questions, pay careful attention while they work on you and make sure a supervisor is nearby.

EXERCISE ON YOUR OWN - Work out on your own if money is an issue. If you are disciplined, focused and creative, you can get the physical exercise you need to keep yourself in shape, stay healthy and look good. Put a daily routine together and stick to it. Jog around your neighborhood, buy exercise DVDs and work out with them, stretch, create your own weight workout, do sit-ups and push-ups, etc. Change your workout every four-to-eight weeks to keep motivated. Maybe get a fitness magazine and try a new regimen that is featured. It takes commitment but it's for your health and well-being.

BUY CLOTHES AT THRIFT, CHARITY, OUTLET AND DISCOUNT STORES AS WELL AS GARAGE SALES - You can save lots of money and get great clothes (even designer fashions) when you shop at thrift, charity, outlet and discount stores and garage sales. There are stores in New York and Los Angeles that specialize in wardrobe that was bought for actors (and not always worn) in films, TV shows and commercials. Many times it is designer clothing and costs half of what is charged in department and specialty stores. You may have to hunt around and sometimes do some alterations, but the money you save is often worth the time.

BUY GROCERIES, GASOLINE AND HOME NECESSITIES AT MEMBERSHIP CLUBS - Membership clubs like Costco and Sam's Club offer incredible savings on groceries, gasoline and many necessities as well as clothes. Most items are sold in large quantities. I suggest you divide your purchases among room-mates or friends. There is an annual membership fee, but it is only a fraction of the money you will save. Maybe the fee could be split up among those sharing your purchases.

PUT COUPONS TO WORK - In newspapers, magazines, mailings, handouts and on numerous websites (e.g. couponcabin.com and coupons.com) you can find coupons that can be used to save money on all kinds of items. Cut the ones out for things you need and use them. It might surprise you how much money you can save.

UTILIZE REFERRAL DISCOUNTS - Often acting teachers, photographers, photo duplicators, etc., give discounts to agency clients, organization members, students, etc. Check with people and businesses that you are already affili-ated with to see if they have referral discounts set up for a class or service you want. But don't let a discount be the main criterion for choosing a class or service. You only save if it's something you truly want. If not, you're wasting money.

UTILIZE THE INTERNET TO SAVE MONEY - There are several websites that list the best online businesses to buy almost any product at great prices, e.g., nextag. com, shopzilla.com and pricegrabber.com. Be sure to factor in the shipping and handling fees when determining how much you are really saving. Sites like craigslist.com have saved people lots of money on previously owned products.

 WARNING: When there is a problem with the products purchased from website businesses, it is sometimes difficult to get good customer service. Research the customer ratings and return policies on any online business you plan to purchase from and always make sure they are a credit-card-secure site.

TAKE ADVANTAGE OF THE PUBLIC LIBRARY - Join the library, which is free, and check out copies of books, movie DVDs or scripts. Libraries also have copi-ers and often Internet access.

MONEY SAVING WARNINGS

Most of us look for a bargain or creative opportunities to save money. It is crucial to weigh what you are getting against what you might be saving. Many times an attempt to save will cost more money or valuable time. Here are specific examples:

- Saving rent money on a house or apartment that is a long distance from where you work, study and audition is not really saving. The expense of gasoline as well as wear and tear on your car will often end up costing you a lot more than the higher-priced apartment or home closer to the hub of your activities. Plus, the time driving (usually in traffic) could be used working at your "survival" job making more money so that you can afford the higher priced abode closer to where you need to be.

I always suggest to actors looking to make the move to L.A., to consider finding a place to live in between Hollywood and Burbank, as most of the theatrical auditions center around these two areas. Sure, there are satellite offices located twenty to forty miles from those areas, but the bulk of auditions are usually found in Burbank and Hollywood. **TODD JUSTICE,** Talent Representative @ Marshak/Zachary

- Choosing teachers only because they are less expensive, willing to barter, or willing to make you a class assistant could end up costing you time; more importantly it could take a toll on your talent development. A deal only benefits you if it truly serves you. Select teachers who you would be willing to pay, not just any teacher who would be willing to make you a deal.

- Taking breaks in your training is not a good place to save money. Your training is making you an actor. Don't jeopardize your craft. Doing so could postpone when you will start earning money doing acting work.

- Networking groups are about building careers. Even though I did suggest starting your own to save money, realize that professional groups with their established contacts, tried-and-true tactics and established networking opportunities are definitely more valuable, if you can afford it. A reputable networking/entertainment business guidance organization will be able to move your career along faster (especially after eighteen months into my plan) and should help you to help yourself find more acting work.

- Saving money with a less expensive photographer does not always work. Do your research and if you find that a more expensive photographer is the one you truly prefer then wait a little longer, save the necessary money and shoot with your first choice. If you go with a photographer primarily because he/she is inexpensive and don't get photos that serve you then you will need to shoot again with a better photographer (usually the one that you wanted in the first place). In an attempt to save money, you will have spent almost twice the amount.

Your pictures are nothing to skimp on. Bad photos waste your time, your agent's and manager's time and cost you more in the long run. **ABBY GIRVIN,** Owner of DDO Agency

These are just a few examples of mistakes actors make when they try to save money. So, look at what you are getting for what you are saving. And save wisely.

EARNING

Okay, now that you know how much money you could be spending and saving, let's take a look at occupations and part-time jobs. During the first year or so of my plan, you should have a full-time job or several jobs that

- earns you enough money for living expenses and classes as well as enough to save for marketing your career in the second year
- provides time flexibility so you can audition and do acting work
- offers a positive environment that helps develop, not undermine, your confidence
- you feel good about the work.

  If you are in a job that you hate just to make money, you might take that negativity into your acting work or even give up your career in order to stop doing the "survival" job. When your job(s) is interesting and nurturing, you are inspired to succeed and make good money.

  Acting is your avocation. Let it be the work you do from the heart. Trust me, you are going to need a vocation. It took me five years before I was able to completely support myself with acting. That seems to be the number when I talk to other actors – and we are the lucky ones. The goal is for your avocation to become your vocation. **LESLIE JORDAN**, Emmy-Award-Winning Actor

ACTOR-FRIENDLY JOBS

Having a job that provides a good salary and that you enjoy with an accommodating company or starting your own small business creates a work situation that gives you security, freedom and flexibility, and can help you feel successful. Choose your job(s) or second career carefully. The following are the more popular jobs because they are conducive to actors pursuing a career:

BOOKKEEPER AND TAX PREPARER - Both require training and certification and can be ideal, well-paying jobs. It is essential to work for a company that can be flexible with your hours. Temp agencies do find work for bookkeepers. It can be even better if you have your own personal clients.

CAB DRIVER/LIMOUSINE DRIVER - Both require a chauffeur's license. If you want to drive a cab, you can work for an established company. Or you can buy a medallion (which is fairly expensive) and a cab, get a business license and work for yourself. The rates are set but additional money is made in gratuities. To drive a limousine you can either work for a company and draw a salary (the gratuities are yours) or own your business medallion and limo and establish your own rates.

CASTING POSITIONS:

- Casting Assistant: They assist commercial and theatrical casting directors with everything from running errands, sorting through pictures, setting appointments and writing letters to running a casting session's waiting room. This job normally pays between $100 and $150 a day.

- Casting Camera Operator: Almost every commercial casting session and many theatrical ones are recorded on video and thus a camera operator is necessary. Knowledge of and experience with video equipment, lighting and editing are prerequisites for this work. Camera operators usually earn $125 to $175 a day.

- Session Director: They direct actors at the auditions for the CDs, supervise the camera operator, and do the paperwork as well as oversee the shipping of DVDs and paperwork. Session directors make $150 to $200 a day.

- Camera Operator/Session Director: Often the camera operator and the session director are the same person. When doing both jobs for the same session, he/she will earn from $200 to $350 a day.

A great way to get these jobs is to intern or work for free for a month or two with a CD with whom you would like to seek employment. Once you prove yourself and when there is an opening, you have a strong chance of getting hired. Most will start you as an assistant. Once you are assisting, if you choose, you can usually arrange to get training as a camera operator and/or a session director.

After becoming proficient and experienced, most assistants, camera operators and session directors work for several casting directors. Two great perks: often actors are invited to audition for parts that are appropriate for them when they are working at the sessions or because they have a relationship with the CDs; and because there is a network of actors doing this work, it is usually easy to get yourself covered if you have to leave for an audition or acting job. Unfortunately, this work is not consistent for most so it could mean that you would need another job.

CLUB AND PARTY DOOR GUARD/BOUNCER - This work entails ousting problem patrons at nightclubs and parties or standing at the door and checking that guests are on the invitation list. This is normally a nighttime and/or week-end job that hires good-looking, well-built, strong men. There are businesses that supply guys for these positions. Or if you know someone associated with the club or party or happen to be at the right place at the right time, you could get the job on your own. The money is set or can be negotiable, based on the club's popularity or the clout of the organization that sets up the guards.

COMMERCIAL PRINT WORK - You don't have to be a model or even an actor to do commercial print work. All types at any age can do it. You will need an agent to be considered for the majority of this work. (There are some print jobs that you can submit yourself for online.) When you get an appointment, you go to the office of the client's photographer or the advertising agency to meet those in charge and shoot one or two audition photos. Sometimes print jobs are booked off your headshot(s) without an audition. The fee you earn for this work is based on what your agent negotiates per hour, day, or week or for the whole job; if product exclusivity is required; and whether or not travel is involved. Most actors can, at best, make a supplemental income doing commercial print jobs.

DOG-WALKER AND CAT CARETAKER - If you are good with animals and enjoy taking care of them, this job might be right for you. Animal owners who work long hours or go out of town often need help with their pets.

- With dogs you could be required to feed them, walk them around the neighborhood, take them to a public dog park or trail, pick up after them and, if needed, give medications and take and pick them up at the veterinarian.

- Cats need to be fed, cared for, played with, their litter box cleaned once or twice daily and if needed, given medications and taken to and picked up at the vet.

The money earned is based on experience, the number of pets, whether walking dogs or looking after cats, certifications, if it is a regular gig, a few days or weeks and, of course, what is negotiated. Normally, they earn from $15 to $45 an hour. Often dog-walkers walk a few dogs at a time, which means they can make more per hour. If there is house-sitting involved while caring for the pet(s), add an additional $25 to $60 a day depending on whether you are staying the night or the number of times you visit a day.

EXTRA WORK - Extras are the people with no dialogue who fill the background in TV shows, movies, commercials, music videos and industrial films. It may seem easy, but this can be tedious work, with lengthy periods of waiting-to-work (often in uncomfortable situations), long, late hours and lots of standing, sitting or walking when the shooting starts. Once registered with a "Call In" service, if you are right for the kind of extras they are hiring, you will be contacted and booked for a day, week, month or longer. For more information on doing "extra" work, check sag.org and aftra.org.

FIREMAN AND AIRLINE ATTENDANT - Many actors are firemen or airline attendants. They often work a two- or three-day shift and have the rest of the week to pursue acting work. These jobs require training and certification(s), pay well and have health benefits. I believe both jobs are probably better for those pursuing acting as a hobby because it can take years to accrue the seniority necessary to arrange schedules that are conducive to pursuing an acting career.

HOUSE PAINTER, HANDYMAN AND CONSTRUCTION WORKER - Lots of actors work as painters, handymen and construction workers. Many work for companies or contractors and some have their own businesses. It is physically demanding and can be creatively satisfying. It averages from $15 to $45 an hour or from $100 to $600 a day. The money earned depends on the clients, your experience and level of expertise and, if you are in business for yourself, your ability to market yourself.

 WARNING: Extras are often told that they will only be needed for a few hours and then have to stay on the set well into the evening. If you have a class, are in a play or have something you must do that evening, play it safe and turn down that day's work. There will be other opportunities to work as an extra.

Money earned for doing "extra" work:

- Non-union extras are paid a minimum of $50 (for an eight-hour day) plus overtime.

- SAG extras make a minimum of $130 for film and TV shows and $291.80 a day for commercials: plus there is the possibility of earning overtime and penalties.

- AFTRA extras earn a minimum of $130 when working on TV soap operas and $119 for other AFTRA television programs.

MASSEUSE, MASSEUR, FACIALIST OR PHYSICAL THERAPIST - These jobs require a training program, certification(s) and a license. Once this is accomplished, masseuses, facialists and physical therapists can make anywhere from $25 to $150 a session (plus gratuities) depending on their clientele, service offered, location and whether they work at a spa, a facility or for themselves.

NANNY - A nanny (female or male) assists with the care of a baby or young children during the day or evening. This job usually requires references and often certifications and a license. Most families hire licensed nannies through employment agencies. It is best for new actors only during the initial training period – when responsible for childcare it is impossible to get away for auditions. A weekend nanny would be a good job after the first eighteen months of my plan. The money is negotiated and depends on the hours, certifications, number of kids, responsibilities, if you live-in and the clients. If you do a live-in situation, you save money on food, gas and lodgings.

NIGHT-SHIFT EMPLOYEES - Hospitals, hotels, police stations, grocery stores and many corporate businesses have night-shift employees, e.g., customer service agents, data-entry people, restockers, security, receptionists, orderlies and nurses. Sometimes nighttime employees will get more per hour than those doing the same job during the day.

OUTSIDE SALES - Doing outside-the-office sales work can be an ideal job because you are usually able to schedule most of your client appointments around your auditions and acting work. The amount of money you can make depends on the product, the territory, your contacts and your skill as a salesperson. Many sales jobs are minimum wage plus commissions and normally include expenses. Specialized sales jobs, depending on the product, require a certification(s) and/or training. Some examples: selling medical supplies requires an academic degree and a license; real estate brokers must take a course and pass a test; some sales jobs, e.g. magazine advertising and multi-level marketing, require training from the company.

 When selecting a product to sell I recommend you choose one that you believe in, really understand and feel good about selling.

PARTY OR CLUB DJ'S - This job offers a chance to work with music, socialize, network, be in the center of the party scene and work nights and weekends. The money earned depends on the club or party planner doing the hiring. It is an enjoyable, creative job that (for most) supplies additional income.

PERSONAL ASSISTANT - Being a personal assistant can involve all kinds of tasks: errands, phone calls, writing letters, mailings, general office work, research, overseeing workers, shopping, walking dogs, changing cat litter, making signs, putting together scrapbooks, organizing projects, data-entry – whatever is needed at the moment or on a regular basis. The pay ranges from $10 to $35 an hour depending on references, skills, number of hours and clientele. There are agencies that find jobs for personal assistants.

After the first eighteen months, when you start going out on auditions, I strongly suggest that you do not work as a personal assistant for a celebrity, corporate executive or major businessperson. Working for high-profile clients will earn you more money but it is usually impossible to pursue your career. Once you are auditioning regularly, only do assistant work with clients who will be flexible with your schedule.

PERSONAL SHOPPER - If you love shopping, have excellent (as well as trendy, creative and sophisticated) taste in clothes, gifts, food, etc., you may want to investigate earning an income as a personal shopper for individual clients and businesses. (You must be willing to adapt your tastes to serve the preferences of others.) The challenging part is getting the clients. You can start by working for an established "shopping" business or high-end department store and once you have the experience and contacts, move out on your own.

PHONE SALES - There are two main types of phone sales jobs:
• Telemarketers make unsolicited calls to encourage people to buy

products or services. They can work from any location as long as they have a phone and a computer. Normally they receive a base salary with commissions.

- Incoming phone sales employees receive calls from those interested in the products or services being offered. This job usually entails working in an office. They earn a base salary and sometimes commissions.

Income depends on the product(s), call volume, amount of time working and sales ability.

PHOTOGRAPHER - Many top photographers are or were actors. Most photographers earn $200 to $400 for a shoot that takes, on average, three hours. Even with the great ones, the hardest part of being successful is getting clients on a consistent basis.

PHYSICAL TRAINER, YOGA, AEROBICS OR DANCE TEACHER - These jobs require a committed training program and/or certifications. You can earn from $20 to $100 an hour depending on whether you work for a company or for yourself, give classes or do private sessions, and the number of certifications completed. In the major entertainment cities there is an abundance of dancers, athletes, actors and others who opt for this kind of work. It can be very competitive and therefore slow to build a clientele.

PRODUCT PROMOTIONS - Actors are hired to speak (either scripted or impromptu) about companies and products and/or do product demonstrations at various venues such as conventions, special events, bars and parties. The money earned depends on the job, venue, company, amount of time and travel required and the person's training, experience, expertise and how long or how often they have worked for a company. Most actors can't count on these jobs for a steady income: however it is great work to supplement earnings. Once positioned with agents, companies, party planners, etc., you will be able to work fairly frequently and make good money for a day or a week or two at a time. Many jobs are local but some require travel – occasionally out of the country. You can choose to take only the jobs that work for your schedule.

RETAIL SALES - Sales positions in department and specialty stores or in car dealerships are good if there is an understanding boss and others who can fill in on short notice. Retail sales jobs offer a salary and/or a commission. The amount of money to be made depends on the product, location, clientele, commission structure and sales ability.

SINGER, DANCER, FASHION MODEL OR HOST - Actors who sing, dance, model or do hosting can get work through agents who specialize in each of these fields. So with proper skills, the right look, marketing and representation, you could make a full or supplemental income doing any of these jobs while preparing for or pursuing an acting career.

WARNING: Be careful not to accept too many out of town jobs or jobs that take you on the road for extended periods of time. It is extremely difficult to build your acting foundation or create career momentum if you are constantly interrupting the process.

SPECIALIZED SKILLS TEACHER - If you have a strong knowledge or talent in a specialized skill, such as computers, arts and crafts, dog training, languages, photography, feng shui, golf, tennis, baseball, cooking, quilting, etc.,and have an ability to communicate that skill, you can make either a living or supplement your income teaching your skill. There are people, sometimes lots of them, who would like to learn what you know. It's a matter of locating them or them finding you. With a business plan, advertising, word of mouth and/or a good location, finding potential students to start your own teaching business is doable. You can secure a job with an established teaching institution and when you are ready, move out on your own. The income is determined by the complexity of your skill and the demand.

SUBSTITUTE SCHOOL TEACHER - This job requires an academic degree and a certification. Substitute teachers get their work calls either the night before or very early on the morning they are needed. If actors don't have auditions or acting work, they take the job. It is usually a 9 a.m. to 3 p.m. job. For six hours of work, the pay is approximately $120.

SWAP MEET, STREET FAIR AND FLEA MARKET VENDOR - Selling products at weekend markets that you either make or buy wholesale is another option. There is normally a market venue to be found (within a reasonable driving distance) every weekend in the major entertainment cities. If they have a desirable product(s) at a good price, are good salespeople and secure a good location, many actors make enough money in two days so that they don't have to work another job. You will need to get a business and resale license and you must make sure your paperwork is accurate and your taxes are paid so you can avoid problems with the IRS. During the week, at their convenience, those doing this work can handle the restocking and paperwork of running their own little business.

TEMP WORK - Those skilled in data entry, computer research, letter writing, research, receptionist work, and other clerical skills can apply with a temp agency (or several) to do daily, weekly or monthly work. Sometimes these temp jobs can lead to a permanent position (if you want). The salary for this work is based on skills, the going rate for specific services, and the fee the agency has negotiated.

WAITER AND BARTENDER - These are appealing jobs because most shifts are in the evening or are flexible, which leaves the time for auditions and classes. The shifts are scheduled in advance and if the actor needs to go to an audition or do an acting job, he/she can usually get someone to cover or switch. Plus, the money earned can be pretty good, especially if you work for a popular restaurant or club. Depending on the cost of the meals and drinks, actors can make from $10 to $35 an hour in gratuities (sometimes more) in addition to the minimum wage. Caterers and party planners also hire servers and bartenders for parties and events, which will create additional income.

TIP Finding work as a waiter or bartender is not always as easy as one might think because the major entertainment cities are saturated with lots of actors who want to support themselves doing this work. So, if you are thinking about supporting your acting career as a waiter or a bartender, before moving to Los Angeles, New York or Chicago, start working for a corporate restaurant that has locations in one of the three cities in which you are planning to move. When you are ready to move, ask for a transfer so that you will probably have a job when you get to your destination.

MORE JOBS - Additional actor-friendly jobs and occupations that can provide a substantial living for actors.

web designer	online business owner	astrologer
golf or tennis pro	graphic/art designer	acupuncturist
cabinetmaker	hypnotherapist	accountant
business consultant	animal groomer	publicist
tutor	script reader	event planner
house cleaner	Internet marketer	hair colorist/stylist
artist	interior decorator	jewelry maker
landscaper/gardener	security officer	eyebrow shaper
book/copy editor	body waxer	valet
day trader (stocks)	mobile auto detailer	resume writer
personal chef	real estate salesperson	consultant
notary	artist's model	mystery shopper
computer technician	computer programmer	messenger
kids' party entertainer	car valet	translator

preproduction and post-production work for TV/films/commercials

Choose wisely. The money you make from your job(s) facilitates and sometimes can dictate the course of your career as well as make it possible to have a comfortable life.

I don't believe in a fallback plan for actors. An actor needs survival skills, whether it is bartending, dog walking, data entry, whatever will pay the rent and fund classes. But an "if this doesn't work out I can always go back to being a lawyer" mentality doesn't just reduce the possibility of a successful acting career, it dampens the commitment needed to push through the tough times. Do you want your surgeon hoping this medicine thing works out, but if not, she can always pick up her job at the bank? **ALICIA RUSKIN,**
Commercial Agent & Partner, KSA Talent Agency

THE BOTTOM LINE

There are services and jobs you perform to make a living and then there are occupations that are careers and require your full focus. You work to earn money while pursuing an acting profession but it is nearly impossible to pursue a full-on business career and an acting career simultaneously. If you want to be a business professional then being an actor can be a hobby. Also, it is possible but extremely difficult to work, for example, a government job or be a doctor, lawyer, schoolteacher, psychiatrist, executive in the corporate world or even a full-time receptionist. Jobs that are structured for a 9-to-5 day, five days a week and require overtime are not conducive for actors except during the training year(s). Once again, those pursuing acting work need to have a job with flexible hours that is not heavy with responsibility or should own their small business maybe with a partner. It is essential to prioritize your goals and serve one career at a time. It will help you to focus your time, money and energy efficiently, thus producing more results.

I strongly suggest that during your training years, you start positioning yourself for whatever avocation(s) interest you. Then you will be ready to move into one or two of them once you start pursuing acting work full time. If you eventually decide that acting is not for you or is a hobby, the job(s) you choose can help you to develop a business or skill that you might want to take on as a career.

PACKAGING YOUR PRODUCT

TYPING

So far we have covered talent development, which clearly needs to be your first focus. Next comes learning how to package your product – <u>you</u>. As an actor, you are the product. You are not selling shoes, houses, computers or widgets; it is your talent and image that are developed, packaged and marketed. To create your package, you must first know who you are, your "type."

> TYPE: *Refers to an actor's physical image and identifying qualities that suggest the kinds of characters and roles for which they can be cast.*

When you start to work as an actor in film, TV and commercials, you will probably be cast by type. In most scripts, the roles have specific descriptions of the types needed to play them. It's the job of CDs to find actors with the look, essence, age, talent and ability to play the designated characters. The main categories for adult actors are: Ingénue, Young Leading Woman, Young Leading Man, Leading Woman, Leading Man and Character/Comedienne. Then there is more specific typing of the main classifications: Young Character, Character Leading Man and Woman, Upscale, Country, Hip/Trendy, Urban, etc.

A big mistake many new actors make is to think that they can play any role. In theatre, actors perform at a distance from the audience so, with the help of makeup, wigs and wardrobe, they can play a range of characters and ages. Because of the close-ups in film, TV and commercials, actors must truly look the part. So actors are cast because of their look as well as personality, essence and talent. Many of the actors auditioning are trained and talented so it often comes down to a look. For example, a 20-year-old, bleached-blonde, California-surfer-girl type would probably never be cast to play a 30-year-old corporate attorney; or a mid-50s, overweight, character man wouldn't be considered for an early-40s surgeon. Being clear on your type helps you to know what roles you should pursue and which ones not to. It is beneficial for actors to determine their type, essence and persona, and then create a physical look (hair, makeup, wardrobe, etc.) to match that image.

> *I was photographing an actor for commercial work and said, "You're a great spokesperson type." He got quite upset and said,*

"I'm not a type, - I'm an actor." I tried to explain that theatrically you may have more time to develop your character with a substantial role. Commercials are very short and aimed at specific target markets. You have to be an instant read. There's no time to develop a character. They're looking for types: power business executives, blue-collar workers, grandparents, newlyweds, surfers, etc. In a ten-to-fifteen second commercial you may only get one to two seconds to establish who you are and what you're doing. So actors must have a good sense of who they are and what category or markets they fit into – their type. **RAY BENGSTON,** Eyekool Photography

An actor should be aware of his age range, sense of comedy or drama and general persona (such as serious, playful or grounded). Other than that, he should concentrate on being the best actor he can and let the CD, producer or director decide on more specific types. **TERRY BERLAND,** Commercial CD & Author

THE VALUE

Many new actors resist the idea of being a type. They feel it is limiting to their talent. I believe it is necessary in order to <u>start</u> getting work. Knowing your type is not a limitation. It is a distinction that gives you parameters within which to play. There is only one of you and if you are a good actor, you can do all kinds of roles that are <u>you</u>. Once an actor has a body of respected work, then he/she can experiment. Put in the time and effort to discover your type. Here are a few reasons why having this insight will help your career:

- An understanding of the roles you are right for can help build confidence. Most feel frustrated and disappointed when they audition for roles they are wrong for and don't book (unless doing it as a practice audition). Constant frustration and disappointment can undermine confidence. Auditioning for roles that you are right for will improve your chances of getting them. Booking a decent percentage of the roles for which you audition tends to build confidence.

- When shooting your headshots, you will know the quality and attitudes that you want to capture as well as the kind of wardrobe and hairstyles that you should utilize. You will have a better chance of getting pictures that will market you successfully.

WARNING: It is not good business to solicit auditions with glamorous pictures that are not truly representative or ones that make you look much younger. They might get you auditions but once you are there, you may not stack up against the really beautiful/handsome or younger/older people. You will be wasting the casting director's time, which does not make them happy with you.

- For your auditions and interviews, you will save time and money when choosing your hairstyles, hair color, makeup and wardrobe because you will have a good idea of how to package yourself. Determining all the elements available for you to hone your look will be covered later in this chapter.

- Your talent can be fairly judged. Actors get most auditions based on their pictures and resumes. Pictures that represent you incorrectly, because they are presenting an image that you can't support when you walk in, could be problematic. CDs see lots of actors and it is hard for them to remember the quality of each one's performance. If you audition several times for a CD and don't get a callback or a booking, he/she might forget that you were not right for the roles and make negative assumptions about your talent. Or he/she might not know when to bring you in for something you <u>are</u> right for.

- If you "get" you, you will help industry pros to "get" you. During interviews with industry pros, when asked about "how you see yourself," you will be able to answer intelligently and sound like a professional. And with this insight, you can help them better represent you.

- The sooner you get <u>your</u> distinction (after your initial training), the quicker you might start getting work. Don't let the jobs you do or don't book make the decision for you – you might burn a lot of bridges and waste valuable time.

For the most part, your type is a constant but it can be altered somewhat. How much depends on each actor's talent, look and experience. Within your type you are distinctly still <u>you</u> and better at doing <u>you</u> than anyone else. I believe there is real value in understanding that you are a type and knowing what it is. Hopefully you agree. If not, I strongly suggest that you at least remain open to the possibility.

If you have a problem playing a type in which you can most obviously be cast, you'd better reconcile yourself to the idea because that is how you are going to get work. If you don't, someone else who has no problem being a certain type will book the jobs you are creating resistance around getting. Embrace that you can get work playing a specific type. It doesn't mean that's all you are. It doesn't have to define you. It doesn't mean that you won't be given the opportunity to play other roles as your career progresses – but if you want to get your foot in the door, you better know what your type is and then go out there and live it better than anyone else. The sooner you realize this the better off you will be.

ANTHONY MEINDL, Los Angeles, Acting Teacher

IDENTIFYING YOURSELF

Wondering what your type is? Is it difficult to be objective about yourself? I suggest you wait to investigate this subject until you have completed a minimum six months of acting training. You will need your initial training period to discover the kinds of roles that fit you. Classes are very helpful in understanding your type because

- acting classes will expose you to a variety of characters

- the on-camera work will give you a good opportunity to see yourself and study "who you are" as well as become better acquainted with your qualities

- improvisation classes will teach you to trust your instincts and work through your blocks, which will help to free you up so <u>you</u> are present

- most scene-study and commercial-audition-technique teachers will have either talked about or cast you in roles that are indicative of your look and personality strengths.

 EXCEPTION: Often teachers will give you roles to play as a stretch. So be clear about the intentions of their assignments in regards to figuring out your type.

MAIN DETERMINANTS

The main determinants to employ when identifying your type are age, physical appearance, personality and essence/style.

Age: The conventional age ranges referenced when casting roles are: babies, toddlers, kids, preteens, teens, late teens; early, mid- and late 20s; early, mid- and late 30s; early, mid- and late 40s; 50s; 60s; 70s; and 80s. The age range of the characters that actors are right for and their real ages are not always the same. What age can you honestly play? Sometimes our egos make it difficult to be honest. For instance, there are people, in their mid-20s, who believe they can play teenagers. Friends or people in the industry have even told them so. Most could possibly look like one – as long as they are not standing next to real teenagers. At a casting session with real teens, the age and essence difference between actual teenagers and those who can possibly play one is usually noticeable. Then there are actors who appear more mature and older than their real age. It is nothing to fret about. It just is what it is. Don't work against it. Either way, make your "age look" work for you.

 EXCEPTION: Age is sometimes relative to what someone looks like next to people who are working opposite them. On certain TV shows and movies, if everyone who is playing a teenager is actually in their early to mid-20s, it becomes accepted that they are all teenagers. If most of the actors are in their 40s and they are playing roles in their 30s (and kind of look it), then that is the accepted age.

Physical Appearance: The physical attributes of your face, hairstyle, teeth, ethnicity or nationality, body type, weight, bone structure and the quality of your skin all go into determining your "look." Are you a character, slightly character, cute, wholesome, good-looking, handsome, pretty, or incredibly beautiful? This can be a sensitive issue. What you, your spouse or your parents see is not what CDs, producers, clients, directors and agents might see. Most actors find it difficult to label themselves slightly character or a character type because they think it means they are unattractive. In the entertainment business, being considered good-looking or incredibly attractive is relative, for the most part, to how someone's looks compare to models or movie and TV beauties or leading men. I once knew a good actress who was a big girl with a strong character face who insisted on playing sexy ingénues. When she did get auditions for roles she was physically right for, she approached them with the image she preferred of herself. Imagine a tough prison guard reading as if she were a sexy ingénue. As a result she never got acting work. You need to own what you look like and make it work for you. There is acting work for all kinds of physical types.

The perception of your look as well as your age and sometimes your essence/style can be somewhat altered or honed. I will provide information on these options later in this chapter.

Personality:

PERSONALITY: *The totality of qualities and traits, as of character or behavior, that is peculiar to a specific person.*

Many believe that because they are actors they can adjust to any personality type. Some can. Yet, in the entertainment world especially, when you first start, your "quality" – to which your personality is intrinsic – is a label used to describe you. Therefore, it often determines the kind of parts for which you will be considered. What is your core personality in terms of your type? Do you have the quality to play: the vulnerable, confused or powerful one; the comedy relief or the bad guy/girl; the leader or the follower; the quirky, funny, serious or intense character? I understand that all of us have multiple facets to our personalities depending on the people we are with, our moods and where we are situated. For example, we may have a different persona when we are the boss as opposed to when we are the employee, the teacher or the student, the parent or the child, or when we are with our best friend or with someone we love, like, dislike or barely know.

Most people have not given much thought to how they occur to others. If you are not clear and want to understand how to see yourself objectively, try the following exercise:

- Think about or observe several friends or maybe people you barely know.

- Write down or verbalize their personalities in a few words. Here are a few sample indicators you might use: energetic, funny, dull, serious, playful, shy, emotional, quirky, calm, friendly, verbally and physically expressive, introverted or extroverted and somber.

- Then objectively use labels to describe yourself as others might see you.

With the survey that is in the Questionnaire section of this chapter, you will get more feedback that will help you define your core personality type.

Essence/Style:

> ESSENCE: *The intrinsic or indispensable properties that serve to characterize or identify something or someone.*

Your essence is that difficult-to-verbalize "something" that describes you. It is not your age, personality or your looks and yet includes them. Subliminal qualities create essence. Some of the essence descriptions used for actors are: sexy, strong, powerful, weak, spirited, arrogant, cool, crazed, sophisticated, vulnerable, fragile, offbeat, contemporary, spontaneous, lower class, middle class, upper class, city, suburban, country, executive or working class, intelligent, intense, competent, independent, soft, hard, winner and loser. The difference between personality and essence is subtle. I believe personality can be found in what we do and is external. Essence is found in who we are and is therefore internal. To me, your "essence" is a unique combination of your voice quality, speech rhythm, facial expressions, body language, the way you sit, stand and walk, laugh, etc. Like with determining personality types, I suggest you talk to others before you attempt to label your own essence.

"TYPE" QUESTIONNAIRE

If you would like either assistance or clarity in determining your type, I suggest you pose the following questions in the upcoming questionnaire to teachers, friends and especially a few strangers. Strangers you meet at a party, waiting in line, on a plane, etc., can often be more objective about you.

YOUR QUESTIONNAIRE

This questionnaire is designed to help determine <u>your</u> type. Customize each of the following generic questions with <u>your</u> specific three-to-five multiple-choice suggestions that best describe you. The personalized choices you insert should be derived from your teachers and honest friends as well as careful observations of yourself during your on-camera work. Once you have tailored this questionnaire, give it to those providing their input so that they can make their choices – and leave them alone to do so. When interviewing strangers, note for them their perceptions where indicated. Interview at least a dozen people.

> *I recommend that actors ask these "type" questions to people they don't know. It is a valuable exercise to help understand what roles they should pursue at the beginning of their careers. I would suggest taking it one step further. Go out twice more, each time in a different set of wardrobe, accessories and hairstyles and ask the same questions of strangers. You might get different answers. Then look to see the similarities and the differences. This should help further define your type as well as give you an idea of your range.* **MICHAEL DONOVAN,** Casting Director Commercial, Film and Theatre

In order for you to get the most value from this research, you must put your ego on hold. Let the people you question know that you would like <u>straight</u> answers and that you need their honesty. Don't try to sway the person to give you the answers you would prefer. Treat the answers as if they were about someone else – not you.

TYPING QUESTIONNAIRE

- **AGE**

  – What age range do you honestly feel I look like I can play?
  {Give 3-5 choices that are appropriate for you.}

    Example: If you are 21 years old, you might offer these choices: late teens, early-, mid- or late 20s. Also ask, "Or do you think I am younger or older than the choices I just offered?"

- **PHYSICAL APPEARANCE**
  {Give 3-5 choices and ask them for their ideas with each question.}

  – What ethnic or nationality types (if any) do you see me playing?

    Example: If you have olive skin, brown hair and brown eyes, you might offer such choices as Hispanic, Greek, Italian, American Indian or French. Follow by asking, "Or what other ethnicities do I look like?"

  – Describe my facial appearance.
    Sample choices: cute, attractive, nice-looking, pretty, handsome, beautiful, character, average

  – Describe my body type.
    Sample choices: slender, toned, average, overweight, "hot," gawky, skinny

  – Would I play the…
    hero/heroine or the villain/antagonist?
    troublemaker or the do-gooder?
    lead in a movie or the friend of the lead?
    comedic character or the serious/romantic lead?
    hooker or the nun?
    boss or the assistant?
    policeman or criminal?
    teacher, corporate executive, surfer, artist, doctor, student, etc.?

    Then ask what other character/roles do you think I could play?

  – Which celebrities or movie/television stars do I resemble?
    (You don't need to give examples with this question.)

- **PERSONALITY**
  {Give 3-5 choices and ask them for their ideas with each question.}

  – Would you describe my personality as…
    Samples: cute, friendly, powerful, shy, quirky, outgoing, playful

- Do you see me as...
    Samples: leader or follower, extrovert or introvert, cool or intense, athletic or sedentary, type A or "slacker"

- Which celebrities or movie/television stars is my personality similar to? *(No examples are necessary.)*

• ESSENCE / STYLE

- Would you describe me as...
    strong, rugged or fragile?
    powerful or sensitive and shy?
    sophisticated or earthy?
    sexy, sensual, subdued or straight-laced?
    warm and friendly or aloof?
    lower, middle or upper class?
    urban, suburban or country?
    an executive or laborer?
    an authority or someone who needs help?
    responsible or irresponsible?
    competent or incompetent?
    emotional or unemotional?

    Follow by asking, "Or what other descriptions would you use to depict me?

- How would you describe my voice?
    {Give 3-5 appropriate choices.}

    Samples: Soft, strong, sexy, irritating, pleasant, dumb, young, mature

I often ask a new client: "If you could replace an actor similar in type on a television show, whom would you replace?" It helps me to see if we are on the same page. And sometimes gives me an insight as to how to pitch them better. **TODD JUSTICE**, Talent Representative @ Marshak/Zachary

If the responses from the majority of people you question add up to a view of yourself that is different from what you thought, you must accept it for now. With time and experience, it can and often does change. It is important to understand that often responses are based on society's subjective conditioning of what certain physical types have come to represent. For example, blondes are vulnerable and brunettes are strong; guys who are short and thin are weak, whereas tall, well-built guys are tough. Bottom line: Don't take anything personally.

Merge The Answers: Once all your questionnaires are completed, check for the similar responses for each question and merge them. A pattern should materialize that will give you an idea of your type. It might be a generic label. For example

- Early 20s, Caucasian, middle American, attractive, ingénue, urban, warm, sensual – young Keira Knightly.

- Mid-30s, Afro-American, urban, nice-looking character, edgy, well-built – Jamie Foxx type.

Or it might be more specific. A similar person might read

- Early to mid-20s, Caucasian, middle American, (possibly Nordic, Swedish or German), average to nice-looking ingénue with an athletic body, shy, aloof, quirky, intelligent, vulnerable – Keira Knightly type.

- Early to mid-thirties, Afro-American male, urban street type (New York, Detroit, Chicago) with education or has become successful, rugged, sexy, wise guy, strong and playful personality, athletic body, cool – younger Eddie Murphy.

Understand that with these typing descriptions, you are not going to pigeonhole yourself into a rigid category. There is usually a range in each type. How big a range depends on the person.

The Benefits: Have fun with this whole typing process. The description you create with the information in the questionnaire will give you an understanding of your distinct type – the way industry professionals will see and cast you. This information is empowering. Also, it is a great opportunity to study yourself like you probably have never done. You are a unique individual, worth exploring. If you are still not sure of your type, at least you should be clear about what kinds of roles you are not right for.

If you choose not to adopt your typing label and create with it, then you are denying the obvious and building a major hurdle for yourself. When you become a star, you can pretty much do any kind of role you want, but until then utilize who you are. It will maximize the possibilities of getting you cast now.

COMMERCIAL TYPES

TV and Internet commercials run, at the most, thirty seconds. Understand that both have target markets (or specific segments of the population) that they need to appeal to so that those people will buy their products. That is why typecasting here is even more important than with theatrical projects. When an actor is hired for a substantial role in a film, soap, sitcom, episodic show or movie of the week, there is enough on-screen time for the audience to get to know his or her character. She/he has to be in the ballpark of what is physically required (but there is room for some creative casting). With commercials, the actor must look like and be the character because there is no time for development or getting to know him or her. He/she has to physically represent someone that target market aspires to be or someone they can identify with. This may sound like subjective stereotypical physical labeling. You're right, it is, but it must be that way in commercials. The clients, advertising agencies, directors and casting directors must have typing considerations for the actors they choose to cast. Depending on the scenario and products being advertised, these are some of the subjective determinants that are considered:

- Does this person look like someone who
    - has the information (the authority) or needs the information?
    - is working, middle or upper class?
    - is urban, suburban or country?
    - is a businessman or creative type?
    - is the boss or employee?
    - is single, dating or married?
    - has kids? How many and what age(s)?
    - is in high school, college, graduate school, in the work-force or retired?

- Would this person
    - drive a motorcycle, under-$20,000 car, mid-priced car, SUV, truck, or Rolls Royce?
    - drink coffee, bottled water, tea, soda, beer or hard liquor?
    - eat junk food, health food or expensive cuisine?
    - shop at grocery stores, discount stores, outlet stores, major department stores or upscale boutiques?
    - do his or her own laundry and housework or have a maid to do it for him?
    - take heartburn, arthritis or blood pressure medicine or vitamins?
    - play a sport, do yoga, exercise, hike, play chess, etc.?
    - vacation in Disneyland, New York, Europe, Africa, Las Vegas, on a cruise, camping in the mountains, etc.?

- What is his/her occupation?
  - CEO, vice-president, assistant, secretary, doctor, lawyer, camp counselor, waitress, cab driver, construction worker, fireman, pilot, teacher, policeman, detective, librarian, etc.?

You can add these questions to your questionnaire or just ask your friends or teachers. The responses will help you understand the kind of commercial roles and products for which you might realistically be considered.

THE "OTHER WAY TO GO" FACTOR

Often when casting for a role, the CD, director, producer or client will have a very distinct type in mind at the start of the process. After seeing the "right types" audition, sometimes they are not satisfied with what they thought would work, or if an actor comes in with a unique interpretation but was not what the "powers that be" were originally looking for then they could change their minds about the look, personality, essence, age, or sometimes even the gender. This does not diminish the value of knowing your type. It becomes more important because you will know what you can bring to a role. Don't lose your unique interpretation in an effort to be what you think they want. They don't always know what they want until they see it. When I do commercial casting, half of the actors I bring in are exactly what was requested, some are variations on that type, and I always add a few who can put a unique spin on the role. So, at auditions, when you see that the others trying out for the same role as you are a different physical type, don't assume that you are wrong for the job. You or they might be "the other way to go" and can influence a change in the casting of a role.

> *I've had several clients book jobs when they were not the exact type being cast. I've even had actors get jobs when they didn't even fit the category.* **HUGH LEON,** Commercial Agent with Coast to Coast

If there is a role that you truly believe you could play but the character description doesn't really fit, go ahead and work to get an audition. In order to maintain credibility, be very sure that it is a role that you are confident you can do. You might end up booking it because you are the "other way to go." If not, you will have given those industry pros a good look at who you are and your distinctive talent. Then hopefully they will remember you the next time there is a role right for you.

CREATING YOUR PACKAGE

Okay, now that you have a better idea of your type, it's time to hone your "look" and image (if it needs work). First, research the elements that will comprise the physical look you want to create. These are the steps I suggest:

1. Download or cut out of magazines dozens of pictures of the actors,

celebrities and others who have the look that you have determined is your type.

2. Download or cut out pictures of hairstyles, hair colors, wardrobe, glasses, jewelry and makeup (for women) and facial hair (for men) that might work for you and your type.

3. Narrow your choices way down, then show them to several industry pros whose opinions you respect to see if your selections of prototypes and elements work for you.

After you have determined your type and have a good idea of the elements and physical changes needed, you should consult or work with some of the following professionals:

HAIR STYLISTS - Hair is a primary defining factor. It is important to have a hairstyle that works for you and for most of the roles for which you will audition. To help you choose the right look, take the six or eight pictures of hairstyles and hair colors that you like and go to several hair stylists. It is helpful to get at least three opinions. Ask each stylist which styles and colors are right for your skin tone, hair type and facial structure. If the majority agree on a style and/or color, that makes the choice easier. Then select the person you felt the best connection with and whose ideas you like or return to your regular stylist with the new hairstyle ideas.

- Ladies: Wigs are a way to experiment with various styles and colors. Go to a well-stocked wig salon and try on several wigs. If possible, bring a friend whose feedback you can trust. A friend with good taste can sometimes select styles that you may overlook because of your current self-image. Try to take some pictures so you can refer to them when you consult with your hair stylist. (Proprietors don't usually like you to shoot photos – be careful.)

  I always recommend to ingénues who are new to the business to find a complimentary hairstyle that is unique and will separate them from the rest of their competition. ABBY GIRVIN, Owner of DDO Agency

- Men: Experiment with a mustache, partial or full beard, or stubble. Facial hair or no facial hair can add to, detract from, or create a man's image. Or you can alter the length of your hair and/or sideburns to change or enhance a look.

WARDROBE SPECIALISTS - Wardrobe also helps to define your image. Often we know what we like and what looks good but not necessarily what would serve us as an actor. (If you carefully study the wardrobe of the characters you could be playing in commercials, films and TV shows, it might give you some wardrobe insights.) You can get valuable wardrobe input by either working with a personal shopper at a major department store or a color/style specialist.

- Department store personal shoppers don't charge a fee. There is an expectation that you purchase clothes at that store, but it is not required. Show them your pictures and ask their opinions on which of the styles and colors will work for your coloring, body structure and age.

- Color/style specialists will teach you about the wardrobe colors that work for your skin tone and hair color. They can also help with the right styles for your body structure, age-appropriate clothes, fabrics, jewelry, fashion, and metals that best serve you, as well as those to avoid. These specialists charge a fee but the information can be invaluable and will serve you for years. Their input can help you to stop buying clothes that "for some reason" you never wear and thus save you money. There should be no expectation to buy wardrobe from these professionals.

MAKEUP ARTIST - Women understand the value of makeup to look better but not necessarily as a tool to create their image. Makeup specialists teach the application and kind(s) of product that would assist or create a "look." The wrong makeup or the over-application or lack of it, can detract from or negatively affect the impact of what you are trying to achieve. Seek out the professionals in this arena. You can find artists working for corporate makeup companies in department stores and at businesses that specialize in actor makeup who do free consultations. There is an expectation that you will purchase the products that they have demonstrated on you, but it is not always required. There are also makeup classes you can take. They charge a fee and you will have to purchase the makeup, but the knowledge (depending on the quality of the instruction) can well be worth the cost.

EYEBROW SHAPER - Eyebrows frame your eyes. Badly shaped or overgrown brows distract. I have seen the look of many actors, especially men, change dramatically for the better after getting their eyebrows shaped. Women usually do this for themselves (even though the pros often do a better job). Men tend to be reluctant to have their brows shaped because they don't understand the necessity of it, don't want to be waxed or plucked or don't want to bother with the upkeep. However, once most men have done it and get compliments, they are encouraged to continue. If your brows need attention, check into getting them cleaned up or shaped and see if it serves you.

 WARNING: Men, be very careful not to have too much hair removed the first time you try this. If it is, you may look strange, which could turn you off. The first time, have the brow-shaper remove less brow hair than probably needed. If additional shaping is needed, they can remove more the next session. Work with a professional, not a friend.

SPEECH AND DICTION TEACHER - No matter what your type, good speech and diction are important. If you have received feedback indicating that your voice or speech needs work, consult with several speech or diction teachers. Select one and train with him/her. It is an important investment not only for you as an actor but also for your life.

> *For actors who have already taken voice lessons or done Shakespearean training classes, taking speech and diction might be a waste of their time, as they already excel in those areas.*
> **BERNARD TELSEY,** New York Theatre and Film Casting Director

PHYSICAL ENHANCEMENTS

Actors who audition primarily for ingénues, young leading women, young leading men, leading women or leading men usually strive for physical perfection in order to compete in these categories. They often work with professionals who help reduce or eliminate flaws and imperfections that might distract from their physical image.

FACIALISTS OR DERMATOLOGISTS - Most working actors must have great skin. Problem skin and growths, unless you are a character person, can be a distraction especially in commercials, on high-definition TV and on the movie screen. Depending on the condition of your skin, facialists and dermatologists can help resolve problems.

TRAINER/DIETICIAN - Body conscious actors who need a slender and physically fit physique usually watch their weight and work out. If they have trouble doing it on their own then they often seek out trainers and maybe a dietician.

COSMETIC DENTISTS - Good-looking teeth are important. If whitening, bonding, caps, braces, etc., are needed then you will want to see a cosmetic dentist. It may seem like expensive fine-tuning for some, but for those in the above-mentioned categories whose teeth are a distraction, it is a necessity.

OPTICAL SPECIALIST - Most ingénues, young leading women or men or leading women or men do not usually wear glasses on-camera unless they are doing a character part. If these actors actually need glasses, many will find an optical specialist to be fitted for contact lenses or opt for surgery to correct their vision. When choosing to wear glasses they buy ones that are contemporary and are attractive.

PLASTIC SURGEON - If and when an actor is ready to make major changes to his or her face or body, they consider surgery. We have all seen the dramatic changes that can be achieved to make people more attractive and younger-looking. Cosmetic surgery is an expensive process with a lengthy recovery period and is a major and permanent commitment to change. One should consider carefully all the pros and cons. If you elect to have the surgery, I strongly urge you to get recommendations and interview several doctors before proceeding. I also strongly suggest you examine your reasons. Make sure the purpose(s) is valid. Be honest with yourself. Is the operation going to really help you with your physical appearance and thus your acting career? Or do you want to compensate for self-esteem issues? If you are considering cosmetic surgery, take the time to do your research and some introspection. You will have a better chance of getting the results you desire.

IMAGE CONSULTANT - Image consultants are trained professionals who will work one-on-one to create an individual's look or image. They oversee and often choose hair stylists, wardrobe specialists, makeup artists, eyebrow shapers, cosmetic dentists, opticians and sometimes plastic surgeons. Prominent image consultants are costly. With research, taste, forethought, and substantive input from respected friends and industry pros, most actors can be their own image consultants.

....

The experts mentioned above are not included in the actor's expenses outlined in Chapter Six. Therefore, if any of these specialists are utilized, additional money will be needed.

ADDITIONAL INVESTIGATION BENEFITS

There are numerous career benefits in knowing the elements, process and professionals to successfully package your image, but there are additional rewards. The time and effort you invest can give you an intimate knowledge of these basics so that they can be utilized to develop different looks for various characters within your type for film, TV and commercial work. For example, let's utilize our earlier prototype of *an early to mid-20s, Caucasian, middle American, (possibly Nordic, Swedish or German), pretty with an athletic body, shy, aloof, quirky, sexy, unemotional, warm, intelligent, vulnerable – Keira Knightly type.* The various characters she could easily play are: an English, Swedish, or German girl (depending on her ability with accents), college student, nanny, waitress, research assistant, yoga teacher, personal assistant or artist. Our prototype could, within her type, easily do these various roles and stay true to herself by employing various hairstyles and hair colors, wardrobe styles, accessories, jewelry, makeup (or lack thereof), eyebrow shapes, body alterations (weight gains or losses, muscle mass changes), contacts and/or glasses. And men using the same elements (plus facial hair) can alter their appearance to suggest a range of characters within their type.

In addition, this process is a compelling voyage of self-discovery. When you see yourself as others see you, you will understand yourself better. You might also perceive other actors, friends and business associates in a new light. I believe these insights can serve you for the rest of your life. There is a lot to learn in this packaging phase. Enjoy the trip.

PICTURES

There are <u>too</u> many actors who want what you want: great representation and a successful career. Granted, you are not in competition with every other actor – just the hundreds or thousands who are your age and type. To compete, you must utilize a variety of effective marketing tools and devices to promote your visibility, secure auditions and get work. Headshots are your single most effective marketing tool. Other than being requested by someone involved with the project who knows your talent or because of a personal relationship you or your representative has with the "powers that be," headshots and resumes are the primary tools that actors use to be considered for a part. To get auditions and meetings, your representative or you submit photos online or hard copies to casting directors.

> *Today, commercial casting is conducted almost exclusively online and theatrical is rapidly catching on. Casting directors often have only hours to prep and set up a casting session. They will go online and scroll through screen upon screen of hundreds of thumbnail photo submissions. Your pictures have to stand out, say something and look like you. I've always looked at the actor's headshot as his/her first audition, especially now. A weak, nonspecific, unprofessional headshot is like having a weak, nonspecific, unprofessional first audition. The object is to have your pictures get you called in so you can show them your work. You want to get auditions for roles you're truly right for, thus maximizing your chances of getting a callback and booking work.*
> **RAY BENGSTON,** Eyekool Photography

EFFECTIVE PHOTOS

Since pictures are so important, obviously you must get the best. This takes research, preparation and good judgment. There are several significant steps to getting effective photos.

KNOW WHAT YOU WANT TO CAPTURE

Before you choose a photographer, do the research to identify your type and essence (which is covered in Chapter Seven). Talk to agents, managers, professional actors, friends in the business and casting directors whom you know about what kinds of looks you should capture in your photos. Study the hair, makeup and wardrobe of actors in TV shows, commercials, movies, and print ads who are your type and in your age range. Also, study headshots to educate yourself about what kinds of poses, face and body angles, lighting, colors, expressions, etc., would work best in your photos. There are numerous online casting websites where you can view thousands of headshots and most photographers have photo galleries on their websites. Contemplate what could work and what wouldn't work for you. Discuss what you want to capture in your headshots with the photographers you interview. The clearer you are on who you are, your qualities, looks and the roles you are right for, the better job the photographer can do.

PHOTO CATEGORIES

There are several photo categories for actors' pictures. Each is distinct and has its own look, feel and purpose:

COMMERCIAL PHOTOGRAPHS are submitted primarily for TV-commercial and often for sitcom auditions. Actors will have a primary headshot that is usually upbeat, capturing the playful personality or spirit of the actor. Also included in this category are secondary shots that depict various commercial roles for which he/she would be considered.

> *Generic photos for specific character roles that are submitted online can be overlooked because of the large number of actors submitting and the size of the thumbnail shots.*
> **HUGH LEON,** Commercial Agent @ Coast to Coast Agency

Many feel that commercial photos are better when the actor is smiling but I don't believe it is always a necessity. Headshots can work with or without a "teeth-showing" smile as long as the actor displays an authentic positive or playful look or a quirky, cute expression.

> *"Smiley" shots that don't feel believable look stiff and tend to have a yearbook or driver's license feel.*
> **HUGH LEON,** Commercial Agent @ Coast to Coast Agency

THEATRICAL SHOTS are submitted primarily for films, episodic TV shows, soap operas and sometimes for sitcoms. They should capture the essence, character and/or power of the actor, – often a somewhat dramatic quality. The actor is not normally smiling in these photos, but a relaxed smile can work depending on the person's essence.

INDUSTRIAL/CONVENTION PHOTOS are submitted for live, recorded or filmed industrial sales videos, convention shows or product projects. Most depict the actor's business persona and are often, but not always, smiling shots. For this venue, tight headshots can be used but a loose headshot and/or a ¾ shot is the norm.

MODEL PHOTOS are submitted mainly for print, TV commercials and runway work that advertises or demonstrates clothing, makeup, skin and hair products, fragrances, jewelry and luxury items. Female and male model photos show a variety of beauty/fashion looks. There are two categories of these photos:

- Fashion: Utilized primarily by statuesque, extremely beautiful or handsome, high fashion, exotic, and (mostly) young male and female models.

- Model: These typically are for glamorous, "artsy," trendy, sometimes "grungy" or character, and often provocative, extremely attractive, young men and women models.

For submission purposes, several model photos (tight headshots and full body shots) are arranged then reproduced on two sides of a piece of 4 x 8 inch card stock. This presentation is referred to as a Zed card and is the model's business card. Models also put together books and often a website of their photos and print ads in which they were featured. The cards, books and websites are shown to photographers, CDs, advertising agencies and clients when soliciting work.

COMMERCIAL PRINT PICTURES feature a full range of people, types, sizes, shapes, ages, ethnicities and appearances. Commercial photo advertisements are not usually high fashion or ultra-glamorous. Advertisers use these kinds of ads to sell <u>everything</u> from ant spray to zinc supplements and can include clothing, makeup, skin and hair products and fragrances, as well as beauty and luxury items. For commercial print, actor/models or their representatives submit commercial headshots and/or pictures showing them in various activities or occupations. Like fashion models, print actors often use Zed cards as well as books and websites of their photos and ads to promote themselves.

DANCE PICTURES are submitted for a range of dance work: movies, commercials, TV shows, music videos, concerts, theatre, amusement parks, etc. These photos mostly tend to be full body shots that suggest the dancer's personality, specialty or style. Like models, many dancers have Zed cards that display a range of their looks as well as books and websites that exhibit pictures of them in various costumes and dance presentations.

 SUGGESTION: In an effort to be considered for most dance work, it is important that dancers and actor/dancers have photos that show a strong, slender and toned body. There are exceptions when character types are needed: then dancers who are heavier, shorter, taller, bald, and older, etc., will be considered.

THEATRE PHOTOGRAPHS range from headshots to full body photos, personality to dramatic shots. Usually actors submit their theatrical headshot (maybe their commercial picture) and sometimes a photo that captures one of the characters they can play. What they submit depends on the actors, the image they are intending to sell, the venue and the role.

SPECIALTY PHOTOS feature people with special talents or skills or who excel in various sports as well as variety acts and stunt people. These photos are submitted for film, TV, commercial, theatre or venue work. They are usually ¾ or full body shots, posed or in action, holding their specialty or performance instrument and/or dressed in a uniform or costume.

....

Determine the type of photo(s) you need. If you want two or three types, then by studying and understanding the distinctions of each category, you will have a good chance of getting what you specifically need in each.

PHOTO CATEGORY SIMILARITIES - Although these various photo categories have differences, they do share these aspects:
  • The framing is primarily a tight or loose headshot, ¾ or full body shot.

TIGHT HEADSHOT: *A photo framing from the lower neck to the top of the head*

LOOSE HEADSHOT: *A photo framing from the chest to the top of the head*

¾ SHOT: *A photo framing from the mid-thighs to the top of the head*

  • Color pictures are the industry preference in all of the photo categories.
  • The primary headshot (excluding dance, model and specialty photos) will be fairly generic. It doesn't present actors in a specific role, but captures their essence and possibly suggests roles they could play. The exceptions are actors who specialize in specific kinds of roles or characters, e.g., Santa Claus, doctors, hillbillies, celebrity look-alikes, etc.
  • The actor/performer usually is looking directly into the camera (except for most action and some theatre pictures).

    I like a photo with eyes facing forward. I want to see depth and layers of personality from what I see in the eyes and attitude.
    TERRY BERLAND, Commercial Casting Director & Author

CHOOSING YOUR PHOTOGRAPHER

RESEARCH

Many top photographers don't advertise. So, finding one through advertisements is not really doing research. Get recommendations from acting coaches, industry professionals and actor friends. If you are signed with an agent or manager, they will usually have a list of photographers whom they strongly recommend. Your representation usually has a relationship with them and trusts their work <u>but</u> you must connect and feel confident with one of them. If not, find another photographer that you believe will do the best job for you.

 WARNING: Be wary of agents or managers who only suggest one photographer. They should recommend at least three to select from.

If you don't have representation, call several talent agencies and ask about the photographers they recommend. The names that have multiple recommendations are the ones I suggest you check out. Most every professional photographer has a website. View their pictures, prices, recommendations, locations and how professional the site itself looks. Make sure that the photographer's specialty or main body of work matches the type of photo(s) you are looking to get. For example, if most of the better pictures on his/her website are of models and dancers and you need theatrical photos, then he/she might not be the right choice.

INTERVIEWING PHOTOGRAPHERS

Once you have narrowed your choices to three or four names, set up interviews. When you meet, experience how you connect with each one. Most photo shoots take from three to four hours. That is a short amount of time to create a connection. So, it is important to be aware of how you feel with each photographer whom you are considering. You must be comfortable with and trust the person whom you are expecting to capture not only what you look like but also your personality and essence.

Ask Questions: I strongly suggest that you ask the photographer:
- Do you shoot film or digital photos?
- Do you shoot color?

   I'll have clients say to me "Everyone is doing color: I want to be different and do black and white." The problem with that is, on a page full of color thumbnail photos, the black and white ones get lost and are often overlooked. **RAY BENGSTON,** Eyekool Photography

- How much does the shoot cost and what does it include?
   - Approximately how many photos do you shoot?
   - With film, how many rolls of film?
   - With digital, how many "looks," changes of clothes or setups, are included?

- What is your payment policy?

  – However you are asked to pay, do not pay in full before the shoot and/or until you receive or can see your photos.

- How do <u>you</u> define a "look"?

  A "look" is usually considered a hair/wardrobe, location and/ or makeup change. (Some photographers will say a "look" is a character change.) You should be able to capture several qualities within each "look" category or character from theatrical to commercial and comedic to serious. **RAY BENGSTON,** Eyekool Photography

- Do you have a monitor so that I can see the digital pictures during the photo shoot?

  – It has been my experience that when I can see what has been shot and have input, I will get a greater number of pictures that I like, which gives me lots of choices.

- Do you do the hair and makeup?

  – If not, and most don't, whom do you work with and how much do they charge? (Having someone to do your hair and makeup is a choice, not a necessity.)

TIP ▶ At this time Sephora and some cosmetic lines featured at department stores do not charge to do makeup. (They do intend for you buy their products but it is not mandatory.) Girls who would like to have their makeup done for the shoot and can't afford a makeup artist could go to a makeup counter at a department store and have them do it (under the pretense of being interested in the products). Men who need a foundation to cover problem skin should request a makeup artist or go to a makeup place, get matched for an on-camera foundation and buy it then bring it to their shoot.

Some people don't need makeup, especially men. Often a touch-up in Photoshop is all that's needed. Guys who have heavy five o'clock shadows or oily or bad skin may want to do a subtle touch-up but the makeup shouldn't be noticeable in their photos. I'll almost ALWAYS recommend makeup to women. Some women do quite well without a person to do it for them. There was a time when it was all about being glamorous. Today, "real" is the thing. It's about looking like you on a good day. It's not about how much a makeup artist puts on. Sometimes it's about what they leave off. Don't go too heavy. There is a place for that but most women wouldn't wear the same makeup for a night on the town as they would for exercising, taking care of the kids or working in an office. **RAY BENGSTON,** Eyekool Photography

- Do you shoot in a studio and/or on location?

  – If you shoot on location, where do you go? One location or several?

- How do you control the light on location?

  – Even with outdoor photos the lighting can be helped with bounce cards or controlled with placement.

- Do you recommend and help select wardrobe?

- How much time do you allot for the session?

- How long after the shoot until I receive or can see the proofs? The CD? The final prints?

- Do I receive proof sheets, 4 x 6 prints, a CD and/or see the proofs on a website?

- Are 8 x 10 finished prints included in the price? How many?

- Do you do the retouching? If you do, is there an additional fee? What is it?

- If I am not pleased with the photos, what options do you offer?

- What ideas do you have on how to shoot me?

- What qualities in me do you want to capture?

- What types of roles could I play that my pictures should capture?

Be specific about what you want. Do your homework so you can be clear on your type and what you can play. Don't rely solely on the photographer to package you. I ask actors that I am about to shoot what they are looking for to make sure we're both on the same page when it comes to market, category, what we're doing and how we're going to go about doing it. I believe it should be a collaborative effort. It's not about my art and me. I need to serve the actor. Make sure you can have a say in the process and the final product. **RAY BENGSTON,** Eyekool Photography

There are really no right answers for these questions. The information you gather and the way the photographer answers your inquiries will help you to know what you're getting and assist you in deciding who is the right one for you.

Don't skimp on photos. I have seen too many actors waste time and money when they shoot with a friend or someone who may shoot well in a different medium. It is okay if actors choose to experiment with a friend who isn't charging in order to get an

idea of what might work for them. Get quality photos from professional photographers who understand what works in the current market for any submission purposes. HUGH LEON, Commercial Agent @ Coast to Coast Agency

Evaluate The Photographer's Work: Ask to see photo samples of their work. Most photographers will show them to you on their computers. Ask to see numerous photos from a single shoot because sometimes a photographer might get lucky with a picture or two. You want to see consistency in his/her work and the quantity of good pictures others had to choose from. For the untrained eye, it is difficult to know exactly what to look for when judging sample photos. I suggest you evaluate if the

- photos capture authentic personalities; subjects are not trying too hard to portray something that does not appear comfortable
- subject is in focus and the background is subtle or out of focus – not distracting
- lighting is flattering and the photos are not overexposed, too dark or have distracting shadows
- facial expressions are engaging and natural and capture different aspects of each subject's personality, whether it is playful, pensive, warm, sexy, vulnerable, authoritative, etc.
- eyes have life, are not fixed or lifeless
- smiles are authentic, not forced or posed
- poses are comfortable and flattering to the body
- angles from which the photos are shot are becoming to the face and body
- poses, setups and backgrounds have variety
- hair and makeup are not distracting, messy or overdone
- wardrobe is appropriate. It does not distract or emphasize areas of the body that are not flattering. The colors are rich without being distracting.

Be wary of celebrity photographers. The reason some actors are famous is that it's impossible to get a bad picture of them. Look for the unknown faces in the photographer's portfolio – do these people look interesting, "aspirational" and dynamic? ALICIA RUSKIN, Commercial Agent & Partner, KSA Talent Agency

Check Out the Setup: If he/she is shooting your photos indoors, check out his/her studio: lighting equipment, monitor, camera(s) and the place where you will be changing outfits and fixing your hair and makeup. You probably won't know what you are looking at when inspecting the equipment but you should have a sense of whether it is a professional setup.

PREPARING FOR YOUR SHOOT

To get the photos that will best serve you, you must show up to the shoot physically prepared and with all the necessary elements.

WARDROBE

- For the <u>primary</u> commercial and/or theatrical headshot, have at least three sets of wardrobe, e.g., a nice shirt or top, sweater, suit, jacket and upscale casual attire. For the secondary pictures, have a variety of wardrobe choices (mainly shirts) and maybe some accessories suggesting the various looks you want to capture and the roles you can play.

    Commercial casting directors often receive thousands of submissions for one role. We tend to get actors more auditions when they have a photo that suggests the type of role they are being submitted for. For example, if the actor is wearing a suit, he has a better chance of getting the call for a business role. ABBY GIRVIN, Owner of DDO Agency

    I like a variety of wardrobe that represents the characters the actor can play, e.g., corporate vs. cubicle office worker, suburban mom vs. waitress, etc. **HUGH LEON,** Commercial Agent @ Coast to Coast Agency

- For <u>industrial/convention</u> photos, bring a suit or clothing that creates a business or host image. Younger actors doing industrial or convention work for youth-oriented products may use a somewhat more casual business wardrobe.

- <u>Fashion and model</u> photos utilize various outfits, makeup and hairstyles to show versatility and to display a full range of qualities, styles and appearances.

- <u>Actor/models</u> doing commercial print shots need wardrobe that depicts the various occupations, activities or roles they can play.

- <u>Dance, sports or specialty photos,</u> be prepared with the clothing, uniforms or costumes that best shows off the body and/or captures the activity. Bring any specialty instrument used in your sport or specialty (e.g., a golf club, tennis racquet, musical instrument, ventriloquist's dummy, magician's or juggler's paraphernalia, etc.).

<u>Avoid</u> wardrobe that is black or white as well as bright colors that may upstage you, turtle or mock neck collars, clothes that may show too much cleavage or men's body hair and garments with busy prints/patterns. Also, don't wear

jewelry unless it is a very simple necklace or bracelet with a non-shiny finish.

You probably won't use the all the wardrobe you bring but it's important to give yourself and the photographer choices. Wardrobe tips are offered in the "You Are What You Wear" section of Chapter Fourteen.

HAIR/MAKEUP

For women (sometimes for men), prepare for several hairstyles. Bring the necessary hair accessories and products as well as your makeup. Men who have beards might try different lengths and then being clean-shaven. If you hire a hair and/or makeup person for the shoot, be sure to have your own ideas but be open to their suggestions.

SECONDARY PHOTOS

In addition to the main headshot, actors pursuing commercials and/or theatrical work need secondary photos that depict a range of roles that they can truthfully and authentically portray. I suggest a minimum of three and a maximum of seven secondary looks. (When more than that are posted on a casting website, it can be difficult to focus on any of them.) Be prepared with wardrobe, makeup and hair accessories and products to shoot the following secondary types of photos (<u>whichever types best fit you</u>):

Actors Under 25

- Personality/Character – captures a unique, humorous or playful personality. "Nice-casual" shirts are usually worn.

- Student – the clothes a student would wear to school – can either have a trendy or somewhat conservative feel.

- Trendy or "Cool" – captures a contemporary look. Usual attire is jeans and a funky or casual T-shirt.

- Sports/Dance/Outdoors/Body Conscious – an action look that features the body. Attire depends on what the actor wants to feature, e.g., uniforms, leotards and tights, bathing suits, sport outfits.

- Party/Dressy – a "dress-up" outfit – for a party or special occasion.

- Job – the wardrobe worn if working at a job or in an office.

Actors Over 25

- Professional – captures a business quality – usually in a suit or jacket, maybe wearing a pair of glasses. If actors want to be considered for assistants or office employees, this look would be less conservative, e.g., shirt and tie without a jacket or a tailored shirt or dress for women.

- Personality/Character – The wardrobe would be "nice-casual" shirts or character wardrobe, e.g., a Hawaiian shirt.

- Mom/Dad/Grandparents – features the approachable, warm and genuine side of the mature actor – the person you would see with kids or grandchildren. Ultra-conservative, simple wardrobe works best – cardigan or sweater vest might be worn.

- Out-of-doors – captures a farmer, rancher, hiker, camper, gardener, etc., type of look. Attire is usually fall/winter shirts, jean shirts or jackets, sweatshirts, sweaters, and jeans.

- Upscale – usually glamorous, sexy, tailored or sophisticated wardrobe.

- Sports/Dance/Outdoors/Body Conscious – needs wardrobe that features the body and can frame the actor in action.

 SUGGESTION: Actors who want to do semi-clothed or nude photos need to understand that they're competing with some of the best bodies in the world. Consider this before choosing to show off your body.

You will not be right for <u>all</u> of the suggested categories. If you have an agent and/or manager, strategize and get the secondary photos that he/she requests.

PHYSICAL PREPARATION

On my CD program, *The Actor's Guide to Getting the Job,* Terri Hanauer, a top photographer, offers this advice about preparing for the photo shoot:

> *It's important to feel really good about yourself, so work out, take a relaxing walk, get plenty of sleep, drink lots of water. It's very important not to have alcohol at least 24 hours beforehand because alcohol seems to puff up your face. Also, free up your calendar two hours before your shoot and two hours after, just in case it runs over, so that you're relaxed. Then, create some magic with your photographer.*

THE PHOTO SHOOT

> *It can be hard to get time with a popular photographer, but do not show up to a photo shoot after a bad breakup, stomach flu, allergy attack, etc. Makeup cannot hide your discomfort and the camera sees everything. Better to pay a partial cancellation fee than waste the whole fee when your agent asks you to reshoot after seeing the (predictably awful) results.* **ALICIA RUSKIN,** Commercial Agent & Partner, KSA Talent Agency

To get the specific looks that you want or those requested by your representation, before you start, let the photographer know the setups you want and what you want to accomplish. If the photographer thinks it is too ambitious, come to an agreement. For insurance, I suggest you keep track of time. If the photographer is taking too long in a certain setup, you might want to nicely remind him/her of your plan. If the photographer feels that he/she hasn't gotten your best photos in this setup and you trust his judgment, allow him to shoot more.

> *There is nothing worse than shooting one "look" and having 200-300 of the same pose, lighting, background, and expression. What's the point? You may end up with a thousand shots but technically you've only gotten two or three different looks. It's not about quantity - it's about quality! Also, don't over-prop it or over-wardrobe it – keep it simple. With very little effort an actor can achieve quite a few categories within one setup. One example for ladies: Wearing a nice shirt can read quirky or confident secretary. Add a jacket, and you might get a realtor, boss, lawyer, or businesswoman look. Change the hair, add some glasses, and you could be a power executive or the owner of an ad agency. Men can achieve several "looks" using just a shirt and tie, a razor for changing a short scruffy beard to a clean-shaven face, and/or combing the hair differently. Start off with a shirt, sleeves rolled up, scruffy, and a loose tie, and a guy could look like a detective. Shave and the same person becomes quirky computer/used car salesman, or cubical guy. Throw on a jacket, tighten tie, comb hair and he might get a lawyer, corporate businessman, boss or power-broker look.* **RAY BENGSTON,** Eyekool Photography

The most important picture to get from your photo shoot is your main headshot. Frequently actors and performers will want to get their key pictures plus all the aforementioned secondary photos from one photo shoot. I suggest you focus on your main shot and several but not every secondary photo. If you do try to get all of them, you may not get the primary one(s) that would serve you best. It is much better to take the time to get great photos in fewer setups than to rush and get mediocre ones in numerous wardrobe and hair changes and location setups. With digital, you can ask to see the pictures that the photographer is shooting; then you are the one who decides and is ultimately in charge if you are complete in each setup.

 If you have dark hair, request that the photographer shoot you against a lighter background and vice versa. This will help you to stand out from the background as opposed to blending into it.

Don't be concerned about little things that might occur, e.g., a crease in your shirt, a blemish, forgetting an accessory, etc. Most every minor problem can be worked around or touched-up. Being distracted or frustrated is a waste of energy, time and money. I recommend that you choose to have a great time at your photo shoot. It is a choice. You have chosen a photographer with whom you are confident and comfortable. If you can truly enjoy this process, the quality of your photos will probably be better.

> *The key is for the actor to connect with the camera. Think about someone: the person behind the camera, a friend, family member, girlfriend, boyfriend, husband, wife, etc. Allow yourself to experience the relationship with that person and how you feel about him or her. MAKE IT PERSONAL and commit. It's not brain surgery. You should be having fun! Being present and in the moment can turn a mediocre picture into a great one. This is not the time to be thinking: "I don't like taking pictures," or, "I have no idea what I'm doing."* **RAY BENGSTON**, Eyekool Photography

PHOTO SELECTION

Many professional photographers post all the photos from your shoot on a website for you to view. Others will either give or send you proof sheets, paper prints, 4 x 6 inch proof prints or a CD. Go through the pictures carefully. Put aside a time when you can give this selection process your full attention. When making your choices, be sure that the pictures you favor

- are in focus
- are well lit – not too bright or dark. (Most of the time the color in proof prints is not professional quality so the lighting, colors and textures may not be accurate.)

PROOF PRINTS: *Low quality 4 X 6 inch prints of the pictures from a photo session – used to narrow down and choose the final pictures that will be used for headshots and posting on the casting websites.*

- capture your essence and personality
- contain nothing that distracts from you, e.g., jewelry, background, messy hair or bad makeup, unbecoming face or body angles, crumpled clothing, too much body hair or cleavage, etc.

Also check that

- you look as good as you can
- your face is expressive and your eyes are alive
- your body is relaxed not posed
- the picture is compelling to look at
- the secondary shots capture different expressions and looks so that you have variety.

During the first viewing, mark or separate out the photos you like. In a few hours or a day or two, review just the selected pictures. Use the above criteria and narrow down your choices to a maximum of 30 or 40 pictures depending on the number of "looks." If you are having trouble making the final selections, separate out the ones you are pretty sure of and put away the rest. Come back at another time to pare down your "selects" (the photos you favor). After looking at pictures for a long time, it is hard to focus on and evaluate every detail. It has been my experience during the selection process that multiple viewings – a minimum of three – spread out over hours or days, help me to make better choices. Choosing your photos is an important decision. Take your time.

> *Forget "model" looks (you know, those looks we secretly give the mirror when alone) unless you are a model shooting modeling pictures. Save the "model" looks for your mirror. Keep it real. I personally like teeth... a natural smile... shot in natural light. And find someone you TRUST to help you pick out the right shots for you.* **LESLIE JORDAN**, Emmy-Award-Winning Actor

If you don't already have them, develop 4 x 6 inch proof prints. Show your "selects" to friends, family members and, most importantly (if possible), agents, CDs, working actors and industry pros and get their opinions. To keep track of everyone's favorites, mark the back of the photos with the initials of the people who selected each. Your best photos become obvious when a majority of those being polled are drawn to the same one(s). If you have an or agent or manager, he/she will likely want to see more than your top choices, in case you missed any that he/she might like. So, when you meet with your representation to make the final picture selections, bring your favorites along with all your proof prints, CD of the shoot or proof sheets.

If you don't have representation, and after you have everyone's opinions, choose one (or two) primary headshot(s) for each of the areas you are pursuing – these are ones you plan to duplicate as well as post as your main photo(s) on the casting websites. Then, choose your secondary photos for the casting sites and/or for print or modeling cards, books and/or personal websites.

 SUGGESTION: On the online submission sites, most actors post a minimum of three pictures that suggest the range of roles they could be considered for. Since the online pictures are fairly small, make the main picture (the one that is displayed first) a tight or loose headshot.

RETOUCHING

If you or your representation likes the selected pictures just as they are, there is no reason to have any work done on them. Yet often there are improvements that could be made on the picture(s), whether it is to remove facial distractions, e.g., blemishes, scars, moles, wrinkles; to enhance colors, lighting, textures, hair or facial features; or to blend or change colors, designs or textures. In that case, photos can be corrected or "retouched." With digital photography these corrections can be fixed or enhanced by many photographers. If the photographer doesn't do corrections, then find a retoucher.

Be careful that in an attempt to rid the photo of the perceived imperfections you don't take out too many of the lines in your face that give you character and expression. Don't try to make yourself look much younger or more beautiful or handsome. You need to look like your picture. Otherwise, when you show up for the audition that your picture secured, you are not what it represented. You will be wasting your time and that of the CD. With a picture that really looks like you (with a few subtle improvements), you will get called in for roles that you are physically appropriate for and thus have a better chance of booking.

TIP With digital color photos, actors who for any reason want a different hair color in their favorite photo can request from the photographer or the retoucher an additional photo(s) with the color change. It can be useful depending on the roles for which actors will be auditioning or if they decide to change their hair color. This is a fairly simple process and usually inexpensive.

The prices for retouching work varies, so check fees with recommended retouchers and your photographer. Most photo duplication businesses also offer retouching work, so you have options. Whoever you choose, make sure to see samples of their work.

DUPLICATION

Once you have made your photo choice(s) and possibly have had retouching done, you are ready to get duplications. Take the CD with the JPEG files of your selected pictures or the finished 8 x 10 prints to a professional duplication lab. There are two main types of duplications: photographs and lithographs. The jury is still out on which is more beneficial. Photographs are somewhat better quality (cleaner and sharper) as well as more expensive. I can't really tell the difference, but there are many industry pros who are adamant about their preference for photographs. If you want to play it safe, I suggest you get photographs for your theatrical pictures because fewer actors are seen for theatrical auditions than commercial ones so each picture is being scrutinized for a longer period of time during the casting process. At your commercial auditions, they will already have the video of you and the pictures they shot at the session or the downloaded photo(s) or those on your bar code card. So, if they want a headshot, lithographs will be fine.

Usually the lab will produce and show you an 8 x 10 inch photograph or lithograph proof print(s) that you will approve before they start the duplication. If they don't show you one, insist on it or find another lab. Proof prints are a good way to make sure you didn't miss any distracting details and that you are totally satisfied with the original before they do the duplications.

> *Don't use glossy paper for your headshot reproductions. A good pearl-matte or semi-gloss will keep light from bouncing off the picture. You don't want casting people to overlook your picture when sorting through hundreds because the glare was so bad they quickly passed over it.* **TODD JUSTICE,** Talent Representative @ Marshak/Zachary

THE NUMBER OF DUPLICATIONS

Wondering, "How many photos or lithos should you get duplicated?" I suggest you get enough for at least a year by factoring the following into your decision:

- PRICE: Often, for a minimum increase in price, you can get many more pictures. Don't let the savings be the main determining factor. Make sure the photo is working for you before you purchase a large quantity, or you might end up throwing away hundreds of photos that are not getting you results or photos that no longer look like you because you are either older, have changed your hairstyle or hair color and/or gained or lost weight.

- REPRESENTATION: If you have theatrical representation, they will usually submit 50 to 100 pictures every six months.

- ONLINE SUBMISSIONS: If you are submitting primarily online, then you need fewer duplicated pictures.

- FREQUENCY OF SUBMISSIONS AND AUDITIONS: If you are pursuing acting as a career, you will do more submissions and have more auditions so you will want more photos duplicated than if it were an investigation or a hobby.

- COMMERCIAL AND/OR THEATRICAL SUBMISSIONS: Most actors will audition, on the average, for five times as many commercials as theatrical jobs. But even though you may be going out on more commercial auditions, you should need the same number of pictures as for theatrical auditions because most commercial submissions are done online. You will only need to bring photos to the few commercial auditions that are not using the bar code or download systems (but always have them with you).

Several Internet companies offer actors the opportunity to upload their photos, size information and resumes so that all of it can be put on a bar code card and given to the actor or downloaded by the camera operator at the session. So at most commercial auditions instead of giving pictures and resumes and filling out size information sheets, actors simply swipe their cards or their pictures and actor information is downloaded. This procedure is prevalent now with commercial auditions but I am sure that it will also soon be employed for TV and film. The reason I am mentioning this here is because between the online submissions, the bar code system and downloads, there will be less of a need for large numbers of commercial photos to be duplicated.

- **ADDITIONAL ACTING / PERFORMANCE-WORK SUBMISSIONS:** When you choose to pursue other types of acting or performance work, e.g., dance, modeling, singing, theatre, industrial, variety or conventions, the number and variety of photos you need increase proportionately for each category.

- **NEXT PHOTO SHOOT:** When preparing to do a second or third run of duplications, keep in mind when you plan to shoot new photos. Guesstimate how many you might need before your next photo shoot and add on 10 percent. Better to have a few old ones that you might not use than to run out and miss job opportunities.

If you are still unsure, I suggest that you order a minimum of 100 commercial and 100 theatrical headshots, especially when first starting. For those also pursuing other types of acting or performance work, get 50 duplications of the photos you will be submitting for each of the venues. After you give out your initial duplications, you can determine whether the photos are working and/or how many you need for future orders. In the not to distant future, when all the casting directors start using the online submissions, barcodes and download systems, actors will need far fewer photo duplications.

YOUR NEXT PHOTO SHOOT

Photographer Terri Hanauer (from *The Actor's Guide to Getting The Job*) offers this advice about your next photo shoot:

> *Usually every two years you might want to reshoot photos. You want to keep current because having a shot that looks out of date is not valuable. Also, as you grow as an actor and human being, you want that captured in your photo. Please note, if you cut or grow out your hair, shave or grow a mustache, you need new pictures...a $60 hair cut, between new pictures and reproductions, could cost you $700.*

When you are ready for your next session, you can return to your initial photographer if you loved the pictures, they worked for you and you enjoyed the experience. If not, find a new one. Each photography session experience will teach you how to get better pictures.

> *Make sure your pictures are current. Some people are operating with pictures from 10 years ago. Ladies especially, you cannot fool anybody. Your picture is your calling card. If you come in not looking like your picture, you probably will be discounted right there.* **LESLIE JORDAN,** Emmy-Award-Winning Actor

RESUMES

After pictures, the second most important marketing tool for actors is their resume. When industry professionals look at a picture and want to know more about the actor, they view his or her resume. It needs to persuade them to bring the actor in to meet for representation, to audition or to hire him/her for a job.

> *Some actors do not think it is important to have a resume for commercials. It is disrespectful to you as an actor and to a casting director not to include one. As a CD, I want to know what you are all about. My clients expect me to know the actors I bring into my auditions. At callbacks, I take your photo and resume and introduce you to the creative team. Nine times right out of ten, even if you are just there for a part that is only requiring the right "look," the "creatives" will look at your resume to see who they are potentially hiring.* **TERRY BERLAND,** Commercial CD and Author

Resumes present your credits, training and pertinent information and should convey that you are an intelligent professional. In order to create the most effective resume, it is important to address both acting credits and format.

CREDITS

The term "credits" has come to describe a listing of jobs that actors have been hired to do in theatre, film, TV, commercials, concerts, etc. In my opinion, the real value of credits is to give "the powers that be" the confidence to bring you in and/or hire you. I surmise that they believe that if others whose work they know or respect have hired you, you must be good enough to be considered or booked for their job. Yet frequently I have been impressed by the talent of an actor with an anemic resume and conversely disappointed with an actor who has a rather strong one. Granted, the resume is not always an accurate indicator of talent and professionalism (or lack thereof), but it is the one most commonly used because it is usually the most indicative.

THE COMPONENTS

The three main credit components are: 1) Title, 2) Role and 3) Company,

Network, Studio, Theatre, Producer, Director or Internet address (whichever is the most impressive).

Titles: The first thing that is checked is the title of the project, film, TV show, theatrical production or Internet show because it is the most recognizable entity. If it is familiar, industry pros will usually go on to read about the role and production information. If it isn't, sometimes they don't.

 Understandably, the credits of many new actors might not be impressive, but they document camera and/or stage experience to date. As your resume fills, replace unknown credits with each new, higher-profile job you do.

Roles: The second piece of information listed is the role description or character name for theatre credits. This denotes the type and size of roles that actors have previously been hired to do and suggests how much of a role he/she is experienced enough to handle. For example

- if there are numerous lead roles on a resume (depending on the prominence of the productions), those casting a TV show or film might feel confident having an actor audition for or book a supporting or leading role.

- if a prestigious production is being cast, an actor with leading credits in recognizable but not necessarily first-class productions could be considered for at least a smaller role.

- if the majority of credits are smaller roles in lesser or obscure productions, the actor will possibly only be considered for minor roles in films or TV shows.

- when the credits are for small or featured roles in major/successful productions, those in charge of less prestigious projects might consider the actor for a larger role in their production.

- if actors have both major and minor role credits, depending on the prominence of the production, industry pros could consider them for a full range of parts.

And these examples are not always the rule – there are often exceptions. As you acquire starring and co-starring credits, eliminate smaller role credits on your resume, unless they are with a major director, producer or in a prestigious production.

Company, Studio, Theatre, Producer, Director or Internet Address: One or two of these entities occupies the third spot on the credit line. This component represents at what echelon in the industry the actor has been hired. Those who make casting decisions might not know the productions/

shows listed, but they might recognize the producers, directors, networks, theatres, studios, companies and/or .com addresses, especially if they have standing in the entertainment industry.

CREDIT PERCEPTION

I believe there is an unspoken "caste" system at work in the casting process. Industry pros (in my opinion) have a good idea of their position in the societal pecking order of the entertainment business. They tend to respect the choices of those who are considered more successful. This can also explain why some decision-makers are often afraid to take a chance on actors with anemic resumes and why other (sometimes less-talented) actors with stronger credits work all the time.

Strong, notable credits are extremely beneficial, but all credits show experience – no matter what they are. They show that you have worked. New actors need not be concerned that they don't have impressive credits yet. That is not always an indication of their talent. It is usually a benchmark of where they are in their careers. With time, training, perseverance and hard work, resumes will pack a bigger wallop. Be proud of what you have accomplished as you accomplish it. Even though there are many who have more significant and plentiful credits than you, I guarantee that there are countless new actors who don't have as many as you do. Don't frustrate yourself with what you don't have. Let your desire to accomplish more motivate you.

ROLE BREAKDOWNS

There are established terms used by the industry to describe the size and value of a role. They are used in casting, for negotiations and on show and movie credits – and thus on resumes. Each of the major mediums has its own specific role labels. Before I explain how to put a resume together, it is important to define each. However, since there is not an ironclad definition for the designated labels, I have put together a consensus definition of the terms (integrating the union's role descriptions) that best describe the size and value of the various acting roles.

FILMS (Motion Pictures, Television Miniseries and Movies Made for Television)

STAR - Largest part(s) in the film. The movie is either about this character or he/she is essential to the story. There can be one to four stars in a film. With an ensemble cast there are five or more.

CO-STARRING - The second largest roles. These actors are involved with the star or are the antagonists and are integral to either the main or the secondary plot(s). Generally there are four to eight co-stars.

SUPPORTING - These roles have one or several scenes (at least two pages of dialogue), usually with the star(s) or antagonist(s). They can be but are not always essential to the main story. Most films have numerous "supporting" roles.

EXCEPTION: Often, with negotiations, credit descriptions might not be accurate. For example, if a celebrity/name actor wants to do a co-starring or supporting role in a film or TV show, he or she might request and get a starring credit.

FEATURED - Roles with a minimum of one line or a significant piece of business. They can have more to do or say but, bottom line, it is a small part that supports the plot but is not vital to it. There are an unlimited number of "featured" roles in a film.

 WARNING: Often actors who do "extra" work in films and TV shows give themselves a "feature" credit. This is incorrect. SAG has its designations as to what is a "feature" role. It is easy for industry pros to check this out if they are so inclined. If a credit is found to be false, it can be embarrassing.

TELEVISION EPISODICS AND SITCOMS

SERIES STAR - The actor(s) who plays the pivotal character in a series. The stories revolve primarily around this character(s). There can be one or a few stars. With ensemble shows, there can be as many as twelve.

SERIES REGULAR - These actors play secondary roles, e.g., the spouse, boss, coworker, friend, neighbor, or relative of the series star(s). They appear on most episodes and can have their own storylines once or more in a season. The format of the show determines the number of series regulars, but there is usually a minimum of four.

RECURRING REGULAR - These peripheral roles, with character names, appear in ten to sixty percent of the episodes in a season. These parts can range from a few lines to several short scenes.

GUEST STAR - These characters traditionally have a major impact on the plot. They have a character name and several big scenes. They will appear in one or a number of episodes and usually have their own storylines.

CO-STAR - With a costar role, there is a character name and several lines or a few short scenes with the series star(s) or one of the regulars. Their participation usually assists the storyline but doesn't fuel it.

FEATURED - The featured actor is hired as a principal but he/she does not usually have a character name. Featured actors can either have physical business with no dialogue or have one line or a few lines and can appear in one or several scenes.

SOAP OPERAS

CONTRACT ACTOR - Most daytime soaps have numerous characters and revolving storylines. Several characters, for a designated time, will have the major focus and others will have supporting roles. Then often those doing the supporting roles will get the major storyline and those who were primary actors will have secondary roles. Most contract soap actors are considered series "stars." The length of an actor's contract depends on the storyline and whatever is negotiated. Roles can run for several months or years. When designating a contract actor's soap participation on a resume, most present it this way:

Love Lost   Lawrence Caldwell (2 yrs)   ABC

SUPPORTING -These characters support the storyline for the contract princi-pals. Their roles can play out over a few episodes or much longer, and they will usually have one or several scenes each show they work. The amount of time an actor worked on a soap might give this credit more power but only if it is for a substantial amount of time. I think the minimum employment length worth noting would be two months. Their credit might look like this:

Love Lost   Supporting (2 months)   ABC

RECURRING REGULAR - These roles have a character name and appear in a minimum of two shows. Some have been known to recur for years and may even have a contract. They will be involved in one or several scenes per epi-sode, appearing with a contract principal or supporting actor(s) or another recurring character.

PRINCIPAL - This actor is traditionally hired for a day or a few days, will ap-pear in one or several scenes, has more than five lines and may or may not have a character name.

UNDER-5 - Just like the name indicates, this actor has a role that has five lines or less and does not usually have a name – just a role description, e.g., nurse, detective, teacher. He/she usually works for one or more days and may recur.

CAMEO - A well-known actor or a celebrity plays himself or herself or a one-time character in one or several scenes. Their parts can work for one or more days.

THEATRE

LEAD - The largest role(s) in the theatrical production. The story is either about this character or he/she plays the major role. There are two to six leads in most shows. With ensemble casts, there may be more.

FEATURED - Those playing a secondary role have "featured" credits (which is a different use of this description than in film, TV and soaps). They have character names, appear in multiple scenes and have strong focal moments in a theatrical production.

MULTIPLE - This credit describes an actor who plays numerous small roles in a play or musical. Some of the characters will have names and others may not. Two or three of the characters that the actor portrays can be listed on a resume instead of using "Multiple."

ENSEMBLE - Actors who appear as background players or as part of group scenes get an "ensemble" credit. They sometimes have a few lines. In musicals, "ensemble" usually refers to singers and dancers.

> *Virtually all theatre roles have a name. If not, that's the ONLY reason to put "Ensemble." It's MUCH better to list a name if there is one, no matter how tiny the role. For musicals, you should put "Singer/Dancer" or "Dancer/Singer."* **MICHAEL DONOVAN,**
> Casting Director, Commercial, Film and Theatre

UNDERSTUDY / SWING: Actors who understudy the lead, a featured actor or multiple small roles. Some understudies for smaller roles will also perform in the ensemble. In most major productions, those understudying leads and featured performers are not in the ensemble. The swing actors do not perform in the show – they fill in when needed for ensemble members.

FORMAT

Credits have the power to get actors auditions and representation especially when they are presented effectively and professionally. Your resume layout can either make you look like an amateur or a pro whether you have lots of credits or just a few. The basic acting resume format normally fits on one page. Although there are differing points of view on the ideal format, the one used by the majority of actors is shown here:

ACTOR'S NAME *1
UNION AFFILIATION (if any) *2

AGENT and/or MANAGER *3
Address
City & Zip Code
Agent/Manager or Actor's Contact Phone Number

*4 Height:
Weight, Hair Color:
Eye Color:

<u>FILM CREDITS</u> *5

<u>TELEVISION CREDITS</u> *6

<u>THEATRE CREDITS</u> *7

<u>WEB CREDITS</u> *8

<u>COMMERCIAL CREDITS</u> *9

<u>ACTING TRAINING</u> *10
    Acting/Scene Study
    Improvisation
    Cold-reading
    Commercial
    Specialty

<u>SKILLS</u> *11

MANAGER'S PHONE NUMBER, SPEED REEL INFO, and/or WEBSITE # *12

At first glance this format looks rather simple, but there are many intricacies. The following pages will offer tips, delineations and clarifications that will help you put together a professional resume.

*1 Name - Your name is obviously important. But do you like it and plan to use it for your career? If you want a different one for any reason, before you start to seek work might be the ideal time to make a change. I once had a student whose name was Sara <u>Poor</u>. She hated the name and didn't feel good about it when she introduced herself, so she changed her name to Sara <u>Rich</u>.

Before you invest in anything as an actor with your name on it, be sure to check with all three unions to see if another actor has registered your name. In order to avoid confusion in the industry, the unions don't allow two actors to have the same name. If yours is taken, you should change or alter it before you put it on your resume and industry pros start to identify you with it.

*2 Union Affiliation - Acting work falls into two major categories:

- Union: Jobs that require actors to belong to one of the acting unions. When a job is under a union contract, only union members, SAG-eligible actors or those with a Taft-Hartley status have the opportunity to audition, but there are exceptions.

TAFT HARTLEY STATUS: *Once an actor works a union job, they have 30 days during which he/she can do non-union and union work before having to join SAG. After 30 days, if an actor intends to book more SAG work, membership is mandatory.*

- Non-union: Only actors who are <u>not</u> union members can audition or work these jobs. The exceptions are actors who are Financial Core or SAG eligible or have a Taft-Hartley status. (Financial Core and SAG-e are covered in Chapter Thirteen).

It is important that your resume displays your union affiliations, e.g., SAG (Screen Actor's Guild), SAG-e (SAG-eligible), AFTRA (American Federation of Television and Radio Artists), AEA (Actors' Equity Association), or ACTRA (The Alliance of Canadian Cinema, Television and Radio Artists). Your union affiliation(s) makes a strong statement about where you are in your career. On the other hand, if you are not a member, it will say that you are a new actor and you are eligible for the non-union jobs.

> *I can often tell when actors are SAG from a quick glance at their resume. If they have several soaps listed, they are obviously AFTRA. If they have a list of TV guest star credits, the CDs and agents will know they are SAG. The big theatrical agencies remove it. Only put SAG or AFTRA on your resume if it is rather sparse or when your credits are not well-known.* **TODD JUSTICE,**
> Talent Representative @ Marshak/Zachary

Under your name, list the union(s) to which you belong. I suggest using a smaller font than your name. For example, if you are

- A member of one union:

    YOUR NAME

    AEA

- A member of several unions:

    YOUR NAME

    SAG, AFTRA, AEA, ACTRA

- Eligible for membership in the Screen Actor's Guild (meaning you have a Taft-Hartley status or are SAG eligible) but have chosen not to join yet:

YOUR NAME

SAG eligible

- SAG Financial Core:

YOUR NAME

SAG FiCore

I suggest never listing Financial Core on a resume. There is controversy associated with this legal wrinkle in the union contracts in America. If you wish to be FiCore, I suggest it is a conversation to be had with the producers of a project, AFTER they've called you in and wish to hire you for a non-union job.

KEVIN E. WEST, President of The Actor's Network

 For those who are Financial Core, I suggest having two separate resumes: one that you submit for non-union jobs with "SAG FiCore" listed, another for union work where "SAG" is posted (without the FiCore). Those doing union jobs just need to know that you are a SAG member. However, those casting non-union projects might be impressed to know that you are an experienced SAG actor and eligible to do their job.

If you are not a member of any of the actors' unions, leave this space open.

*3 Agent and/or Manager or Actor's Contact Number -

Placement: Ideally, you want to be contacted for representation through your manager (if you have one), and for auditions through your agent or manager (if represented). Their contact info needs to be easy to spot, preferably in this position. Some like to put the agent or manager info at the bottom. (It's your style choice or your representation's preference.) It just needs to be prominently positioned. This designated section should include the name, address, phone number and possibly the logo of your representative and presented like this:

AGENT or MANAGER NAME (or Logo)
Agent's Address
City & Zip Code
Agent's Phone #

When you have an agent or two and a manager, and you choose to list all of them on your resume, I suggest you place the agent on the left side and the manager on the right, - or the theatrical agent on the left and the commercial one on the right and the manager at the bottom.

AGENT NAME (or Logo)   MANAGER'S NAME (or Logo)
Agent's Address   Manager's Address
Agent's Phone #   Manager's Phone #

If you have a few specialty agents, position them across the page in this area:

COMMERCIAL AGENT (or Logo)	HOSTING AGENT (or Logo)	MANAGER'S NAME (or Logo)
Agent's Address	Agent's Address	Manager's Address
Agent's Phone #	Agent's Phone #	Manager's Phone #

When you position any of your representatives on the right, then place your (*4) height, weight, hair and eye color under their info.

No Representation: Put your business contact information in this section if you don't have representation. I suggest a designated pager or cell phone number. Put the number in bold print and in a 12-point or larger font size, e.g., Contact # (333) 444-5555

 WARNING: For security purposes, <u>never</u> put your home address or phone number on your resume.

<u>Creating Representation:</u> Many actors create the appearance of having representation by devising a company as their contact entity. They will make up a name like A-1 Talent, Premiere Group, Barry & Company, Omni Group, Talent Corp or Blossom Management, etc. (If you choose to do this, be sure to do a Google name search to make sure your representation name is not taken by an established business.) A designated phone line or a second cell phone with voice mail or an answering machine is needed for such a business entity. Whenever actors receive calls on this designated line, they always answer with the name of the created company and speak as if they represent actors (themselves). If they want to post an address, they get a post office box and present it like an office address.

If actors decide to create the appearance of representation, this area might look like this:

A-1 TALENT

555 5th St.
Suite 205 *(instead of P.O. Box #205)*
Hollywood, CA 90046
(333) 444-5555

Putting the name of a fake agency on your resume is not something I support, though I know it is becoming increasingly common. There will inevitably be that awkward moment when you have to explain to a producer that the person taking your appointments and negotiating your rate is you (unless it's fun for you to switch voices and keep up the ruse). I'd save the theatrics for the camera.
ALICIA RUSKIN, Commercial Agent & Partner, KSA Talent Agency

*4 Height / Weight / Hair Color / Eye Color: This section is rather straightforward. <u>Accurately</u> list your height, weight, hair and eye color – not what you might like them to be. Sometimes short or very tall actors believe that their height might limit the roles they will be considered for so they "fudge" their statistics. Those actors might get more auditions, but it is going to be a problem because once they arrive, their height is apparent. Worse, they will miss auditions where their size would be an asset. The same is true with your weight, hair and eye color, especially for commercial auditions. Misrepresenting yourself is bad press for you and your representation and upsetting to the casting director.

> *Don't state height and weight on your theatrical resume. What if the casting director or agent really likes your picture but sees you're short and decides not to call you in? Wouldn't it be better to get in the room first and let your talent speak for itself?* **TODD JUSTICE,**
> Talent Representative @ Marshak/Zachary

> *Do not put your physical stats on a theatrical resume – in my opinion. This is the job of your representative, in terms of pitching you. Theatrical auditions are about ten times more difficult to get than commercial ones. Film and TV CDs look for reasons not to audition actors – and physical stats are a great reason. They want someone 6' tall, and you're 5'10, yet if they read you, you might just kill the audition and they put you in shoes with a larger heel.*
> **KEVIN E. WEST,** President of The Actor's Network

Hair color is often important in commercials and sometimes an issue in TV and film casting. With color photos, hair color is obvious so it may not need to be stated. If there is a change, be sure to report it in this section and possibly put a sticker on the photo itself stating the current color. If you do a major hair change, I strongly suggest new headshots, or you could be going out for the wrong roles and missing out on the ones you would be right for.

 Often actors create two resumes: a complete one utilizing everything presented here that is used for commercial submissions and a slightly altered one for TV, films and theatre work. For the theatrical one, these physical statistics, the commercial agency and (maybe) the "*9 Commercial Credits" section are deleted.

*5 Film Credits: Film work is usually positioned first in the credits section, especially when marketing oneself theatrically. I would venture to guess that this is because these credits are considered the most prestigious (except for student films) since often they are more difficult to get.

- Layout: This is the preferred layout:

  (A) Film   (B) Lead, Supporting,   (C) Studio or Production
                    Principal or Featured   Company, Director or Network

  (A) The name of the film is placed first.

  (B) Lead, supporting, principal or featured are the role labels utilized for film credits and are normally determined by the size or significance of the part. They are placed to the right of the film title.

  WARNING: Often actors list the name of the character or part instead of "lead," "supporting," "principal" or "featured" in the film and TV credits section. It's amateurish to list a character name as a role description here. Ask yourself, how does an industry pro know the size of the role that character played in that film or show? Also, when actors list parts like mom, doctor, security guard, waitress, cab driver, teacher, etc., it looks as if they are creating an acting credit from background work. Use the labels relevant to each medium. It is the professional and accurate way to describe a role.

  (C) On the far right, list the studio, network, production company, director or Internet address (when listing Internet shows), whichever is the more prominent or prestigious. Understanding that resumes are meant to impress, it makes sense to select the name that has the most impact. If your film credits are student films, you might want to list the university (if it is an established institution). If none of the names or companies is notable, I suggest you choose the one that might appear the most impressive.

  If theatre is your main focus, then position your theatre credits instead of film credits here. In the theatre credits section I will offer additional options.

- Order: When deciding the order of your film credits, you have two choices:

  (1) The traditional mode is to list the credits in <u>reverse chronological order</u>, the most current at the top, especially when all the credits are strong.

  (2) List the <u>most impressive credits first</u>. I believe that the decision-makers, at first, look quickly at resumes and don't read all the credits. If your strongest ones are at the top, they should be motivated to read more. Also, this way it looks as if the level of the work and size of the roles are on the upswing.

*6 Television Credits: All television credits – soap operas, sitcoms, episodics, made-for-TV movies and miniseries – are listed under this section heading.

- <u>Layout:</u> This is the preference for mounting TV credits:

(A) Show	(B) Series Regular, Recurring Series Regular, Guest Star, Co-star or Featured	(C) Studio, Production Company, Director or Network

This layout is quite similar to the one for film credits except the classifications utilized to describe the role size/status are different. Television credit descriptions are "series regular," "recurring," "guest star," "co-star" or "featured." (These role descriptions are in the "Role Breakdown" section early in this chapter.) On the far right, choose either the studio, production company, director or TV network – whichever would be the most recognizable or impressive.

- <u>Order:</u> TV credits should be in reverse chronological order, with the most recent shows listed first. It is impressive to see that the actor has recently been employed.

*7 Theatre Credits: Theatre roles are normally positioned next. Those who cast film and TV usually look at the theatrical credits first and then view the theatre credits. Both musicals and plays are listed under the "Theatre" heading. It is not usually necessary to delineate whether it is a play or a musical unless theatre work is the majority or all of your credits. Then it might behoove you to list "Plays" and "Musicals" as sub-categories under "Theatre."

- <u>Layout:</u>

(A) Show	(B) Character Name and/or Lead, Featured, Multiple Characters or Ensemble	(C) Theatre, Director, or Company or Location, Celebrity/Star

(A) The show title is positioned first and to the left.

(B) Next list the character name. Next to the name, in parentheses, to clarify the size of the role, state the appropriate role classification: "lead," "featured," "multiple characters" or "ensemble." Many industry professionals, especially those who are or have been involved in theatre, prefer the traditional listing where only the character is stated, not the role classification. It's been my experience that most TV and film CDs are not versed in theatre. If an actor were to list *The Glass Menagerie* as the play and "Laura" as the role, I would give you odds that many (especially younger) film and TV industry pros won't know that "Laura" is the lead. This is why I suggest listing the role label (especially if it is a lead) in parentheses next to the character's name. For example:

Glass Menagerie   **Laura** (Lead)   **Firefox Theatre, NYC**

Just list the name of the character. If the casting director isn't sophisticated enough to know the play/roles, it isn't an actor's problem. Also, when I see play credits with "star" instead of "lead" or "supporting" instead of "featured,"right away I think the actor is an amateur for mixing his classifications. **MELISSA MARTIN,** Commercial Casting Director

I strongly believe that actors should use the character's name. The only time 'lead' should be used is if it's an obscure play .e.g., Carolyne's Carriage   Boopsie (lead)   Hooterville Players. **MICHAEL DONOVAN,** Casting Director, Commercial, Film and Theatre

(C) In the last position on the right, list either the name of the theatre, theatre company, city, director or maybe the star.

• Alternative Credit Listing: Depending on the prominence of your theatre work and in lieu of film and TV work, substitute as credit headings either

Broadway, Off-Broadway, Regional or National Tours;

OR – New York, Los Angeles, Chicago, Toronto Theatre, etc.

For example, instead of film credits, use the heading: BROADWAY or maybe NEW YORK THEATRE. And instead of television credits you might use that section for the second most prominent listing of theatre work or the next well-known area, e.g., REGIONAL THEATRE or LOS ANGELES THEATRE. If you have another set of prestigious theatre credits, e.g., NATIONAL TOURS or CHICAGO THEATRE, use that heading for the third sector where the theatre credits would normally go. If not, present two separate sections of theatre credits and list whatever video or film credits you have in the third sector.

• Order: List the show credits either in reverse chronological order or the most impressive ones first. If you are using the alternative section headings for your theatre credits (instead of TV and film headings,) place the theatre cities in the order of their prominence.

*8 Web Credits: Acting work that is produced for and runs on the Internet is listed here. The role descriptions, layout and order would be the same as for TV credits except the Web address, production company or director is stated in the far right position.

*9 Commercial Credits: Under the commercial credits heading, most actors who have either done many commercials or none state: *"Commercial conflicts upon request."* This statement saves actors from listing their commercials and thus safeguards them from being disqualified from auditioning for or booking conflicts.

CONFLICTS: *The products for which actors have shot TV commercials and that either are running on TV, the Internet or in movie theatres or are being held by the advertising agency. Actors can't audition for commercials for products for which they have a current conflict. For example, if you shot a commercial for Coca Cola, you can't do a spot for Pepsi, Guinness Beer or Lipton Tea. Usually your agent is*

When commercials that you booked and shot in the past have been discontinued, they are <u>not</u> considered conflicts, therefore, actors can audition for similar products.

 WARNING: Sometimes commercial conflicts may be hard to determine. Pay attention to potential conflicts when you get an audition. Agents and managers have been known to set actors up for auditions for which they have a conflict. Your representation will keep track of your active commercials, but ultimately you are responsible. If unsure, ask – e.g., "Is this car audition a conflict with the tractor commercial that I have running?" Don't ever think that if you do shoot a conflict commercial that it won't be noticed and you can get away with it. Many actors who tried have been caught, penalized and ordered to reimburse the advertising agency for the shoot.

Some of the reasons that the statement *"Commercial conflicts upon request"* protects actors:

- Often, the clients and advertising agencies don't want actors who are associated with other products even if they aren't conflicts.
- Many decision-makers think an actor is overexposed in the commercial world when he/she presents a list of spots in which they have appeared.
- One of the listed commercial products may be perceived as a conflict with their product but is not a real conflict.
- And the decision-makers don't know whether an actor's commercials ran years ago, are currently on the air or will be running in the future.

Many new actors use this statement to indicate that they've been in TV commercials even if they have not. It suggests credits and experience without technically lying. I don't recommend utilizing it for this purpose because if asked about your conflicts, then you are put in a position of having to fabricate. I consider this a meaningless category, but to give your resume a professional appearance, include it.

> *The only time to list your commercials is on resumes that you are sending to commercial agents.* **ALICIA RUSKIN,** Commercial Agent & Partner, KSA Talent Agency

*10 Training: Whether you have numerous credits, few or none, your training provides important information about you and your background. Your training is a continuation of your credits. With whom, where and how long you have studied improvisation, cold-reading, commercial technique, specialties and especially acting/scene study is not only informative but can be impressive. Most agents and casting directors know the reputable schools and teachers in their market. If you have chosen to train with those who are highly regarded or those who are not considered respectable, it is a reflection on your judgment. (Understand that there is a major difference between teachers who are not known and those who are not reputable. So don't hesitate to study with a great teacher if he/she is not a major name yet.)

- Layout: The following is the format I suggest for the training section layout:

TRAINING

Type of Training (Acting, Improv, etc)	Name of the Teacher or School	When You Studied or How Long	City or Special Info

- Order: I suggest that you list your workshops in this order:
  Acting/Scene Study
  Improvisation
  Cold-reading/Auditioning
  Commercial Audition Technique
  Specialty Training (e.g., Shakespeare, sitcom, soap opera, dialects, etc.)

Acting/scene study is normally listed first because it is considered the fundamental acting training and the foundation of the craft, and thus the most respected. The listing order of the other types of training is somewhat arbitrary. I do believe that most industry professionals would consider the sequence listed here to be the best way to present your training. If you have not yet done some of the above-listed workshops, (e.g., commercial audition technique or Shakespeare), it is nothing to be concerned about. The good training that you have done is an asset and is a positive reflection on you. Actors choose different types of classes because of what is needed, personal preference, cost and/or availability. Your training as well as the rest of your resume is a work in progress. Here is an example of how this section should lay out:

TRAINING

Scene Study	Shirley Angel	2008 – present	Los Angeles
	Synergy Theatre Lab	2006 - 2007	LA/Resident member
	Todd Teacher	2005 - 2006	Los Angeles
Improvisation	Ed Instructor	2009 - present	Improvocative Brigade
Cold-reading	Nail It Studios	6-month program	Los Angeles
Commercial	Barry Booker	Inter & Adv Level	Los Angeles
Shakespeare	Drama Institute	Invitational program w/Marjorie McStar	San Francisco
Theatre Arts Major		Graduated 2005	Michigan University

If you have trained in a city other than the one where you are currently seeking acting work and the teacher or the institution is respected, you could specify locations in the training section. Always put the larger theatrical market first. For example:

TRAINING

LOS ANGELES

Scene Study	Shirley Angel	2008 - present	Professional Lab
	Todd Teacher	2006 - 2007	Thespian Work-Out
Improvisation	The Freedom Lab	2007 Summer Session	The Institute
Cold-reading	Kevin Jobs	2008 Intro & Intermediate	Westside Players

DALLAS, TEXAS

Intro to Acting	Steven Best	2005 – 2006	Sage Actor's Group
Shakespeare	Thomas Theatricum	2006 Summer	Session Artists Repertory
Theatre Arts Major		Graduated 2005	University of Texas

 WARNING: If you list numerous acting teachers for short periods of time, this could convey that you are not disciplined or dedicated to the craft. Do your research and choose teachers whose process you want to dedicate yourself to.

*11 Skills: There are many commercials and theatrical roles that require actors with specific abilities. Skills can be a deciding factor for booking jobs, especially when actors are first starting.

> *SKILLS: Your ability to do anything from racing cars to horseback riding, drawing to computer abilities, singing to dialects, languages to playing a musical instrument, collecting salt and pepper shakers to being the president of a celebrity's fan club, performing all kinds of dances as well as participating in various sports activities. Just about anything in which you excel, do well or have some experience can be listed under "Skills."*

In the skills section of your resume, it is important to list <u>all</u> the skills that you have and include hobbies. You never know what a role might require. Don't list skills or activities that you think you might be able to do, tried once, are not good at or are just putting on your resume to get up for more roles. The goal is to get the auditions you are truly right for, not to get a lot of auditions. There is nothing worse than an actor showing up for an audition that requires a particular ability and he/she can't do it. It is embarrassing for the actor and frustrating to those running the audition.

• <u>Layout</u>: Skills are listed in a one-paragraph format. Here is an example of the way most professional actors present them:

SKILLS (or SPECIAL SKILLS)
Roller-blading (state champion), singing (mezzo soprano, two-octave range), French (fluent), Spanish and Italian accents, volleyball (B-rated), swing dancing (competitive), experienced dog breeder, excellent cook, intermediate guitarist, miniature doll house expert,

choral director, collector of McKnight lithographs, trained in firearms, juggling, basic martial arts, crew rowing, Jeopardy contestant, balloon sculpting, valid drivers license and passport

If you are good at or have mastered certain skills, state your level of proficiency because it can be more impressive. Some of the words you might use to describe your expertise are basic, experienced, intermediate, excellent, professional, rated, competitive, fluent, trained, collector, expert, certified and recognition received or awards won – or whatever is descriptive and appropriate for you. It can also work to simply list a skill without describing the proficiency because many roles may not need an expert, just someone with experience. In addition, put passport info and any licenses and foreign citizenship that you might have at the end of the paragraph.

Actors sometimes list personality traits like "good with children," "calm under pressure," "strong communicator," etc. I don't recommend this even though it has been helpful for some. In my opinion, it feels like an actor trying to compensate for a lack of credits or skills.

> *Skills that are unique or silly can capture attention or show personality as well as can be conversation starters when interviewing with an agent or CD, e.g., "can cross eyes and wiggle ears at the same time" or "can make the best shrimp Creole in the world."* **HUGH LEON,** Commercial Agent @ Coast to Coast Agency

The more skills, hobbies, talents and life experiences you have and sports you participate in, the more roles you could be up for. It is a good career strategy to have a full life.

• Order: I suggest that you start with your most proficient skills and then those for which there might be a greater demand. Then follow with the ones you have less experience doing or the more obscure skills or hobbies. The "skills" example above should give you a good idea of the order you might employ.

*12 Manager, Speed Reel info and/or Website: If you have used
area #3 for a second type of representation, if you have a manager, a website and/or a speed reel, state one or more of these pieces of contact information at the bottom of your resume.

 SUGGESTION: Create an e-mail and website address that you plan to keep. It will always be a reliable way for industry people to reach you if you have changes of representation or in case of an emergency.

Often actors feel that if their agent(s) and/or manager's data are on the resume, there is no reason to list business contact info. I believe it is important to include because

- agents and managers move and phone numbers change, but personal contact information should remain constant
- industry professionals, under a deadline, frequently prep casting on the weekends or after hours on weekdays and they may not be able to reach the representation
  - A website is a good way for them to find out more about an actor and see his or her work when there is a reel on his or her website.
- there are times when an industry professional doesn't have a good working relationship with the representation but still wants to bring the actor in
  - This gives them a way to contact the actor directly. It is not an ideal situation but is better than not getting the audition.
  - Agents and managers often will put their contact information stickers on the actor's resumes which have been known to fall off

Have a resume copied with the agent's sticker on it then make the copies from the initial resume – this way there is no danger of stickers falling off. **HUGH LEON,** Commercial Agent @ Coast to Coast Agency

- actors with websites look like dedicated and established professionals.

Don't list your address or personal contact numbers. Your website address, representation info, IMDB.com and any union with which you are affiliated provide plenty of ways for you to be contacted. I've had actors stalked because their personal numbers were available. **TODD JUSTICE,** Talent Representative @ Marshak/Zachary

- Order: There is no established order, although the number of sources does affect the layout. If you have one, I like to see it in the middle of the bottom of the resume. If you have two contact sources, I suggest:

hero@aleyactor.com   aleyactor.com

FIRST RESUME TIPS

For those with strong credits, I suggest you utilize the tips I offered in the previous "Format" section to make it more impressive. This information is for those who are just starting and don't have many entry-level credits. Here are suggestions that could give some muscle to a resume when there are little or no film or television credits.

This template is obviously a simplified version of the earlier one in this chapter. It utilizes the same information and offers substitutions in lieu of the credits that are yet to be attained.

Union Affiliation or Representation: If you do not belong to an acting union, one should not be stated. It does you no good to lie and frequently can lose you work and alienate industry contacts. Not being a member is beneficial information for those doing non-union acting jobs.

Height, Weight, Hair and Eye Color: State this accurately. Depending on the role, this information can help if you are truthful and be a problem if you are not.

Video / Film Projects and Music Videos: No matter how small the video or film projects you have done (whether for friends, school or local cable), list them. Also, music videos are viable credits. They help fill the page and show that you have done some on-camera work. Utilize the credit psychology I laid out in the *5 Film Credits section earlier in this chapter.

Theatre: List theatrical productions in which you have appeared, including your junior high, high school and college, as well as community theatre work. Some actors feel that these credits don't have any value. Well, they have some value. They show that you have had a little experience versus no experience.

Web: "Webisodes" and Web programs are respectable credits for a resume. Use the same layout in *8 Web Credits section.

Training: If acting training is the core of your resume, it becomes an important indication of abilities and dedication. So be sure to use the tips I presented in the *10 Training section earlier in this chapter to make this area as impressive as possible.

Skills: There are many commercials and theatrical roles that can be booked by less-experienced actors who are proficient at special skills. When a unique activity or ability is crucial to the role, e.g., elephant riding, specific sports or the ability to speak a language, that is when the CD looks carefully at the "Skills" section on the resume of the actors who are physically right for a role. Be sure to use the tips I offered in the *11 Skills section to best capitalize on your talents and abilities.

Your Contact Info: For all the reasons I previously stated, posting your business contact information and website here can be helpful in securing auditions.

RESUME BOOSTERS

In an effort to make a new actor's resume look somewhat impressive, there are liberties that many actors have been known to take. These tricks to enhance the effectiveness of a first resume can be called lies, padding or, as I like to refer to them, "boosters." Most industry professionals will tell you that they frown on this practice and would be upset with me for even mentioning it. But many actors will take liberties on their first resumes even when discouraged from doing so.

> *I have heard way too many stories about people who were caught either in a meeting with an agent who knew the credits were bogus or with a casting director who happened to have cast the project the actor "claimed" he worked on. Have integrity and honesty as a foundation in your career. Padding and lying on the resume is a BIG violation of those qualities.* **LAURI JOHNSON,**
> Entertainment Industry Life Coach

I strongly suggest you <u>don't</u> do it, but <u>if</u> you choose to do some "boosting," be very, very careful. Do it minimally and intelligently: then remove these deceptive declarations as soon as you have legitimate credits. Some of the liberties that I know have been employed:

For Representation: In the "Creating Representation" section under the *3 Agent or Manager segment, I offer the way to create the impression that the unrepresented actor has representation.

For Credits: In order to embellish their resumes with additional credits or make acting credits more impressive, actors often

• create titles of projects or films as well as bogus directors or production companies and list them as independent or graduate films. For example:

| Day Off | Lead | Crescent Limited Productions |
| | | Or Indiana University (Graduate Film) |

> If actors are asked about it, they can say that the project was not released, never completed or was only screened at the college and they never got a copy.

• up the role. When an actor has done a small role in a project or film that was not in wide release or wasn't completed, he/she sometimes lists it as a lead or co-starring part.

> If questioned about it, they will say that their role had been edited a lot.

• list a featured or an understudy credit in theatrical productions where the actor did not appear but worked at the theatre in some other capacity.

> If questioned, they can talk knowledgeably about the production and the actors and say they were only in the show for a short time.

• list as theatre credits the scenes that were done for a class. In other words, the actor is basically declaring that he/she was in a full production of a play, not just one scene. Then he/she has to get creative with the name of the theatre or where it was produced.

> This "booster" credit necessitates a lot of fabrication, especially when dealing with industry professionals who are well versed in theatre. If you choose to employ this "booster," always check to see if the CD, producer or director who is auditioning you has a theatre background.

> *Theatre people know most other theatres and theatre professionals at most theatres that an actor might use to fabricate his resume – it's SO easy to check, and they do! I've personally busted several actors for this.* **MICHAEL DONOVAN,** Casting Director, Commercial, Film and Theatre

One might think, "Who keeps track of actors' credits?" The IMDB, "Internet Movie Database," has listings of almost every credit for most every actor as well as other industry professionals who have ever done a professional film or television production – not commercials or theatre. This website is highly respected and referenced regularly by casting directors, producers and writers. All kinds of information is readily available to anyone who logs on to IMDB. com and does a search. If you insist on still doing some resume "boosting," consider <u>only</u> the ways that I have conveyed. Remove the "booster" credits as soon as you can replace them with real credits, and take the necessary precautions – otherwise you could cause major problems for yourself.

. . . .

In these last two chapters you have been presented with information, tips and insights to produce your pictures and resume – your best marketing tools. I believe these instructions will guide you in creating the most professional, accurate and impressive presentation of who you are and where you are at any given time and thus help you get the auditions that are right for you.

READY, SET, GO

READY

Actors can't wait until they can start booking work in films, on TV and in the theatre. They want to work on sets with directors and professional actors and get paid. The majority must audition to get the work. Yet most only get hired for a small percentage of the jobs for which they audition because auditioning is a competition. Many participate but only one wins each role.

There are a lot of actors and want-to-be actors but not much competition. I define the "competition" as those who are talented (often gifted), who have done their research, training, preparation, packaging and marketing, and who continue to develop their craft. This is a lot to accomplish and it takes time, but it is crucial in order to compete. Be part of the competition, not an actor without direction, dedication, or the right training.

NOTE Auditioning is not the end of your training. When you are prepared and confident, it is the next step in your development. And when you stay in class, the experience you get from auditioning and working will augment your training and help you become a better actor.

Are you ready? Don't gamble with your career by starting to audition before you are ready. Agents and casting directors have a limited number of actors whom they can see at any given time. If you audition prematurely and do mediocre or bad work, industry pros may choose not to see you again. This is why I am passionate about actors being truly prepared before seeking representation and work. You may ask, "When is the right time to start?" This is an important question. Contemplate it. Don't let your enthusiasm overwhelm your logic. In Chapter Five, I have laid out a course of action that should adequately prepare and guide you.

> *Casting directors have memories like elephants. If you were to audition for one before you were ready, it could have disastrous results. If your name came up years later when you were operating at the top of your game, trust me, that casting director would remember your weak audition and not have you in. Find someone*

you trust and let him/her tell you when they think you are ready.
LESLIE JORDAN, Emmy-Award-Winning Actor

If you are not confident in your work, then don't stress about the "time factor." It takes some people longer than others to hit their stride, know who they are, discover their strengths and weaknesses, and be consistently authentic in their work. You are on your own journey and your path will unfold in its own time frame. In the big scheme, a year or two years – or even five years – isn't that long if you are still finding your way. Don't let agents or anyone else tell you that you need to be doing it now or it's never going to happen. Everyone's career is different. **ANTHONY MEINDL,**
Los Angeles Acting Teacher

If you are unsure or choose not to follow The Plan, then I suggest you ask your acting teacher if you are ready and/or do a few "practice auditions." Practice auditions for "safe people" will give you feedback regarding your preparedness without exposure to the mainstream industry pros. I talk about this later in more detail in the Experience and Confidence section of this chapter.

SET

You've done <u>at least</u> nine months to a year of concentrated, professional training and you honestly believe you are ready to audition. What now? What can you do to jump-start your career (while continuing your training)? What information do you need? Where can you learn what to do so that you don't waste time and money or make irreconcilable mistakes? I strongly suggest you take a few months, before you start auditioning, to do the groundwork that will facilitate the audition process. The following are my suggestions, insights and tools to prepare you.

INTERN

It is important at this juncture to understand the business of acting. Before seeking representation or auditioning, I strongly encourage actors to intern, if at all possible, with an agent, manager or a CD. The valuable experience and knowledge gained usually make up for the money you are not getting paid because

- you learn about the <u>business</u> of being an actor
- the insights acquired can decrease the number of audition and career mistakes
- it is an opportunity to be part of and thus truly understand the casting process – so as to do smart auditions
- you get first-hand knowledge of what it takes to create the promotional materials, personal packaging and marketing strategy that produce results

- it is a great networking opportunity

  - Actors often secure representation or acting work during or shortly after interning as a result of the relationships that were established with those they assisted and other contacts that were made.

- often, internships lead to part-time jobs that help support your career.

An internship should not be viewed as a work possibility. Focus on the learning experience – anything beyond that is gravy. **HUGH LEON,** Commercial Agent @ Coast to Coast Agency

Do one internship with an agent or manager and one with a CD. It doesn't matter which is first. Doing one of each will expose you to both sides of the casting process. The knowledge gained with an agent or manager helps when you intern with a casting director and vice versa. After assisting one, he/she may help place you with the other.

Decide with whom you want to intern and find a way, if at all possible, to meet him or her. Many college and university Fine Arts programs give "credits" for doing internships and might even help find you placement. Most CDs, managers and agents are open to taking on interns, but each has his own acceptance protocol. Some need recommendations; others don't. Many have scheduling restrictions while others don't. A few have waiting lists, and many can start you immediately. It may involve writing a letter or finding someone to introduce you. It may take several letters and a few people to put in a good word for you.

Although the benefits of interning are numerous, really understand that there can be negative consequences if you don't approach the job as a professional commitment. Here are suggestions that can keep you from making common mistakes:

- Clearly understand the time required, the period you are signing up for, the tasks you will be performing and the intern policies. Honor the expectations of this commitment. If not, you could be turning a great opportunity into a bad relationship.

- Treat this opportunity as if it were a paid job. Be a professional. Just because no money is being earned, that does not allow you to slack off or miss work. Agents, managers and casting directors can always get interns. You need this learning experience more then they need you.

- While interning, <u>don't</u> ask to audition unless they need an actor to fill in and it is your true desire to help. They know you would love to get acting work. Manipulation, guilt or pressure is not appreciated. Many will offer if they feel it is right. If not, don't press the issue. It will compromise your relationship. Once your internship is complete, you can approach them.

WARNING: Some actors choose to start the internship earlier than I recommend in The Plan. I strongly suggest waiting until you are truly ready to audition. It often happens that while interning, audition opportunities arise. Actors must be prepared to capitalize on these situations. If you are unprepared and do a so-so read, you may not get another chance to audition with that industry pro.

BUILD AN AUDITION WARDROBE

What you wear for auditions assists those watching to define you as the role and can help you create the feel of the character. Carefully watch commercials, TV and films and study the wardrobe of people who are similar to your type, quality and age. When you understand your type (which is covered in Chapter Seven), and the kinds of roles you will initially be going out for, you should have a good idea of the audition clothes you need. At first, buy a few basic wardrobe pieces that will function for most of the roles for which you will be considered. What is basic will vary from person to person. Additional outfits will be added as you discover the kind of characters for which you are getting seen. (Information and tips on audition wardrobe are offered in the "You Are What You Wear" section of Chapter Fourteen.) The sooner you start building your audition wardrobe, the less it might cost. Since you won't be in a hurry, you will be able to wait for bargains or scout out garage sales.

SHOOT PICTURES AND CREATE A RESUME

As you prepare to start auditioning, it is time to shoot your pictures, get them duplicated and compose your resume. In Chapter Eight and Chapter Nine, I present a step-by-step, comprehensive and effective plan to create both.

> *There is NO excuse EVER for not having a headshot and resume at an audition.* **MICHAEL DONOVAN,** Casting Director, Commercial, Film and Theatre

CREATE A COVER LETTER

When sending your pictures and resume to agents, managers and casting directors, include a cover letter. It is important. Without one, your promotional material seems impersonal. It is like receiving mail addressed to "occupant." Their negative reaction to receiving impersonal mail would probably be the same as yours. If done well, cover letters can create a connection as well as present you in a positive, professional manner. Here are tips to get the best results:

- Make sure you address it to the right person. The correct spelling of names is essential. Ask yourself, Why would anyone bother to read a letter if his name is misspelled or it is addressed to "Ronnie" when his name is "Ronald?" Do your research.

- Start the letter addressing the industry professional as Mr., Miss, Mrs., or Ms. Don't use first names unless you are on a first-name basis with this person. It is unprofessional and disrespectful.

Actors should have accurate info on the people they are submitting to. I see submissions sent to agents who are no longer at our agency or addressed to our commercial agent when they are seeking theatrical representation. It is really unprofessional and tells me this actor did not do his homework. **HUGH LEON,** Commercial Agent @ Coast to Coast Agency

- Keep the cover letter short. Industry pros get massive numbers of solicitations and don't have the time to read long letters. Write a brief letter introducing yourself and what you are seeking, e.g., work, representation or an internship. Succinct letters have a better chance of getting read.

- Make it personal. It can be considered insulting when the letter is generic. It's easy to make each recipient feel as if he/she is the only one to whom you are writing. In a complimentary way, explain why you have chosen to contact them. Don't be insipid with your praise. They've had their "butts" kissed by the thousands and most find it annoying.

- Be specific about who recommended that you contact them or how you know of them. This helps to make a quick connection and entices them to read more.

If you have a recommendation from a CD or someone else I know, have that person call me! You are more likely to get in if someone I respect has called on your behalf. I often get letters mentioning how a casting director I don't know referred me and I just throw it away. **TODD JUSTICE,** Talent Representative @ Marshak/Zachary

- Don't make assumptions, e.g., "I know you will want to work with me." It can sound arrogant and manipulative.

- Don't state the obvious. For example, don't write things like I am an actor. / I am eager to work. / I love acting. / I have lots of experience – or none. (Your resume will tell them this.)

- Make sure you include your contact numbers in the letter in case it gets separated from your picture and resume.

- Keep it light. They don't need to know that you are scared, broke, frustrated, etc. This is potentially a professional relationship, not a personal one.

- Incorporate a line or two that shows a sense of who you are without being cute. This is tricky. Only add it if it doesn't feel forced.

- Don't complain about other industry pros you may know or have worked with. It creates a negative impression and the people you are soliciting may be related to or friends with them.

- You may want to describe yourself using a current or classic actor as a prototype, e.g., "a contemporary Gwyneth Paltrow type with a quirky sense of humor." It can be intriguing, plus helps to give them an idea of your essence or personality that may not be apparent in your photo.

I like to see a cover letter that highlights something worthwhile, e.g., "I booked two national commercials, AT&T and Pizza Hut, this year" or "I am doing the lead in Day's Night at the Serious Theatre." **HUGH LEON,** Commercial Agent @ Coast to Coast Agency

AGENT SAMPLE COVER LETTERS:

With a personal recommendation, this is a sample cover letter that I suggest, as an outline:

Ms. Barry/ Mr. Carroll, *(his or her name)*

My name is____*(your name)*____.____*(contact's name)*____ recommended that I contact you regarding representation. He/She spoke highly of your agency and encouraged me to send my picture and resume. (*Here you might succinctly speak about your contact, e.g., "Jane has been a big supporter and has always guided me in the right direction."*)

As my resume reflects, I have trained for____*(# of years or months)*____ and/or worked at____*(the training institution/ theatre)*____in ____*(city)*____and/or have been a professional actor for____*(# of years)*____ years.

I am dedicated and my commitment to my career keeps growing with every job I do (*or the more I train*). I sincerely hope you are looking for a contemporary Gwyneth Paltrow type with a quirky sense of humor (*use your own prototype and description here*), and find ____*(your contact's name)*____'s recommendation, my picture and resume an incentive to set up a meeting.

I will call your office this week to follow up. Thank you for taking the time to review my materials.

Respectfully,

Your Name (signed*)*

With <u>no recommendation</u>, this sample cover letter could work as an outline:

Ms. Barry/ Mr. Carroll, *(his or her name)*

My name is____*(your name)*____. After doing a good deal of research, (*or* after what I heard *or* read about you from *(the source or publication)*, I was impressed with you and your agency. Your reputation and the successes of your clients motivated me to contact you regarding representation.

As my resume reflects, I have trained for____*(# of years or months)*____ and/or worked at____*(the training institution/ theatre)*____in ____*(city)*____and/or have been a professional actor for____*(# of years)*____ years.

I am dedicated and my commitment to my career keeps growing with every job I do (*or* the more I train).

I hope you are looking for a contemporary Gwyneth Paltrow type with a quirky sense of humor (*use your own prototype and description here*), and find my picture and resume an incentive to set up a meeting.

I will call your office this week to follow up. Thank you for taking the time to review my materials.

Respectfully,

Your Name (signed*)*

The cover letter should reflect you and your personality. Have some fun and put some intention behind it! Also follow up with a phone call. This is professional business behavior. A casting VP once told me that he was astounded by how many letters he got saying that there would be a follow-up call and there never was.
LAURI JOHNSON, Entertainment Industry Life Coach

These letters are <u>samples</u> and <u>only</u> intended as a format. Instead of just filling in the blanks, find your own way to express the pertinent information. Your cover letter will only work when you make it your own. You are a creative person. Create with these samples.

GET EXPERIENCE AND BUILD CONFIDENCE

To audition without confidence and freedom is like operating on a patient without having completed a residency or like starring in a play with no rehearsal. It can be done, but the chance of doing good work consistently and looking like a professional is rather slim.

> *The most important thing to booking work (along with sheer talent) is CONFIDENCE. I can't stress this enough. Too often actors are scared and come off weak at auditions. For a casting director or producer to hire you, they must feel confident that you are the best choice. Walk in and own the room. Say hello, be polite, feel strong, but don't be arrogant. Some actors are so insecure that they go to the opposite extreme and seem defensive. Develop real confidence.* **DAVID SWEENEY,** Los Angeles Talent Manager

Earlier I said, "With experience, confidence is built and with confidence comes freedom in your auditions and acting work." I believe it works like this:

Talent is developed with training.

Training creates experience.
Confidence comes with experience.
Freedom evolves from confidence.
Training, confidence and freedom produce strong auditions.

Before you start auditioning for industry professionals, who probably won't give you a second chance if you don't do a good job the first time, get entry-level audition experience and build your confidence and freedom. My suggestions:

- CLASSES - Being an actor who does strong auditions takes muscle. Like your body's muscles, the more you work them, the stronger they get. Many actors take cold-reading/auditioning classes to learn the necessary tools and to practice and polish their audition and interview skills. This is a cloistered learning environment that does create some pressure when reading in front of the class and the teacher. This form of experience is definitely important and has much value. But it does not produce the same anxiety as reading for strangers in a real audition situation for an actual job.

- PRACTICE GROUPS - Another way to hone your audition skills is to join or organize a practice group. Once a week or twice a month get together with several actors and work on reading scripts and auditioning. This effort is great practice and extremely helpful but, again, does not duplicate the pressure actors impose on themselves at actual auditions.

- INDUSTRY WORKSHOPS - Many believe that one-on-one, industry workshops are good ways to practice, experience audition pressure and get the attention of industry pros. I believe that these types of showcases, selected wisely, can be of value <u>after</u> you have done your foundation and audition training, attained some entry-level experience, and developed confidence.

WARNING: When first starting, it is a bad idea to perform in front of industry pros whom you can't help but want to impress. Mistakes are a crucial part of learning. Most actors try very hard not to make mistakes in front of those who can give them acting jobs. So until you are ready, it is neither the ideal learning opportunity nor the best situation in which to build confidence.

- **ENTRY-LEVEL AUDITION EXPERIENCE** - Get entry-level audition experience and build self-assurance by auditioning for acting work you don't want with "safe" people for just a few months. Since this kind of audition has no real career significance, it is a low-stress way to practice and enjoy the process. You can experience taking direction from industry pros as well as dealing with the anxiety of reading for an actual job. Because it is an "experience" audition, there should be little or no pressure. If mistakes are made they can be looked at objectively as a lesson because you know that your reputation has not been damaged. Hence, your confidence won't be undermined.

  - <u>Safe People</u> are those hiring for minor jobs that have no real effect on your career. For example, people casting, producing or directing

    student or graduate films: these are student filmmakers, not career-making professionals working in the entertainment industry (at least at this time)

    small theatre: those doing church, park productions or local theatre in small cities or outside of major markets are usually not directly involved in the industry

    projects or presentations for friends: they are usually supportive.

If you are fuzzy about who the "safe" people are, know that all union and non-union work for which you are being paid as well as theatrical productions in major markets are, in my opinion, not safe places to practice. These people are working pros whom you will probably really want to work for. This process may seem unfair to the people whose time you are wasting during the auditions. It is. But if it weren't such a valuable experience, I wouldn't suggest it. Follow the specific parameters I have laid out and only go out for "safe" auditions for a <u>short</u> time.

  - <u>Work You Don't Want.</u> Are you wondering, "Why go out for acting work you don't want"? My answer: for the practice with little or no pressure to prove yourself. Thus, when you do well, you build confidence. If you fall short, you can view it as a learning experience. The "work that you probably don't want" could be:

> Roles for which you are too young, old, short or tall or are type-wise or ethnically wrong (at open calls).
>
> Theatrical productions that are so far from where you live that it would be impractical and time-consuming to drive to rehearsals and performances.
>
> Student films that you are not interested in doing.
>
> Parts requiring physical attributes that you do not have or skills at which you are not proficient – as long they aren't required at the first audition.

You have to submit your picture and resume to be considered for most auditions (except open calls) so they wouldn't be seeing you unless there was some possibility that you would be considered. But remember, you do not want the role. I know it may be difficult when you have invested the time to prepare and audition, but try not to fall into the trap of hoping to be cast. Instead, acknowledge yourself for your determination to build your confidence.

> – Finding "Experience Auditions". The best way to find "experience" auditions is the same as what you would do to find opportunities for real acting work:
>
>> Listings and advertisements in trade papers like *Backstage East* and *Backstage West*, *Variety* and *The Reporter* (in paper-copy and online)
>>
>> Online actors' registries like Actor's Access, L.A. Casting and Now Casting
>>
>> Networking groups and organizations
>>
>> Acting teachers
>>
>> Friends

THE MAJOR PREREQUISITE: The only way these "experience" auditions are beneficial is if you prepare and endeavor to do your very best. You must do the same investigation and preparation that you would do for a major CD or director. Otherwise this exercise is a waste of everyone's time with no value. Focus on your purpose: to practice your craft and build your confidence muscle so that you will be ready for your career auditions.

WARNING: Callbacks are not part of my "experience" audition scenario. It is unfair and unethical to go to the callback for one of these "safe" jobs unless you have revised your intention. It creates false expectations for those running the audition, and since callbacks are more time consuming, it is a real waste of their time. There is no way to justify it. If you do go in for a callback and book the role, you'd better accept it or you will be making enemies.

If you are asked to return for a callback and choose to go (because you have discovered that it would be a job worth doing for reasons you didn't know at first), the exercise would still have served its purpose.

MOVING ON: I suggest doing no more then ten or twelve practice auditions.

 WARNING: Don't wait <u>too</u> long before starting to do real auditions – you may undermine the confidence you have developed. Fearing rejection, some actors postpone auditioning for so long that they become professional students. The fear only gets worse with time if you keep procrastinating when truly ready.

JOIN OR CREATE AN ACTORS' SUPPORT/NETWORKING GROUP

One of the best ways to do your research and get valuable information is to join an actors' organization. For a membership fee, the well-structured, professional ones offer extensive resources and research materials plus support from the staff and membership. The reputable organizations can teach you who are the best teachers, photographers, makeup people, duplicators, etc.; about audition opportunities; the most productive ways to connect with casting directors, directors, producers, agents and managers; how to promote your career and market yourself; the insider tips from industry professionals who conduct classes; and a lot more. It can save you time and money as well as help you avoid career mistakes.

> *Another great resource is to be a part of a positive, supportive acting studio or theatre company where actors see your potential and wish to help you as they help themselves. Find a place that fosters friendships and supports the work that the entire studio is creating. The understanding is that there is enough work out there for everyone and that everyone's essence is different.* **ANTHONY MEINDL,** Los Angeles Acting Teacher

If you are in a major market, you will probably find several actors' organizations. Many are mediocre or a waste of money. Do your research. The one I strongly suggest in Los Angeles is The Actor's Network. If you don't live there and would like to take advantage of their valuable information, you can join their website program at actors-network.com.

Creating Your Own: If your city doesn't have this type of organization or you absolutely can't afford to join a good one, try to start your own. These are my suggestions that might help you in the formulation and management of a group:

- Choose eight to twenty-five dedicated, responsible, compatible actors who would be willing to participate at 100 percent. <u>All</u> members must be willing to share the responsibilities of running the organization.

- Set up a regular meeting day and time and keep to your schedule.

- A chairperson or administrator needs to be chosen. The position might rotate monthly or several times a year among motivated members.

- Members are assigned to research information that will be presented at the meetings. Suggested topics: representation, productions that are casting in your vicinity, beneficial showcases, teachers, photographers and networking activities.

- Invite industry professionals to be guest speakers. Some will request compensation but there may be a few who will donate their time. Teachers, photographers, image consultants, life coaches, etc., would probably donate an hour or two to speak in order to interest the members in their services.

- Structure the meetings. For example, half an hour to review what was accomplished at the last meeting and "share" members' successes; an hour to ninety minutes to discuss or brainstorm work opportunities and for the members who were assigned research topics to present their findings; one hour or more for the speaker (if one is booked) or an activity, e.g., script reading, practice auditioning, acting-related discussions, etc.; and fifteen minutes to decide on the topics to be researched for the next meeting and assigning the members who will do the jobs. Vary the presentations and activities at each meeting to keep the interest of the members.

- Create a policy regarding bringing in new members and dropping those who have not proven to be responsible, and enforce it. Make this policy clear to members upon joining.

- Establish a monthly membership fee that covers the organization's expenses. Choose a treasurer. This position should rotate so everyone has to be responsible for being the collector.

- When there are disagreements, work them out immediately.

It has been my experience that creating and managing an independent networking group takes a very dedicated group of people. It has been done and is extremely beneficial. But if at all possible join an established one. It is better, easier and usually more productive.

NETWORK

Actors don't get all their auditions or jobs from the traditional submission process. Work opportunities come from many sources. You never know who knows whom and when someone is going to be doing a production that would be right for you. Directors, producers, friends working on productions and CDs often cast actors they know or request them for consideration. As you start to seriously audition, it is time (if you haven't already) to create your network.

Suggestions that will help create your industry network:

- Create social and business relationships with the actors in your classes and your teachers. They can possess a wealth of information and contacts.

- Get involved in or volunteer for charities or organizations where you will meet and work side by side with actors and industry professionals.

- Get a "survival" job where you can work with or have contact with industry pros.

- Support actor and industry friends. Attend their productions and events because

  – they will probably support you

  – it presents more opportunities to make contacts

  – it is the right thing to do.

- Go to industry parties and social functions.

- Keep contact information on <u>all</u> the industry people you meet and work with. Maintain at the least an e-mail relationship with them.

  – Many actors send out entertaining e-mail newsletters several times a year, updating their friends and business contacts about what is happening in their careers. It is an easy, no-cost way to stay in touch and self-promote.

- Every few months, send photo postcards reporting your career progress with a short note to your casting director, director and producer contacts.

- Help out (other than as an actor) in theatre productions, spec projects, AFI films, music videos, low-budget films, etc.

- Maintain friendships outside of the industry. It never ceases to amaze me that in a show business town, by a few degrees of separation, most everyone is related to or connected with industry people. Often non-industry friends want to help actors by introducing them to their relatives in the industry. You never know who can help you.

 WARNING: Friendships created only because of what someone can do for you are frequently counterproductive. First, if you don't truly enjoy being with them, it is a waste of your time and life. Secondly, it is apparent to most industry pros when actors are "users." So if your intent is insincere, being acquainted with influential people could backfire. Create authentic relationships.

Get together, stay in touch with phone calls, postcards and holiday cards and when possible support the endeavors of your friends and contacts. If you are short on time, then communicate through e-mails. E-mail, what did we ever do without it? There is no reason nowadays not to stay connected to your network. It's time-consuming to develop and maintain your network and you are never done. Do it in the right spirit and it is usually fulfilling.

RESEARCH

The information gleaned from doing research will give you valuable insights, knowledge and save you time and money. Knowledge is and will always be power. Here are a few things you can do to help in your acquisition of craft and business information:

- Subscribe to one or more of the industry publications (in print or online).

- Check online actors' chat rooms and bulletin boards when doing research.

- Read books, blogs, websites and articles, watch TV programs and webcasts and listen to podcasts and compact disks for information about acting techniques; the entertainment business; the audition process; industry pros you will be meeting, auditioning for and working with; the hierarchy and politics of theatrical and commercial casting; and the ups and downs of being an actor.

- Send out e-mails to those in your network for input when doing research.

. . . .

I strongly believe in the information presented here. It is now up to you to choose to do all, some or none of it. Seriously contemplate what you have read here, and apply what works for you. Too many actors jump in too soon and/ or unprepared and botch opportunities by making mistakes that could have been avoided if they had done the research and work and, most importantly, built up their confidence. There is something to be said for just jumping in and learning from experience. But there is more to be said for being a well-prepared professional and then jumping in.

GO

You are ready and set. You've done your foundation training and business groundwork and have created your marketing tools. You're hungry to audition and work. Just like with any other career, you have to get to the people with access to the jobs. Agents and managers submit actors for auditions and are intrinsic to most actors' success. Representation and securing it are topics unto themselves, and will be covered in Chapter Eleven. Yet agents and managers are not the only way to get auditions. Today's actors have options and more opportunities than ever.

SUBMIT YOURSELF

Casting notices for commercials, film and TV shows, especially for the larger roles, go out mainly to the agent and manager community when projects are in pre-production. Then the agents (and many managers) submit their actors' pictures and resumes either online, by mail, or by messenger. Sometimes, they call to pitch their actors to the "powers that be." Without representation or knowing the right people, it is challenging for the new actor to be considered for leading roles. But there are all kinds of job opportunities to which unrepresented and new actors do have access. Roles are available in non-union productions, small theatre shows, music videos, spec commercials, industrials, Webisodes, conventions and at theme parks, as well as specialty (appearance or skill-specific) roles or small roles in union commercials, films and TV shows. Plus, with many of the cable networks producing original programming, there are even more work opportunities.

With initiative and perseverance, auditions can be secured by self-submitting. When cast in them, these jobs build resumes, provide experience and help create a network of industry contacts, all of which will make actors more appealing to an agent or manager. With some credits, auditions for more and larger roles can often be attained. Even with representation, lots of motivated actors still submit themselves to secure additional opportunities.

> *Be relentless in trying to get work, but let the pursuit come from the desire to show your WORK. If you are confident and excited about the work you are creating, you should be able get anyone to see it. Passion and persuasion go a long way. But please get your work into shape so that when you entice Steven Spielberg to watch you do a scene, you truly are magnificent. Don't waste anyone's time if you aren't ready to be seen.* **ANTHONY MEINDL,** Los Angeles Acting Teacher

There are several ways to find out about work for which you can submit yourself:

- **Referrals:** When actors hear about jobs from friends, teachers or neighbors, they send a cover letter, picture and resume to the person in charge or the one they have heard is connected with the production.

- **Trade papers:** Listings and ads in the trade papers and their online entities provide audition information for open calls or the mailing or e-mail address where actors can send submission materials.

- **Online submission websites:** The Internet has opened the door for actors to submit themselves for all kinds of work. There are several online casting/submission services. (You will find more details in Chapter Thirteen.)

- **Production information website:** A company called Casting About (which was acquired by Breakdown) is an online casting and production membership website (castingabout.com). It tracks all the major film and TV projects casting in for Los Angeles, New York, Chicago and Vancouver–helping actors to target specific shows and casting directors, and to submit themselves. The casting staff (including associates and assistants), current mailing address and production status for each production can be found online for it's members. The information is updated daily, and can be easily searched.

SHOWCASE YOURSELF

One of the best ways to get meetings with casting directors and other industry professionals is to have them see you work. Creating a theatre or video vehicle with fellow actors and a director is a great showcase for you and your friends plus an incredible learning experience.

THEATRE: CDs and agents often go to theaters to find new talent, so doing a play, especially one you star in, can be great exposure. If you choose to do a theatre showcase for yourself

- research all the costs involved

- collect the necessary money from the actors and others who are funding the show and put it into a designated bank account

- get written permission to do the play

- set a director, producer(s), and stage crew

- organize a production schedule, allocating enough time for casting, pre-production, rehearsals, previews and the number of weeks or months the show will run

- Run your show for at least six weeks so it can be reviewed and so that the industry pros you intend to invite will have multiple opportunities to attend.

- cast any additional actors

- select a theatre
    - Make sure it is a reputable theatre in a safe area of town. Otherwise, people may feel uncomfortable attending

- before the opening and during the run of the show, invite, invite, invite every type of industry pro several times.

    - Even if they don't come, they will see your name and face (if you send a picture postcard), so they should become somewhat familiar with you.

PERSONAL VIDEO PRODUCTIONS: There are a few types of personal video vehicles that can be produced for showcasing: a film (short or full length), short scene footage for your demo reel or a 3-5 minute scene(s).

> DEMO REEL: *A short edited compilation of an actor's best work on a DVD, typically three to five minutes in length.*

Shooting a film is a major undertaking and will require a large investment of money, time and effort – it is an amazing creative endeavor. If this is something that you really want to do talk to people who have done it, take workshops on the subject and purchase books that will guide you through the process. Make sure you are prepared for all that is involved.

If you decide to create video scene footage for your first demo reel, I suggest that you choose three very short scenes that show the different kinds of roles you can play. You only need to shoot a minute of each, then you can edit out the best thirty to forty-five seconds of each scene – scene snippets on a demo reel are only thirty to forty-five seconds at the most. When shooting your short scenes, use different locations, wardrobe and hairstyles so that each one looks like a distinct production and be sure to

- shoot with a <u>professional </u>company that specializes in this venue or find a creative, dependable friend(s) with a good camera(s) and sound equipment

- shoot outside during the day
    - The texture of a location and daylight will give the production a better look

- when shooting with friends, rent professional sound equipment and, if you shoot indoors, get good lighting units

- do a few camera setups for each scene: a master, over-the-shoulder and matching close-ups – then you will have "shot" choices when editing.

If you want to do only one scene, most all this information is applicable. Make it short, no more than four minutes. It will be less expensive to edit and industry pros prefer watching short promotional pieces. It is better to do a short scene(s) in which you have good production values rather than an amateurish-looking longer one.

After you have your video scene footage, take it along with photos and any other film or video you have to a professional who specializes in editing and/ or creating actors' reels. (There is more information on demo reels in Chapter Thirteen.) This first reel is a temporary vehicle until you get professional film and TV footage. Many industry pros might not respect it (depending on the quality) but it can be better than nothing when you need a reel.

WARNING: Once you have your reel, there are companies who will submit it to casting directors and/or agents for a $50 or $60 fee per industry pro. Actors can choose off the company's list the CDs and/or agents who they want to view and write comments about their reel. If this is something you want to do, research and choose a very reputable company – realize that if you submit your reel to several CDs and/or agents for review, it could get expensive and there is absolutely NO guarantee that any of these industry pros will bring you in for a meeting or audition. This is a new practice and with disreputable companies it could be a sham.

Casting Director/Audition Workshops and Industry Showcases Another great way to get exposure to industry pros is to participate in audition workshops or industry showcases. If you impress them with your work, you might be contacted for representation, invited to audition for a specific role they are currently casting, contacted in the future, or remembered when your headshots and resumes are submitted. Once you are ready to showcase your work and seriously start pursuing acting jobs, you might consider participating in one of these venues.

- INDUSTRY SHOWCASES are productions featuring scenes that are directed, rehearsed, then mounted specifically for an industry audience. Usually the show is comprised of ten or more two-person, five-minute scenes with a minimum number of performances at a theatre. If experienced and reputable producers and directors put on the showcase, this can be a great vehicle for actors to be seen by numerous industry pros.

  Industry people come straight from a long day of work to see showcases. Personally, I hate seeing big dramatic scenes involving yelling and crying. It's too "acty" and generally boring. Comedy,

if you can pull it off, makes a better impression. **HUGH LEON,**
Commercial Agent @ Coast to Coast

- **AUDITION WORKSHOPS** normally have sixteen to twenty-five actors doing cold-readings and getting audition tips from casting directors or associate casting directors – sometimes agents or directors. Each speaker participates for one night, and the workshop takes place on the company's premises. The scenes are done in front of the other participants, and every actor gets a critique. The format may change depending on the industry pro. With reputable companies, the guests are working professionals and those participating are high-caliber actors. Many actors have gotten work, under-5 roles as well as leads, from these venues. It is not a guarantee that the CDs you meet will bring you in to their castings. No matter what could happen, these workshops provide an opportunity for actors to garner tips, get insights and feedback, and practice auditioning.

  I like to attend workshops because they allow me to see lots of actors in a short time. In scene showcases actors perform set pieces but in an audition workshop, I can stop and give them direction. I can see what they are really made of. I like knowing that the actors I represent are strong enough to make adjustments. It's surprising to see how many actors can't adapt to direction they haven't prepared for. **TODD JUSTICE,** Talent Representative @ Marshak/Zachary

- **PREPARED SCENE WORKSHOPS** are a new form of showcasing. Ten or more two-person, five-minute scenes are performed for the casting director. At each session, the actors will go to a different CD's office and do their scenes: then they usually get a short critique or interview.

SHOWCASES	AUDITION WORKSHOPS	PREPARED SCENE WORKSHOPS
2 weeks - 2 months (rehearsals & performances)	One night w/CD	One night w/CD (Several rehearsals to prepare)
Exposed to dozens of industry pros	Work one-on-one with one CD, agent or director	Perform for CD and get feedback
Performing in a rehearsed scene	Cold-readings	Performing in a rehearsed scene
Material: mutually agreed upon scenes	Material selected by CD, agent or director	Material: mutually agreed upon scenes
$250 to $600	$25 to $60 per night	Approx. $50 per night

Many choose not to participate because they see these workshops as paying to meet and audition for the people who can get them work. It's a personal and business choice. If you do choose to participate in any of these venues, make sure to check the following:

- the reputation of the company or individuals running the showcase or workshop: Only an elite few of the showcase/workshop providers are selective, ethical, and produce quality venues. Which one(s) you associate with is an indication of your talent level and professionalism.

- the industry pros who are the guest teachers or audience:
  - Are they currently employed and do they cast shows you want to audition for?
  - Are they industry pros or their associates or assistants?

Second-rate companies will bring in the casting assistants and associates, not the CDs or agents. The casting assistants and associates can provide beneficial input and might have the power to bring in actors to audition, but sometimes they don't. It's a gamble. I suggest you only sign up to work with the CD or agent unless you learn that specific assistants or associates have value.

- if auditions are required to participate: When companies don't audition prospective members, they are not being selective. Disreputable providers will allow new and unprepared actors to participate because they don't attract enough strong actors or they want to make more money. When you are seen alongside less than qualified actors, no matter how good you are, it could be a negative statement about your professionalism.

- the talent level and experience of the actors in the workshop: Be in the company of professional actors. The instructors can't help but judge the overall echelon of talent at these workshops.

- the number of participants and the amount of time each actor receives: Don't join a workshop or showcase that takes more than twenty-four participants per night – ideally less. If there are more, you won't have enough time to get the information, feedback and exposure you are paying for.

- the cost and the length of each session.

....

Did you know there were all these options to get work and build careers? If you are resourceful and strongly motivated, you will do the work willingly to get representation and auditions. If you are not, you may want to rethink this as a career. It is not enough just to be talented and trained. Getting work requires a lot of effort, creativity, commitment, money and time. I suggest you love and have fun with this whole process because it will be a large part of your life.

REPRESENTATION

Actors are artists. Most don't want to solicit acting jobs for themselves or deal with negotiations (even though often they have to do it). Actors prefer to act and to continually be developing their craft. They desire representation to deal with the pursuit of work and the business of acting.

> REPRESENTATION (as it pertains to the entertainment industry): *The action of speaking or acting on behalf of someone or the state of being so represented*

TYPES OF REPRESENTATION

The most established forms of representation for actors are agents and managers. There is also a new representation entity that I call (for lack of an established title) "submission groups." Actors are not always clear about the services that are provided by agents, managers and the groups. The confusion is understandable since there are no clear-cut job descriptions beyond "assisting actors in getting work." In an effort to explain their differences and similarities as well as delineate their jobs, I have put together a consensus description.

AGENTS/AGENCIES

The jobs that agents do for their clients and the procedures they follow:

- Submit actors for roles.
- Specialize in commercials, TV and film, theatre, modeling, hosting, commercial print and/or dance. Many represent performers in several of these areas. A few of the midsize and larger agencies cover most every area.
- Negotiate salaries, credits and when appropriate, amenities.
- Focus on getting work rather than building careers – except sometimes for the major theatrical agencies.
- Represent a large number of actors (depending on the size of the agency and number of areas they cover).
    - Commercial agencies represent hundreds and sometimes thousands.

- Theatrical agencies sign dozens to hundreds.
- Major agencies handle upwards of a thousand clients for multiple areas.

- Oversee marketing tools and suggest professionals for development and packaging.
- Collect 10 percent commission on union work and 15 to 20 percent on non-union and print jobs.
- Are licensed by the state and must follow regulations.
- Are affiliated with the Screen Actor's Guild, the Actor's Equity Association and/or the American Federation of Television and Radio Artists and work with their contracts. (Most agencies but not all have chosen to be affiliated with one or more unions.)
- Work with union agency contracts, which have time limits as well as "outs" for the actor.
- Most work in an office and have several agents and assistants. Many boutique agents work independently from offices in their homes.
- Are public businesses and are fairly easy to research.

MANAGERS

The work that managers perform for their clients as well as their business procedures:

- Help find their actors representation.
- Represent all kinds of talent or specialize in one type of performer.
- May do audition submissions, especially when their actors don't have agents.
- Focus mainly on building careers.

    As a former manager, I have to say that they oversee the client's entire career. An agent is interested in sales, so they throw you up against the wall to see if you stick. Having a manager should be viewed as a marriage. They're in it for the long haul. AMY LYNDON, TV & Film Audition/Booking Coach

- Supervise job choices, e.g., when there is a choice or conflict, they may suggest doing a lead role in a prestigious play rather than taking a supporting role in an episodic TV show because the play offers industry exposure and is the better career move (or vice versa).
- Organize their client's auditions and work schedules when they have multiple agents for different mediums.
- Confer with the agent(s) on all business deals. If there is no agent, they sometimes handle the negotiations. Most will work with a lawyer on contracts.

- Handle a small number of actors (depending on the size of their firm).
- Fight their client's battles. The manager handles all problems or disputes with agents, casting directors, directors, producers, etc.
- Work alone or with other managers and a small staff. There are many large management offices with multiple managers and employees, but mostly they are smaller operations than most agencies.
- Are actively involved with the creation of their actors' marketing tools and often oversee craft development and packaging.

 WARNING: I have heard stories of managers who have asked clients to get naked or wear a bathing suit so that they could do a body check to make sure that their bodies were good enough to submit for roles that required "hot" bodies. This is not an accepted practice. If a manager (or agent) ever makes this request of you, report him or her to the authorities.

- Collect commissions varying from 5 percent to 25 percent, with the average being 10 to 15 percent of your gross income. Never pay a manager to work for you.

If a manager tells you they charge a "fee" for their services, e.g., $500/month, then that manager is not legitimate and you need to move on. When you make money, we make money. That's how it works. **DAVID SWEENEY,** Los Angeles Talent Manager

- Are not "affiliated" with SAG and AFTRA. There are conferences and organizations that suggest business practices for managers but it is not mandatory for them to join.
- Information on them is not always accessible because they are small businesses.
- Contracts often have no time limits as well as no "out" clauses unless negotiated then put into the contract. Managers' contracts are designed to favor them, not you.

 WARNING: Often actors have to pay commissions to unscrupulous managers long after they leave them because there were no time limits or stipulations for a release from their contracts. Make sure that if you sign with a manager (or anybody), you fully understand the agreement you are entering into. I suggest bringing it to a knowledgeable industry friend or an attorney before signing.

Manager contracts are hard to dissolve so I would suggest only signing for a year or two maximum and be wary of any manager who takes over 15 percent. **ABBY GIRVIN,** Owner of DDO Agency

When thinking about hiring a manager, factor in

- the amount of their commission
- what you believe they can do for you
- their ability to get you an agent(s) or their working relationship with your agent(s)
- your comfort level with them as an ally
- contract exit provisions
- their clout in the industry
- whether you <u>really need</u> someone to help oversee your development as well as make career decisions.

Consider all the pros and cons, and then determine whether it is beneficial to have a manager at this particular time in your career. If you choose to sign with one, be sure that your contract specifically reflects what they are committed to doing for you. Clearly understand <u>all</u> of their terms.

> *Both agents and managers should guide the actor, help make decisions about what he/she is presenting to the world (e.g., headshot, resume, general look, etc.) and most importantly get the actor seen by casting directors for acting jobs. Expect sometimes to have trouble getting your agent on the phone. If your manager doesn't call you back in the same day, then you need a new manager! Finally, a manager is legally not supposed to negotiate. That is the agent's job. If an actor does not have an agent to negotiate the deal (but has a manager) then the actor must also have an attorney.* **DAVID SWEENEY,** Los Angeles Talent Manager

 SUGGESTION: If you find a manager who is interested in representing you and you already have a commercial agent and are booking a good number of commercials, I recommend you propose: giving them their 10 or 15 percent commission on the commercials you book <u>after</u> you have made, while working with the manager, a minimum of fifty thousand dollars in theatrical work. You don't need their management skills to book commercials. You already have that going for you. If you give them that money, then you are paying them to work for you. Most managers will not go for this, but I really believe it is fair. But you could compromise, and offer them only five percent commission on the commercials you book at the start of your business relationship. It's just something to think about.

SUBMISSION GROUPS AND BUSINESSES

The main difference between agents, managers and "submission groups" is that with the groups, actors are members, not clients, and are charged a fee to be submitted. This type of representation is sometimes appealing to actors who don't have representation or feel they want additional coverage along with their representation. These submission groups often call themselves "management companies" and fall into two main categories:

- 1) A business, run by an individual or a small group, that is paid to submit actors. It is recognized as a "management business" by the online submission companies and legitimately receives the casting breakdowns. The fee/commission for its members varies from group to group. Some take a monthly fee plus expenses. Others have a monthly fee and a commission.

- 2) The other type is a "management group" – a few actors who set themselves up to do their own submissions. The fee charged is just to cover expenses. These groups are not recognized by the online submission businesses and get their breakdowns any way they can. This is not legal and there have been lawsuits, but this practice continues.

Both types of submission groups do the following:

- Submit actors for all kinds of work. Their main focus is film and TV but they often submit for theatre and commercials. Some submit for the full range of acting work that can include music videos, convention work, industrials, web programs, and print.

- Do not help secure representation.

- Work independent of agents and managers.

- Focus on getting work, not building careers.

- Do not negotiate salaries. The majority of them only submit for work that is union "scale" or non-union work – the fees for these jobs are usually a set amount and are often a "buy-out."

SCALE: *This is the minimum amount of money that SAG, AFTRA and AEA actors are paid to work a daily, weekly or contract job.*

BUY-OUT: *The fixed sum the producer pays the actor to own his or her performance for a limited time in a non-union or union commercial, film, project or show.*

- Are not typically involved with their members' marketing, packaging or training.

WARNING: I suggest you avoid submission businesses that require you to hire their photographers, makeup and hair people, photo reproduction companies, teachers, etc., or pay to take their classes. Most of the time, their recommendations turn out to be a waste of money and time.

- Are not affiliated with SAG or AFTRA.

- Normally have monthly agreements that are usually easy to get released from.

- Are difficult to research because they aren't formally recognized businesses.

Submission groups are not recognized or respected by the casting community. **HUGH LEON,** Commercial Agent @ Coast to Coast Agency

Submission groups have only recently come into play because getting representation has become so competitive; they can help get entry-level credits and additional work, which can make actors more attractive to agents and managers; and many new actors as well as professionals choose to work all the avenues to get jobs. I don't necessarily recommend these groups. I am just informing you that they exist as an option.

It is imperative to bear in mind that many things that are illegal or vastly unethical in many United States industries seem to go on regularly in Hollywood without a whisper. This does not make it an intelligent professional business decision and submission groups can be one of those. A union actor does not, under any circumstances, have the right to submit a fellow actor for work. Ask yourself…do you see baseball or football players representing other players…while they're currently playing? Answer: Of course not. This is why most industry professionals do not seriously consider submissions from these groups and fake management companies. **KEVIN E. WEST,** President of The Actor's Network

If belonging to a "submission group" is what you want, I am fairly sure you will find one if you check around. Most actors prefer to have an agent and/or manager to get work and create careers, so I will be focusing on them.

HOW THE PROCESS WORKS

In major markets, there are hundreds of agents and managers. Most are legitimate, but there are many who are not. Attaining legitimate representation is usually rather involved so it is important to understand the process.

Commercial Agents: Most new actors start with a commercial agent. Securing one is typically easier because

- they represent more clients than theatrical agents do. Many more actors go out for commercial roles than for theatrical ones so there are more audition opportunities.
  - Fifty to two hundred people are up for one role in a commercial, whereas five to twenty, on the average, will be seen for most theatrical roles. (The number auditioning for starring roles in films and TV series is much higher.)
- there are more commercial agencies than theatrical agencies.
- they will sign new actors with little or no experience who have a good "commercial look" as well as accomplished professionals.

Theatrical Agents: Unless you are related to or highly recommended by an industry power player, the chances of getting a theatrical agent when you first start are rather slim, but not impossible. (I know you don't want to hear this, but it is true.) There are exceptions, but it usually takes most actors at least two years of development and booking jobs before they secure a respected theatrical agent. The majority of agents prefer you to have numerous credits. If you have chosen to hire a manager first, then he/she could help you get your agent(s).

Managers: Securing a manager can be easy or very difficult. Years ago, they didn't actively seek work for their clients and weren't interested in actors until they had credits. Now there are managers who take people right off the bus, put them in classes, groom and package them and then work to get them representation and acting jobs. Then there are the major ones who will only take established actors who are ready to move to the next level of their careers. The majority of managers represent clients between the two groups.

> *I believe that you don't need a manager until you have a career to manage. The only thing a manager can technically do for the new actor is to help him or her get an agent. But today the lines are becoming blurry between what an agent does as opposed to what a manager does. I currently have a manager and a lawyer handling my career.* **LESLIE JORDAN,** Emmy-Award-Winning Actor

RESEARCH

What do you need to know about the agents and managers you are pursuing? Who might be looking to make you a client? How do you make contact? There are lots of questions and considerations. Like with everything else, start with research:

- Buy updated books that list and describe agents and managers (sold at Samuel French in Los Angeles and New York and the Drama Book Shop in New York, or go online and order from these stores).
- Obtain a list of franchised agents from SAG.

- Go to the website for the Conference of Personal Managers (ncopm. com) and the Talent Managers Conference (talentmanagers.org) to find a directory of members.

There are agents who are not SAG-franchised and many managers who don't belong to a conference. That does not mean they are not reputable. Those who are members are just easier to check out and are accountable to a supervising entity.

- Ask industry pros you know as well as your friends, teachers, relatives, and classmates the following about agents and managers:
  - Whom do they recommend or have heard about with great reputations?
  - Who should be avoided?
  - What is the best way to contact these agents and managers?
  - Is there anyone they know who could help get more information or has an "in"?
  - Would they be willing (with the ones they know) to recommend you? Maybe, ask if they would give your picture and resume to their contacts.
- Go to the websites of those you are considering and read about the company history, the agents, how long they have been in business.
- If you belong to a networking group, check with their members and their records.
  - The more established ones have their members document experiences and information regarding industry pros. Talk to or e-mail the fellow members to see who and what they know. When you have decided which agents and managers you plan to target, ask members who are represented by them if they would be willing to recommend you or take your promotional materials to their office, or if they have suggestions on how you could get in the door at their agency. (It doesn't hurt to ask.) Don't ask someone who is your type to help you get representation – your competition isn't always eager to help.

SUBMIT

Now that you know the reputable agents and managers who are suitable for you, choose those you want to target and submit to them. The size and status of the office you should realistically approach is determined by where you are in your career. When starting, you will find that the small and medium-sized offices are often more receptive to meeting new talent but if you do have an "in" at a major agency or just want to try to get with one, definitely pursue it. If your timing, talent and type are right, you could get lucky.

TIP Once you have a short list, check your choices with the Better Business Bureau. Find out if they have had claims filed against them.

Submit your picture and resume to the representatives you are targeting. Don't mail to one at a time and wait for them to contact you. It is also a waste of money to do a mass mailing to every agent and manager in town. I suggest mailing to a select fifteen or twenty agents (and the same number of managers when you are ready for a manager). For those who have been recommended, I propose you ask your contact if they would advise the agents or managers to expect your submission.

> *Know who you are submitting to at the agency and address the envelope and cover letter accordingly. Do not submit to "To Whom It May Concern," "Agent" or "New Talent Department."*
> **HUGH LEON,** Commercial Agent @ Coast to Coast Agency

> *Often managers will respond to a blind submission if the photo really pops. Your photo is the first thing the potential representative or casting director will judge you by. It is your calling card so it better be good. You'd be shocked to see the bad photos that come into this office on a daily basis.* **DAVID SWEENEY,** Los Angeles Talent Manager

Some agents and managers accept e-mail submissions. But many feel it is an invasion of their privacy. Be sure to check with your contact or their receptionist <u>before</u> e-mailing. If they don't respond, I recommend you not e-mail them again. All operating systems must be able to open your e-mail attachments. You never know how new or old their computers are, the software programs they are running or who has a Mac or a PC. If you don't get a response, it <u>may</u> be because the agent or manager was not able to access your promotional materials.

> *I do not accept e-mail submissions, yet dozens are sent to me every day.* **HUGH LEON,** Commercial Agent @ Coast to Coast Agency

Also, if you belong to a casting website(s), check the agent/manager submissions programs that are offered. When agents and managers look for new clients, they sometimes post on these services: then they contact the member/actors who respond or request that the actors contact them.

 WARNING: Most agents or managers meet with a potential client based on a resume and who they see in the picture. Be sure your picture represents who you are and not what you want to be. If you show up and you are not that person, the agent or manager might be dismissive because it wasn't you they wanted to meet.

Agents and managers are bombarded with actors soliciting them. You might hear from some within a few weeks after you send your submissions. If you don't get any responses, submit to your second choices. Agents and managers will call you for a meeting if they are interested in what they see in your submission. If you get minimal or no response after the second round of submissions, shoot new photos, redo your resume and cover letter and then, in a few months, submit again to your first then second choices. Client rosters often change, making room for an actor who was of no interest just a few weeks earlier.

OPPORTUNITIES TO CONNECT

Auditioning or showcasing your talent in one or more of the following ways provides opportunities to connect with potential representation:

- Commercial Agent Open Calls: Some commercial agents have open calls regularly. Find out when they are scheduled and what is required. Many require recommendations and/or an appointment. Others, actors can just show up on a certain day and time and wait to be seen. They usually have those auditioning prepare commercial copy in their office and then do a read, which is often recorded.

- Theatrical Productions: Performing in a professional theatrical production is a great way to grow as an actor as well as an opportunity to get exposure. Agents, managers and casting directors frequently attend plays to scout for new talent.

TIP ➤ You must be a member of most theatre companies to be cast in their productions. Before auditioning for one, check out the company's members, reviews of previous productions, the theatre's reputation, and their association with industry professionals. Then go audition for the one(s) that feels like the best fit. You want to shine, but not in a second-rate company or production.

- Industry Showcases: The good ones do professional scene presentations and draw a good number of industry pros. (Which agents and how many will attend is always a gamble.) Find detailed information about these showcases in Chapter Ten.

- Agent/Casting Workshops: Many of the companies that produce audition workshops with CDs also offer sessions with agents.

IN THE INTERVIEW

With your research, preparation, submissions and some luck, you now have the interest of one or more agents or managers. It is time for them to meet you.

WHAT AGENTS AND MANAGERS CONSIDER

While interviewing prospective clients, agents and managers will be considering if they want to represent the actors and evaluating if they can sell them. Bottom line, you are a product to them. What are they evaluating and considering? This is a subjective business. Each one will choose clients based on his or her criteria, taste and needs.

The Representation's Determinants:

TALENT: Agents and managers want to know that the actors they sign are talented. They need to believe in an actor and their work so they can submit him/her with assurance to casting directors who in turn can feel confident bringing the actor in to audition for their bosses. Agents and managers use the following to appraise an actor's ability and potential:

- Acting work they have seen in a theatrical production, a TV show, a movie or on a reel.

- A scene done in their office (primarily for theatrical representation).

- A reading of commercial copy, prepared in their office and which is often recorded, for commercial agents and some managers.

- A strong recommendation by someone the agent or manager trusts.

SUGGESTION: There are many commercial agents, smaller theatrical agencies and managers who sign actors based primarily on type, a look and/or personality. Talent is not their main focus. Do you want representation that submits a look or one that represents you and your talent? Encourage them to see you act. If there is nothing to view, invite them to your acting class or, at least, have them speak with your acting coach. Unless you are doing acting as a hobby, it is important for whomever you go with to know your work in order to best represent you. If you are anxious to get a "start-up" agent or acting is a hobby, the distinction of them wanting your type as opposed to you may not be important. If you have choices or can be patient, then signing with someone who appreciates your talent is better for your career.

PHYSICALITY: When you understand that you are the product, you get why your physicality (your type, age, body type, height, weight, hair, etc.) is a big factor. Agents and managers must be confident that there is a product they can sell. Each will look for different physical packages based on what types are needed for their roster.

POTENTIAL AUDITIONS: The amount of work an agent or manager thinks he or she can get for an actor is a factor when choosing clients. There are more roles for the new actors who are seventeen to twenty-six years old and who are beautiful, handsome or unique than there are for character actors and those over forty who are new. Agents and managers are often willing to sign the younger ones who don't have extensive credits because they are more of a commodity and it is easier to get them auditions – then work to build their resumes. This does not mean that everyone else won't get representation. On the contrary, agents and managers need all types and ages. Character people and actors over thirty who are new often have to be more talented and experienced to be considered (unless they are unique characters, have special skills or a celebrity status, or are types in demand).

TYPES NEEDED FOR THEIR CLIENT LIST: In order to submit for a full range of roles, it is necessary for agents and managers to have a variety of actors on their rosters. Most want several leading men and women, ingénues, young leading men, young leading women, younger and older character types, a range of ethnicities, etc. If they are saturated with ingénues, they may not be willing to take on another one, no matter how great she may be. If they are short on young character guys, they would be willing, if not eager, to sign the right talent. Being passed on by an agent or manager is not always a rejection of you or your talent. It is often a business decision to not bring on actors who conflict with their current clients or who are a type that they have too many of. Once you are signed with an agent or manager, they will hopefully be making these kinds of decisions to better represent you.

RESUME POWER: The more credits you have, the more people know your work. The stronger your credits, the more you are respected by CDs, directors and producers. When industry pros know and/or respect your work, it is easier for your representation to get you auditions. Although many agents and managers may be willing to take on new actors, most, especially the mid- and upper-level theatrical ones, prefer not to start careers. It is not cost effective. This does not mean a new actor can't get "heavy hitter" representation. It is just easier with an impressive resume (and even that is not always a guarantee).

REEL: For those actors who have worked in film and TV and have a "reel" of their work, the quality and presentation of that "reel" (or a professional looking starter reel, covered in Chapter Ten) can be an impressive factor as well as a good marketing tool for the agent or manager.

VOICE: An actor's voice is a subjective factor. It is not often discussed but can be influential. If it is charming, sexy, masculine, rich, resonant or cute, it can add to an actor's appeal. If the voice is irritating, withheld, too loud or soft, etc., it can make an actor less appealing. If your voice or speech needs improvement, work on it before starting to look for representation. Information about voice training can be found in Chapter Four.

TIME AND WORK REQUIRED: Agents prefer to do a minimal amount of work preparing new clients to start auditioning. Time and work will need to be invested if actors require pictures, training, additional experience, appropriate wardrobe or a dental, hair or makeup makeover. Depending on the status of an agency and the interest in the actor, some will devote the time but most won't. This is why I stress that it is important to be as prepared as possible before starting to seek an agent. Don't give anyone whom you worked hard to meet any reason for not wanting you. In most cases, you will only get one chance with each person. Be ready.

INDUSTRY CONTACTS: The more industry pros you know, the more know you thus making it easier to get you seen when they are casting. Bring a list of the people with whom you've worked and with whom you have relationships – show it to your potential representation. Having industry contacts demonstrates that you are a dedicated and motivated professional and can make you very attractive.

PERSONALITY: It is important that your potential representation sees your true personality so they know whom they are signing – except don't be sarcastic, negative, moody, silly, introverted or overbearing. It is essential to be respectful, appropriate and YOU.

CONFIDENCE: Do what you need to do to put yourself in a positive and confident state of mind for your meeting. This is a business. Deal with any personal issues another time. No one wants to represent an insecure, non-celebrity actor with personality problems. Would you? On the other hand, do not be cocky or arrogant in order to compensate. Confidence looks different than arrogance.

PROFESSIONALISM: Your professionalism is a subjective factor that is part of their selection criteria. The following are suggestions that will help you look like a professional:
- Dress and groom yourself appropriately for who you are. If you are a contemporary college type, do not dress in a business suit. If you are a sophisticated leading man, don't go in jeans and a tee shirt. Whatever you choose to wear that best shows who you are, make sure it is clean and looks good – this is a business meeting.

- Be on time and be prepared to wait. Having actors wait is not a game or a test. Do not complain. It's usually because there is a problem that needs to be addressed, someone requires their attention, or they are just running late. It's not personal. You're not their priority – yet.

- Make sure your resume, pictures and reel are professionally presented.
    - The resume is either printed on the back of your photo or cut to the size of the picture and neatly glued or stapled.
    - Be sure to bring several pictures. Most don't want to look at proof sheets, but bring them just in case.

- A demo reel (if you have one) should be professionally edited and packaged.

• Know about the agents or managers you are meeting so you will have intelligent questions and topics to discuss that will help you to be personable and professional. Go online and/or talk to industry pros about them. If you know any of their clients, get some pointers about their preferences.

• Be prepared to intelligently talk about and describe yourself: what you've accomplished, what your goals are and what kind of roles you see yourself playing. Smart and motivated actors are very appealing.

• Don't use profanity (even if they do). You never know how your swearing will be perceived. Some think it's cool and others may be offended.

• Be prepared with the audition material.
    - Often, commercial agents will give you audition copy to audition with. Take your time preparing. When you do your audition, commit to your choices and instincts. If they video your audition, look into the camera when you do your read unless they tell you otherwise.
    - Be well-rehearsed when requested to do a scene or monologue for theatrical agents and managers. Whether you have a reel or they have seen you in a theatre production, if you are a new actor, you may be asked to do a monologue or a scene (with a partner) in their office. They may also request a cold reading.

• Don't "badmouth" anyone. First, it is impolite, and second, it can be business suicide. You don't know whether the agent or manager has worked with, is related to, is friends with or knows that person. If he/she "badmouths" someone, be diplomatic but do not contribute to the negativity. (I would not trust and would be hesitant to get involved with anyone who would make negative comments about others at a first meeting.)

WHAT YOU CONSIDER

In most situations, there will be two meetings. In the first, both parties will evaluate each other. Sometimes there will be an offer of representation at that time. Usually, if there is interest, there is a second meeting. Here you might meet other agents or managers in their office, do another audition, show your reel and/or talk further. You are getting to know each other and determining whether it will be a good working relationship. Both scenarios give the agent or manager and you the opportunity to get questions answered. Your questions will give you the information you need to know if an agent or manager is a fit. It should be a rather light inquiry without attitude or judgment.

Questions To Ask:

What types of roles do you see me playing?

> Their answers give you an understanding of how they plan to represent you. Does it match how you see yourself? Do you feel you are right for and can compete for the roles for which they will submit you?

How many actors are in my category?

> Agents have several actors in most every submission category. They must, because although actors may be the same type, it's the individuality that secures auditions and bookings. With commercials there may be product conflicts, and with theatrical work there may be scheduling conflicts. Their answer helps you to understand how much of your competition is with the agency and possibly gives you an idea of where you might be in their submission seniority. Some might be uncomfortable with this question so be aware of the agent/manager's disposition before asking.

> *I hate being asked this question as it insults my agent abilities.*
> **HUGH LEON,** Commercial Agent @ Coast to Coast Agency

How many agents or managers work in the office?

> There are a lot of commercial and theatrical casting directors in the major markets. The larger the staff, usually but not always, the better the coverage is for their clients.

Do all the agents or managers in the office represent all the clients?

> In some offices, each agent or manager represents just their personal clients. In most, every agent or manager represents all the clients. Either way works. This information gives you an understanding of their operation.

How many actors does the office represent?

> There is no perfect ratio of actors to agents/managers. Their response gives you an idea of how much attention you may be getting.

Do you specialize in TV and film, commercials, theatre, print, industrials and/or voice-over?

Do you represent "across the board"? (This question is not usually applicable to managers.)

> ACROSS THE BOARD: *Agents representing clients in all the mediums for which the agency has departments.*

> Many agents focus on one or two of the mediums. Larger offices and some mid-sized ones represent actors for several if not all of them. Those with multiple departments might want you to sign "across the

board" (depending on the prominence of the individual divisions). If asked to sign "across the board," evaluate the strength(s) of the agency. For example, if you're already with a strong commercial agency that is getting you lots of auditions, you may not want to trade that for a good theatrical agent with a low-level commercial division who insists on signing you "across the board." Or then again, you might, depending on your focus. This is a business decision to consider carefully.

 NOTE: Some actors will sign with an agency in one of their departments in hope of eventually being picked up as a client in another. For example, an actor will become a "print client" in order to eventually be invited to join their commercial or voice-over divisions. Or they may sign commercially in hope of getting theatre or theatrical representation with that agency. It works sometimes, but you can't depend on it.

Do you help with photo choices and resumes and do you give training recommendations?

Since your headshot and resume as well as your development are so important, agents or managers will often assist you with them. This answer gives you an idea of their willingness to help their actors.

If an agent or manager strongly suggests one specific photographer or teacher, don't automatically go with that person if it doesn't feel like a fit. You must feel great about the photographer who takes your photos and the teacher(s) who help develop your craft. The agent or manager should suggest at least three people in each category. Check out their choices as well as others whom you have researched: then trust your instincts and choose the professionals you feel good about working with.

What is your commission?

The standard agent commission is 10 percent on union jobs and 15 to 20 percent on non-union jobs and print. Managers range from 5 percent to 25 percent, with the average being 10 to 15 percent. But be sure to ask – don't assume.

What do you expect of me? What can I do to help you?

Their answers will give you an insight into your potential working relationship and might provide you with tips on how to get more work.

AGENTS: Do you work with managers?

Some agents refuse to work with managers. Most have no problem with it. If you have a manager, ask the agent, "How do you prefer to work with a manager?" They will either choose to call your manager, give them your auditions, and the manager will inform you, or the agent will call you and you will inform your manager. The three of you need to work it out.

MANAGERS: Do you set up meetings to get an agent?

It's great to have a manager working for you. It's much better to have a manager and an agent(s). One of your manager's jobs is to help you acquire an agent, change agents or, if you want to, add specialty agents. Most have the resources to help you meet them – at least commercial agents. If they don't, they probably have very little clout.

Actors should ask prospective managers: "Can you help get me auditions? What agents and CDs do you have working relationships with? Can you introduce me to agents?" Don't be afraid to interview the manager. Take some control over the situation, without being bossy or obnoxious. Finally, ask the manager if he/she will be accessible to you. If you sign with a manager and it takes more than two days to return a call – you need a new manager. **DAVID SWEENEY,** Los Angeles Talent Manager

Questions Not To Ask: Don't ask "needy" questions like, "Do you think I am: too old / a good type / pretty / handsome / talented, etc?" These kinds of inquiries make actors seem insecure. It has been my experience that when actors ask needy questions, they don't really want the answers. They are usually worried about these issues and want to hear compliments to quell their concerns. In an attempt to create a relationship, many actors ask questions that can be intrusive, controversial or rude – avoid asking about religion, politics, sexual issues, health or family. If you are confused as to what is appropriate, ask yourself, "How would I feel if a stranger asked me this question?"

DECISION TIME

You probably worked hard to set up your meeting(s) and you may be hungry to get an agent or manager, but make sure that he/she is the <u>right</u> one(s). Believe that you have earned the right to have representation that you are confident will work for you.

It's 90/10. You are doing 90 percent of the work. Agents get 10 percent of the money from the work you do. You are their employer. It's not the other way around. Actors constantly forget this and consequently cede their power to someone who really doesn't have any. Without actors, agents wouldn't have jobs. Without actors, agents wouldn't get paychecks. Without actors, the business would come to a screeching halt. **ANTHONY MEINDL,** Los Angeles Acting Teacher

Once you have met, gathered your pertinent information and have an agent or manager interested in representing you, consider the following before making a commitment:

YOUR DETERMINANTS

PROFESSIONALISM: The way they dress, speak and their office setup are factors that give you a sense of their professionalism. I am not saying it has to be any certain way. They don't have to wear expensive suits with conservative hairstyles, speak with an accent and have contemporary furniture in a fancy office in an exclusive part of town. Their personal presentation just needs to be business-like, and their offices should look professional and fairly organized. Professionalism is also manifested in the way they deal with you as well as others in their office. Some questions to ask yourself:

- If they were late, did they apologize or at least acknowledge their tardiness?
- Did you feel that their questions, input and/or comments were intelligent and had value?
- Were there other agents, managers, assistants or staff, or was the office a one-person operation?
- Did the agent or manager take calls during your meeting?
- Was he/she friendly, business-like and/or respectful to you, the people in their office and on the phone?
- If you did a reading, were the comments valid and/or positive?

There is no definitive way to define "professional," but you certainly would know if the person you are meeting with is not.

NOTE: Small and mid-sized agencies and some managers may choose to "hip pocket" new clients instead of signing them. This means that they will submit these actors for auditions for a period of time and see how they do before making them a client. This could be a factor in your choice of representative.

CHEMISTRY/RELATIONSHIP: Be aware of how you felt during your initial interview. Were you relaxed? Did they listen and appear interested in you and what you said? Did you feel that the person connected with you, recognized your talent and was truly interested in representing you – not just your type? Were you comfortable with the way they spoke to you and how others in their office treated you? You'll be speaking with your representative fairly often so you must feel comfortable. Envision what the real relationship will be, not what you hope it will be.

If an agent makes you feel bad, is unkind, compares you unfairly to others, tries to diminish your spirit in any way, RUN – don't walk. It's better to have no representation than to be with someone who is abusive or doesn't understand your talent or makes you question your choices. There are a lot of people in this business who are frustrated actors. Don't let them project their insecurities onto you. They aren't the ones in power, although they would make you think it so. Why would you want to work with someone who doesn't have your best interest at heart? There are so many wonderful agents out there that you could meet, create positive relationships with and who are excited about you as an artist. Don't waste time with people who don't get you. It's like dating. Why would you go out on a second date with someone you aren't interested in? Don't let a fancy office or title sway you. If you don't feel good about the person you are with, then get out of that relationship. **ANTHONY MEINDL,** Los Angeles Acting Teacher

CLOUT

CLOUT: *The power to direct, shape or otherwise influence. The success of the agent or manager's talent list and their relationships with a large number of top CDs as well as producers and directors, determines their clout.*

Many new actors find their initial representation with smaller agencies (with little clout) – these agents and/or managers usually tend to be supportive and open to establishing new talent, which can be the best move for a budding career. Plus, established actors tend to be time-consuming, which limits the focus larger firms give to the new actors. When actors become successful, some remain with those who first believed in them.

Getting actors auditions often depends on the representation's reputation. Most actors would like to be with a major agency or manager with clout. Unfortunately, most of the majors prefer to represent established actors. It makes their jobs easier. But there are always exceptions, and timing has a lot to do with whether they would be willing to take on a new actor. Go after the "biggies" (if you want) as well as others who would be more realistic representation for where you are in your career. Even if the major ones pass, the connection you create might make it possible to come back to them when you have more credits.

REPUTATION: How respected are they? Check your potential representation's reputation for honesty and commitment to their clients with members in networking organizations, fellow students, teachers, industry pros and the Better Business Bureau, as well as actor chat rooms and any sources whose feedback has merit. Granted you will always find people who find fault with any agency or manager so it's important to check as many sources as possible to get a consensus.

What Is Important:

When beginning a career, it is rare that actors will be able to sign with an agent or manager who ranks high in professionalism, clout and reputation and with whom they have a strong rapport. It does happen, but not often. So it is a matter of what feels best for you. Factor these considerations into your choice of representation:

> Reputation vs. Clout: Some have a reputation for working with new actors but have little clout. Others have lots of connections and are known to work hard for their celebrity clients but minimally for their less established ones. Clout means nothing if it isn't working for you.

> Professionalism vs. Relationship: There are those who are very professional, but you might not feel that they get you or that you connect with them. The flip side is feeling a great connection but not being comfortable with how they do business.

> Clout vs. Relationship: If you don't connect with them or they are just blasé about representing you, then clout won't help you. If there is an eagerness to make your career happen and the office has little or no clout, it's doable but not ideal.

SELECT WISELY

Logically select the agent(s) and/or manager you want to represent you. Unfortunately, when many actors first start, they go with any representation who wants them – this does not serve their careers. If you go with the first person who offers to sign you just to have someone, you might be missing out on an agent or manager who is a better fit and who you could've found if only you had continued searching for a little while. On the other hand, don't be so particular that you put off getting representation for too long. Give yourself a time limit. I suggest no more than four months. Then select the best of whom you have to choose from.

TIP → If agents or managers express interest but you are not sure about them and want to meet others, don't turn them down. You can say that you have other meetings and you will get back to them soon. This could earn you their respect, and maybe they will want you even more because you have options. Or if you sense that the agent or manager's ego could be bruised, you can say that you have to go out of town for a few weeks and you will be contacting them when you return.

AN ACTOR'S LIFE

Unlike most business people who have full and hectic lives, most dedicated actors have both a job(s) where they earn a living <u>and</u> a career that they are preparing for and pursuing. No matter how much is accomplished, there is always more that can be done, which can create frustration, pressure and feeling overwhelmed. One of the biggest complaints I hear from most actors, right behind not having enough money, is not having enough time. Know and accept that this is the way it is. (This is also true for those who don't need to earn a living but who have strong ambitions for an acting career. They will often devote their non-survival-job time to getting more experience, training, showcasing, networking, marketing, etc.). When you are committed, there is so much to do all of the time. That doesn't mean that it won't be creative, fun and exciting. I tell dedicated actors to make friends with feeling overwhelmed and try to have a sense of humor about it.

> *It is NOT a necessity to be overwhelmed. We need to take the drama out of our lives. No drama unless you get PAID for it! An overwhelmed, frenetic, unfocused life will not translate well in the auditioning room. The actor's job is to see that "real life" is as organized and settled as possible. WE can make and create time. Look at your own personal organization. Are you wasting valuable time doing unnecessary things? Hire an organizer if you have to, or seek out a coach to determine how to best utilize your time and remain happy and healthy at the same time!* **LAURI JOHNSON,** Entertainment Industry Life Coach

YOUR DAILY SCHEDULE

If new actors follow my plan and professional actors pursue their careers ambitiously, their schedule can look somewhat like this:

> They will have a 9-to-5 or 10-to-6 o'clock job (with possible overtime) <u>or</u> a job or their own business that has flexible hours during the day. (Time off for auditions or days off for acting jobs are arranged and are a condition of their employment. Often they will make up missed time in the evening or on weekends.) Most every weeknight they either go

to the gym, acting classes, meetings, rehearsals or networking venues for three or four hours. At home, time is spent doing submissions, marketing, exercising, preparing for auditions and getting organized for the next day.

Or actors with night jobs will essentially have the opposite schedule of their daytime counterparts. For those who split work shifts or have two jobs, they will do everything that needs to be accomplished between and after their jobs.

Weekends and any spare time are spent doing craft and career work, plus taking care of family and life errands: laundry, groceries, cleaning, banking, correspondence, working out, religious or spiritual pursuits, etc. Often another job is worked or assignments for the primary survival job are taken care of on the weekends. Social and family time as well as personal obligations are squeezed in wherever possible.

Doesn't sound like the pampered life of the movie stars we read about in the magazines. Those stars do lead more glamorous lives and make a lot of money so they can hire people to do most mundane tasks. But their schedules are equally packed with acting work on sets or in the theatre (which often takes more than nine hours a day), reading scripts, character research, wardrobe preparation, meetings, interviews, promotion and press junkets, as well as personal obligations to their families, friends, themselves and fans.

ORGANIZATION

New actors are not usually prepared for how time-consuming a survival job and an acting career can be. Time is a commodity. Get organized and learn how to schedule yourself efficiently. A calendar is your primary tool for putting your schedule together. I strongly recommend getting an appointment book, a computer calendar program that syncs to a cell phone or an online calendar and use it constantly. There are websites that provide the setup to create an online calendar at no cost. (Calendars and appointment books are assets for tracking deductible expenses when doing your taxes and provide the paper trail to back them up.) Personally, I like a computer calendar program that syncs with my cell phone because I can easily add, change, delete, reschedule or repeat appointments, calls, tasks and notes, etc. and always have it with me. Schedules are easy to read (often color-coded) so nothing gets overlooked.

Some actors write appointments and notes on scraps of paper. There are those who say they feel that too much scheduling stifles spontaneity. I personally think that is an excuse for laziness. Many actors do have some kind of calendar but they don't use it effectively. They record appointments and tasks. They do not schedule them. There is a big difference between recording and scheduling. Most busy people who don't consistently and efficiently schedule and organize themselves usually lead chaotic and less productive lives. Bottom line, lack of scheduling is unprofessional and undermining to any career.

Scheduling your life takes discipline and planning. When each day is thought out, it helps actors from getting overwhelmed. I am no organizational expert, but here are pointers that I use and suggest:

- Periodically, decide on career goals or projects you want to accomplish. At the beginning of each yearly quarter, specifically choose what you want to undertake and accomplish during this time frame. Break down the necessary tasks and activities that lead up to realizing your goals and schedule them over the three months.

- At the beginning of every month divide what needs to be accomplished into each week. Organize tasks and activities in an order that advances your goals.

- At the beginning of each week and always on the same day (Sundays work best for most), choose what you want to complete or steps you plan to take to advance your agenda. Schedule tasks, appointments, errands, activities, workouts, rehearsals, classes and calls that need to get done for your career, work and personal life on each day of that week. Then, schedule times to relax, socialize and accomplish personal "to do's."

- Refer to your calendar a few times a day. Consult and adjust it each time you complete, add, remove or change tasks, calls or appointments. At the end of each day, check to see what you didn't get accomplished. Decide if it is still necessary. If so, reschedule it.

- At the beginning of your next week, look at what was not completed and whatever still has purpose, and then reschedule. There will be tasks and calls that don't get done. Don't get discouraged. Hardly anyone gets it all done.

- At the end of each month, take a good look at what you have consistently postponed or didn't complete. If you have put something off several times, ask yourself if you really want to do it. You have the right to change your mind. It's your career. Once you have given your postponed choices careful consideration, you can recommit, alter or choose not to do them.

- At the start of the next quarter, review your accomplishments and acknowledge yourself for them. Most people are so busy looking at what didn't get done that they don't allow themselves to feel successful about what was accomplished. Feeling good about your successes boosts self-esteem and confidence. Now decide on your subsequent set of goals for the next quarter. Choose the order in which you want to undertake the objectives, schedule them monthly and then break them down weekly and daily.

TIME-MANAGEMENT TIPS

DRIVE TIME

Driving around large cities doing errands for the acting career, job(s) or your life can feel futile and tedious. Traffic wastes more time. Here are a few ways I save time and gas with those "running around" errands:

- When possible, plan your errands in advance to minimize the driving. Do everything you need to do in a specific area of town on one day and on another day do the errands and appointments in another area.

- Partner and divide up your errands or drop-offs with a friend, neighbor, spouse, roommate, significant other, scene partner or networking buddy. They can do some of yours that are convenient for them, and you will do theirs that are convenient for you.

- Try to do errands on the way to and from work so you won't have to make special trips.

- Shop online for suitable items. It can save gas, time and money.

- If possible, arrange to have meetings and rehearsals in your home so that the time you would have spent traveling you can use to get work done.

- Schedule your errands and appointments during times when traffic is light. Go early before the commuter traffic starts, later after the rush, or in the middle of the day.

HOME TIME

I'm sure that you already multi-task in your home. It is almost automatic for most of us, but there could be additional activities you might be able to get done.

- Multi-task, e.g.:
  - While you wash dishes or walk on the treadmill, learn your lines and do laundry.
  - When you eat alone or are waiting for someone, read scripts, organize your schedule or return calls.
  - When you are on your phone, wear headsets so that you can cut your nails, groom the dog, put away the groceries, select wardrobe, water the plants, etc.
  - When you are on the computer waiting for sites to download or documents to print, go through your mail.
- Pay your bills with Online Checking. This not only saves time but money on postage. Manage your expenses with a computer program

like Quickbooks. This will facilitate dealing with your financial records and tax returns – a major time-saver.

- Organize your clothes, paperwork, food pantry, keys, accessories, remote controls and storage spaces and keep them in order so you don't waste time looking for anything. Yes, it will take hours or days to get things organized, but the time spent doing it will save you the time it takes to look for things – which can really add up. Plus, it will reduce the stress that you experience when you are in a hurry and can't find what you need.

- Getting your phone numbers and address book entries organized is a major time-saver. Set up a database on your computer that you can sync with your phone or that you can print out to a constantly "updatable" address book.

- Take very good care of your health. Being sick is not only a bummer but is a major waste of your valuable time. Eat nurturing food, drink plenty of water, take supplements and work out. Get enough sleep, try not to get stressed out and put time aside to relax.

Remember to take a breath and slow it all down from time to time. Your health and well-being involve eliminating and not creating stress. How you handle stress and being overwhelmed is a number one priority, not something you fit in. LAURI JOHNSON, Entertainment Industry Life Coach

If you are standing in line at the bank, holding on for someone on the phone or waiting anywhere for anyone, do something. Not doing something while waiting for anything is a waste of time – unless you choose to do nothing. If you choose to do nothing in order to serve yourself mentally, physically or emotionally, then that is something (a little Zen philosophy).

WORK TIME

Job time is meant to accomplish tasks and produce results for your boss and the business even if it is your own. Yet there are things you can do that can help facilitate your life and career. These suggestions are relevant only if they are appropriate for your job situation:

- Work through lunch occasionally so that when necessary you can leave early or take time off for auditions.

- Access your personal e-mails and text messages on breaks or when you are holding for someone on the phone so you don't have to reply when you go home.

- If you work in an office or do sales, ask your boss if you can sometimes work at home, where you can multi-task your job duties and your acting tasks.

- Make sure to have your business contacts, phone numbers and addresses well organized in some kind of logical system or computer database and your schedules and appointments in a calendar setup. This kind of organization will make you more efficient.

- Create generic draft documents for recurring e-mail and letter correspondence. Letters that you send out regularly don't need to be written from scratch every time they are needed. Create the documents in your computer and leave blanks for the specific information that you will fill in at the time you send it.

SAVING MONEY VS. TIME SAVERS

Time saved gives you time to make more money and do more for your career and health as well as have a fuller social life with friends and family. If the money you spend can save you time, it is usually well spent. Some ways I suggest you can do this:

- Live closer to your job. If your domicile is comparatively inexpensive but is not close to your work or the main vicinity where you pursue your career, it is costing you more in drive time (especially factoring in traffic) and gasoline than you are probably saving.

- Don't live in a residence or drive a car that costs more than you can comfortably earn at your survival job(s). Drive a sensibly priced car and live in a smaller apartment or home. What does it matter in the long run if you drive a "hot" car or where you live as long as it is safe, comfortable and takes care of your needs? You want to spend as much time as possible working on your craft and career. Working more hours or jobs in order to cover high rent and car payments is undermining to your main goal. I have heard of many stars who choose to live in a modest home to avoid the pressure of high mortgage payments. They never had to do projects they didn't believe in just for the money so they were able to make better career choices.

- Have two phones. Many people use their cells as their only phone. I am not sure that is a great idea. I have heard too many stories where actors did not receive important audition or work calls because of problems with their service or voicemail. And often cell phones have service or reception issues. I suggest that you have a home number with voice mail or a message machine. Your message on your home and cell should reference the other number and request audition or work messages be left on both. The few dollars spent on a basic home line will give you the peace of mind of knowing that you will not miss important messages.

- Utilize text messaging, instant messaging, and phone e-mail. What you spend for these services is not as significant as the time it can save you. "Texting" and "IMing" are great tools when you are short on time and only want an answer to a simple question or to receive or deliver a small amount of data. E-mailing on your cell phone when you are out will save time answering e-mails when you get home.

- Buy a washing machine and dryer. Most major appliance stores offer payment plans. The time you spend going to and from as well as waiting for your clothes to wash and dry at the laundromat or at a friend's takes about two hours, two to four times a month. Your own washing machine and dryer will pay for itself within three years and can save you up to eight hours a month. Or you can bring your clothes and linens to the cleaners and pay them to do it.

- Cleaning your house and doing your laundry takes a minimum of four hours a week. Paying bills takes a few hours a month. Running personal errands takes approximately two to five hours a week. Most people really don't enjoy doing any of these chores. If you have a good job that you enjoy and are paid at least $30 an hour, it makes financial sense to have someone charging less than what you make an hour do the work you don't want to do. This way you can help someone else and make more money doing what you enjoy rather then spending time doing stuff that you don't want to do.

If any of these amazing tips don't work for you, find organizational guidance that can fit your lifestyle. There is a huge difference with time between a single actor and one who is married with children – AND, it's all doable if you are committed and unstoppable!
LAURI JOHNSON, Entertainment Industry Life Coach

These suggestions will probably inspire you to think of other ways to create more time by spending a little money. I realize that often the money just isn't there to pay for these devices and services, but if you are creative, you might find ways to afford a few. If not, realize the possibilities so you can opt for them when you can. With time you can make more money. With more money you can pay for help and devices that give you more time to make additional money and to pursue your career and enjoy your life. Time is money and money is time.

HAVE A VERY FULL LIFE

These warnings on how overwhelming an actor's life can be are only intended to help you prepare for them. If you know the hurdles, you will be able to maneuver. Don't think that you won't have time for friends, family, fun activities, sports, exercise, a good social life, love, relationships, relaxation, adventure, and/or religious or spiritual pursuits. They are all very important to you personally and as an actor. You <u>must</u> make time for all these experiences. That is a major reason why I have made these suggestions on how to streamline your life.

> *Don't let acting define you. Take your work seriously (and have LOTS of fun doing it) but have other interests as well. You are more than just an actor. Live as full a life as you can and, coincidentally, it will only help your acting become more exciting, more authentic, and more human.* **ANTHONY MEINDL,** Los Angeles,
> Acting Teacher

Be a passionate and dedicated actor and also have a full life. I'm not an advocate of struggling and depriving yourself. There are some who believe that in order to be a great artist they must suffer. Oh, please, give me a break! Yes, you will have issues, frustrations, and major challenges and you will probably be overwhelmed. You would have that with any career. If you are emotionally fit, healthy, smart, motivated and organized with money and time, you should have a satisfying artistic journey and a great time.

BUSINESS ESSENTIALS

As you have heard, acting is a business. Every business has essentials that are needed for development, launching and growth. The business of being an actor has its own unique and specialized tools as well as the same ones used in many other businesses.

UNION MEMBERSHIP

I consider union membership a primary business <u>essential</u> for most professionals. It affords greater access to higher profile auditions and jobs as well as residuals, insurance and health benefits. Actors can work without being members of SAG, AFTRA and EQUITY, but the job opportunities, money, work conditions, benefits and protection are much better under the jurisdictions of these unions. Being a non-member or staying SAG-eligible for as long as possible does have value depending on where an actor is in his/her career.

SCREEN ACTORS GUILD

Membership in SAG is not a matter of choice. There are three ways to qualify:

1) Actors, while working as background talent in union TV shows, commercials and films, will earn vouchers if they are selected to be featured. When actors receive three vouchers (might go to five), it entitles them to join the union.

VOUCHER: A document that is given to an extra when he/she is featured. It is considered a credit that is registered with SAG, helping to qualify actors for membership.

For specific information on doing background/extra work and getting vouchers, check out these websites:

> www.centralcasting.org
> www.entertainmentcareers.net
> www.extraextracastings.com
> www.idelljamescasting.com

2) When actors are hired for their first union jobs and are cleared by SAG to work that job, they can join. <u>Or, if they choose</u>, they can wait thirty days, during which time they are SAG-eligible and can audition for and work on

both union and non-union jobs. After thirty days, when they book their next SAG job, they must join.

NOTE When an actor books their first union commercial, TV or film job, the CD must write a letter and fill out a form, requesting permission and justifying why the non-union actor should be permitted to book the union job (as opposed to a union actor). Once approved, the actor will become SAG-eligible and can work the job.

3) Members in good standing for at least one year with one of the affiliated performers' unions (ACTRA, AEA, AFTRA, AGMA or AGVA), and who have worked and been paid as a principal at least once in the affiliated union's jurisdiction, are eligible to join SAG. Policies in many "right-to-work states" differ, so check with the unions if you live in one of these states.

RIGHT-TO-WORK STATE: A state in which they have a law that prohibits required union membership of workers

Financial Core

FINANCIAL CORE (also referred to as FI-CORE): Simply stated, actors are "dues paying non-members of SAG" and can work both union and non-union jobs.

Actors usually want to work as much as possible. Union work is the desired way to go, but there are also a lot of non-union jobs that provide exposure, credits and money. For those who want or need the option to do <u>both</u> types of work, SAG permits members to go Financial Core. This status does not affect their insurance or retirement funds that are accrued with money earned on SAG jobs, but fi-core actors <u>can't</u> vote, run for office or have a union card, and they lose member benefits, such as SAG workshops, film screenings, foundation programs and events, strike relief fund benefits and membership in the SAG Conservatory.

PROCEDURE FOR GOING FINANCIAL CORE: In order to opt for this status, union members must first resign their membership and then declare their financial core rights. Those who are not yet members would wait until they were a "must join" and then claim their rights rather than join. Understand that this is <u>not</u> an honorable withdrawal. Someone from the SAG office may call and try to talk you out of your decision because opting for this form of membership understandably weakens the power of the union. Listen carefully to what they have to say. If going Financial Core is a necessity or a choice, send a certified letter to the union. The following is an example of the letter that both members and "must joins" should use:

Dear _____, Executive Director of Screen Actor's Guild
(Name of current Executive Director)

I object to that portion of my compulsory union dues that does not finance the contract process so I hereby resign full constitutional membership in SAG and declare myself a financial core status worker in all jurisdictions of your contracts with employers. I make this declaration within the meaning of "financial core worker" as defined in the series of U.S. Supreme Court decisions culminating in CWA v. BECK. Please recalculate my financial core dues amount owed within the existing SAG union policy and National Labor Relations Board guidelines.

Sign the letter and make sure your address is included. Get a return receipt at the post office when you mail it so there is proof if needed. The union will then send a bill marked "non-member" for the reduced dues. The dues they designate must be paid. Keep your receipt and a copy of your check as proof that you have paid.

REINSTATING SAG MEMBERSHIP: It is vital to know that if an actor changes his mind and wants to become a card-carrying member again, the union board has the right to deny reinstatement. The Screen Actors Guild policy:

> *Resigning union membership is a permanent decision. In accordance with Article IV of the Screen Actors Guild Constitution, members who resign are not eligible for reinstatement to the Guild, however such persons may petition for a waiver of this policy. The reinstatement candidate seeking a waiver of this policy is required to schedule an appearance before the Disciplinary Review Committee and present a petition for reinstatement. The petition for reinstatement must include a list of all non-union work done during the period between resignation and reinstatement.*

Actors who choose to quit and then try to rejoin must expect to justify their situations. SAG contends that making the decision to resign affects not just the member but the entire union membership and the collective ability to enforce existing SAG contracts and to organize more union work. If you ever contemplate this option, be sure to give it serious consideration. I would recommend talking to actors who have gone this route as well as the union advisers in order to understand the benefits, problems and consequences. For important information regarding Financial Core, check out the Screen Actor's Guild website: www.sag.com

ACTORS' EQUITY ASSOCIATION

Joining the Actors' Equity Association is dependent on booking employment under an Equity principal contract. Once an AEA principal job is booked, membership must be applied for during the term of the contract job. Their membership is contingent on additional provisions and exceptions so check their website for details: www.actorsequity.org

AMERICAN FEDERATION OF RADIO AND TELEVISION ARTISTS

Joining AFTRA is a matter of choice. Whenever you want to join, simply contact their office, pay the fee and you will be a member. Their website is www.aftra.org/aftra/aftra.htm

. . . .

Learn more about the different membership qualifications, restrictions and benefits of the unions by researching each of them on their websites. If you have questions, call each union and talk to the person in charge of membership. When you're eligible and when it makes good business sense, join the union(s).

MARKETING

MARKETING: The action or business of promoting or selling a person, service or products.

Marketing introduces and promotes actors and their work to industry pros. There are too many actors who do what you do – but they are not you. Marketing helps to distinguish you from your competition and gives you exposure, which usually generates work opportunities. Photos and resumes are the actor's main marketing tools, and they are discussed thoroughly in Chapters 8 and 9. There are numerous others that are extremely beneficial.

CASTING VEHICLES

No matter how good a type you are or how talented, if industry pros don't see your picture(s) you probably won't get auditions. The online casting websites provide exposure for actors.

Casting Websites: In the major markets, most commercial jobs and more and more TV and film work are cast utilizing online casting websites. Basically, the way it works is

- actors pay a fee and join the site(s), or their agent(s) or manager supervise the posting of their client's pictures and resumes

- the casting website company places the actors' photos and resumes online

- CDs post their casting breakdowns on the casting website.

CASTING BREAKDOWNS: A casting director posts online the descriptions of the roles in a project that they are casting for the agents, managers and/or actors to view then submit. The roles are delineated by gender, age and physical type

- CDs have the option to submit only to the agents and managers or open it up to the actors on that site

- when CDs choose to allow open submissions, actors who are right for a role can submit their photos and resumes thus putting themselves up for consideration

- actors who are deemed appropriate or their representatives will be contacted by phone or e-mail and given an appointment time.

Today there are several of these websites in major markets. Some industry pros prefer using one for a specific kind of job and other sites for different types of casting. It is a marketing necessity for actors to be posted on at least one. In New York and Los Angeles, most actors subscribe to two or three so that they will be able to submit or be found for all the work that might be appropriate for them.

> The major casting websites in Los Angeles are Actors Access, LA Casting and Now Casting.

> The main ones in New York are Actors Access and New York Casting.

> The main casting website in Chicago, San Francisco, Florida, Texas (south central), Southeast U.S., Colorado/Utah, Hawaii, Toronto, and Vancouver is Actors Access.

Showcasing: I consider showcasing in professional venues to be a valuable form of marketing. After all, what is marketing if it does not introduce you and remind as many prospective industry pros, as often as possible, about you and the quality of your acting work? If you choose wisely, showcases, audition workshops and theatrical productions can give you beneficial exposure. Find detailed information on the various showcase venues in Chapter Ten.

Demo Reels: When seeking representation or being considered for TV and film roles, actors will often be asked for their reels. It's a "Catch 22" for new actors. You don't have a professional demo reel unless you have done film and TV work, and it is difficult to get that work until you have a reel. When you have sufficient video on yourself, create your reel – it is a major showcasing tool. (Actors with little or no professional TV and film work can still create viable "starter" reels. Information on how best to produce videos of your acting work for a reel is found in Chapter Ten.)

I would suggest duplicating no more than 25 copies to start since you will be updating your reel periodically. Be sure to create a professional-looking cover for the DVD that includes your contact info and picture.

Personal Websites: Your personal website is a professional showcasing opportunity. It gives industry pros a place to learn more about you and see your photos and short reel(s). Websites don't have to be elaborate or expensive. They should include a professional-looking home page, a number of photos (headshots as well as on-set photos), bio, resume, business contact or representation info and a short edited acting reel. If you do not have on-set photos or a reel when you first create your website, include them when acquired. List your website on all of your promotional materials.

 SUGGESTION: Have your e-mail address be an offshoot of your website then it will always be: "you@you.com." Even if you change Internet providers, you will never need to change your e-mail address.

Online Reels: A great way for industry pros to quickly see a short compilation (similar to a movie trailer) of an actor's work is to watch it on the actor's personal website, the casting sites, and/or sites that feature one-minute demo reels.

PROMOTIONAL TOOLS

Since the name of the game is to get as much exposure as possible, here are more tools that will help industry pros locate and remember you.

Business Cards: Most professionals have business cards. You are a professional and should have them to give to industry people. The card should include a professional color picture, your name, union status (if you are a member), your business phone number or your representation's name and contact info, plus (if you have it) your website address, speed-reel log-in data and/or other pertinent (but not personal) contact information.

Postcards: Postcards can be a valuable way for actors to stay in touch or promote work they have done. The postcard should have a professional headshot or a photo lifted from a job, all business contact info and a note. The message can be hand-written or printed. I strongly suggest that it <u>succinctly</u> reports advances in your career, recent credits or actor-related activities. For example:

- Look for *Your Name* costarring in *Name of Show or Movie* on *Date*
- Just completed shooting *Name of Movie* directed by *Director's Name (especially if prominent)*
- Now represented by *Agent or Manager's Name*
- Studying *Form of Training* with *Teacher's Name*
- You are cordially invited on *Date* to see me in *Name of Showcase or Theatrical Production* .
- Or any combination of the above.

Plus add something personal but short.

> *I look at every postcard that comes in. It is a quick read. Actors send me postcards for years and I start feeling familiar with them. I also know how much work it takes to send these out and I appreciate an actor for taking care of the business end of his or her career.* **TERRY BERLAND,** Commercial Casting Director and Author

WARNING: Be careful not to send out postcards and other materials to the same people too often without a specific promotional purpose. You may alienate those you are intending to impress. It could be annoying or be perceived as desperate when industry pros receive a constant stream of cards or submissions from you. A major pet peeve of many casting directors is getting postcards from actors thanking them for every audition. Expressing gratitude for every opportunity could communicate that you are not getting many auditions. I do think it is a good idea to send a thank-you note to a CD when you have booked a job through their office or a Christmas card to thank them for bringing you in to audition during the year.

Online promotions and advertisements: For a fee, many of the online casting sites will send advertisements and invitations to agents, managers and casting directors promoting showcases and theatrical productions.

Advertising: Advertising in *Variety* and *The Hollywood Reporter* (in the trade papers and online) is a costly form of promotion. It should only be used when promoting a large role in a movie or TV show that is about to be released or aired.

E-mails: Create an e-mail database of all your industry contacts. Every few months send out an e-mail informing them about what is currently happening in your career. Keep it positive, short and fun. Include your picture and a link to your website. This form of promotion does not cost money, only the time it takes to program the database, create the e-mails and send them out.

Drop-offs: Periodically hand-deliver your headshot and resume and/or promotional material to the offices of targeted CDs and/or representation. Most have mail bins or slots for this purpose. You can make special trips or better yet, keep your materials with you and whenever you are in the area, drop it off.

....

It is important to do mailings, drop-offs, e-mails and promotions especially when performing in theatrical productions and showcases or in TV shows and movies. Do several types of promotions and (depending on the costs) repeat at least twice for every project. The majority of people you are contacting will not attend the event or watch the show. However, the purpose is that they see your face and name and know that you are working. Over time, they may get to know who you are even if they have never met you. When submitting for representation or to a CD, the familiarity you have cultivated can influence industry people to take notice of you, as opposed to those where there is no recognition.

BUSINESS TOOLS

REFERENCE MATERIALS

Samuel French in Los Angeles and in New York City (and on their website) sells specialized publications that reference agents, managers, casting directors and teachers. These publications list the individuals and companies specific to each of these categories and give useful data. Most of these booklets are updated three or four times a year and provide the most current information for researching or referencing industry professionals. There are many other beneficial and insightful books written about acting, training, actors and the business that are worth getting so take a look at them.

ORGANIZATION TOOLS

Being organized is a necessity, and there are tools that can be helpful. Keeping records of appointments, expenses, auditions, contacts and events is crucial for taxes, research, referencing, networking, etc. Whether you use a cell phone that syncs with a computer calendar, an online calendar or an appointment book, stay organized. Create or buy (at Samuel French or the Drama Book Shop) an audition book to keep track of your auditions: location, who you saw, what you wore and specific notes. If you have a fairly sophisticated computer software program or online calendar, you will be able to keep all of your audition data there. Also, professionals need to amass numerous documents for referencing. It is important to set up and maintain organized files for audition "sides," scripts, contracts and contact lists. Most but not all of these documents can be kept on computers and compact discs.

MORE ESSENTIALS

PHYSICAL APPEARANCE

The following accessories that alter or change your appearance I consider essentials:

- **Wardrobe:** Appropriate wardrobe for the types of roles you audition for is essential. Once you have a good idea of your type and understand your wardrobe basics, purchase suitable shirts, tops, jackets, outfits, etc.

- **Glasses:** Glasses can be a helpful accessory for actors auditioning for intellectual, character and business roles. The many styles can suggest various characters. The one(s) you acquire should fit your face and type. Be sure that the glass is non-glare so there is no reflection when worn on-camera. Also, they shouldn't cover your eyebrows, have a black frame, or be too wide or too narrow.

- **Makeup:** Most women (and sometimes men) purchase specific makeup for auditions and on-camera jobs. When looking for on-camera makeup, go to a professional film and TV makeup store and have them select what works for you.

- **Wigs, Hair Color and Extensions:**
  - <u>Women</u> with problem hair or who want to have different "looks" might choose to buy wigs, hairpieces or hair extensions. Today's synthetic wigs and extensions look and perform almost as good as the real hair ones and are more affordable. The tricky part is getting them fitted, cut and styled specifically for you, then taking good care of them so they don't look like wigs. Also, hair color is often beneficial for women (and men) in creating their look.

  - <u>Men</u> can change their look with a new haircut or styling. And depending on your type and talent range, you might consider purchasing facial hairpieces, e.g., mustaches, beards and sideburns – they can be helpful in creating characters. (Men can get hair plugs but once implanted are permanent.)

  Experiment with styles, lengths and maybe color but make sure that whatever color, hairpiece and/or hairstyle you choose are right for the roles for which you could be cast. Only work with knowledgeable hair professionals, or you could develop hair and/or scalp problems.

- **Hair Accessories:** When hair length affords versatility, it is smart to have clips, bands, gels, sprays, etc., to assist in creating a range of looks. I suggest that these accessories are kept in a bag that goes with you to your auditions.

....

There are even more tools, specialists, materials and services that can help actors to become working professionals. I recommend many more on my website: carolynebarry.com/recommend.html. I update this section regularly to catalog the best products and the top Los Angeles professionals who provide beneficial training and services for actors. They all have value but they are not all a necessity. The costs do add up, so select those that you can afford and that are beneficial at each step of your career.

COMMERCIAL AUDITIONS

Every audition is an opportunity to be considered for a role, but obviously not a guarantee that you will get the job. No matter how good an actor you are or how long you have trained, successful auditioning requires a combination of preparation, skills, experience, mind-sets and a look – plus luck. It's your responsibility to do a great audition. Then "the powers that be" make a choice from all those who did great auditions.

Most actors start their careers auditioning for TV commercials. In order to do well, it is vital to understand the preparation and process. Here I present essential information, tips and techniques that I am confident will be advantageous in helping you book commercials. (Much of the information in this chapter is also pertinent for TV and film auditions.)

BEFORE AUDITIONS

Audition preparation differentiates the professionals from the amateurs. Here is what professionals do:

Get correct information: When you receive an audition call, text or e-mail, note all the data and/or transfer it to your computer calendar program, online calendar or appointment book. You don't want to go to the wrong place at the wrong time in inappropriate wardrobe. When going to a location for the first time, get specific directions and a phone number. If you don't have GPS, get directions from the Internet or reference a map book.

Confirm appointments: Call, text or e-mail whoever contacted you to confirm your audition. Although this seems like a "no-brainer," you would be surprised how many actors do not. When I am casting and if actors don't confirm, I replace them. If they show up, I often will not have the time to audition them. They could miss out and I might not want to see them again.

Obtain the commercial copy in advance:

COPY: The scripted dialogue in a commercial that is being used for the audition.

Before most dialogue commercial auditions, CDs post the copy on submission websites for the auditioning actors. Join these sites so you have access to your material when posted. Ask your representation if there is copy. If there is, arrange to get it. If it's not up on one of the sites, ask your agent or manager if it can be e-mailed or faxed. If not, get to the audition early. The more time you have with it in a quiet environment, the better your preparation.

Know which role you are reading: You don't want to prepare the wrong part.

Prepare material (when there is copy): Investigate, motivate, find your connection and make choices. Prepare several interpretations. Text preparation will be covered in detail later in this chapter.

> *When doing your commercial or theatrical audition preparation, be sure to rehearse out loud after you have done your investigation. That does not mean practice line readings. It means work with your motivation when you speak your rehearsals.* MICHAEL DONOVAN, Casting Director, Commercial, Film and Theatre

Prepare for cue cards:

> CUE CARD: A large sheet of paper or cardboard on which audition copy is written so that actors can refer to it when needed. It is usually positioned in the casting room near the camera.

Actors often have issues with cue cards because the dialogue is never written out the same as it is on the script that is given out for rehearsal. So inside the casting room it is often difficult to quickly adjust to a new word layout while auditioning. To help become comfortable using cue cards try this preparation: write the copy several times so that in each version the number of words on the lines lays out differently; with every rehearsal, look at a different version so that you don't get locked into seeing the copy only the way it is on the script. This should make it easier to adapt to whatever way it is written on the cue card.

Select wardrobe: Whether the audition is for commercial or theatrical roles, wardrobe helps define the character for the actor and offers a visual image for "the powers that be." On the casting breakdown, in the script, or from your representation, ascertain where the scene(s) takes place and what kind of wardrobe the character could be wearing.

> *Commercial CDs are told by the creative team the wardrobe they want the actors to wear. CDs tell the agents, who inform the actors. Follow those directions. Once, I was auditioning actors for an upscale casino commercial and an actor came in wearing jeans. I asked if he got the wardrobe instructions. He said, "Yes but I don't see why it matters what I wear. My performance should matter." My client asked me why that actor was not*

dressed properly. To my client that actor was unprofessional. Your performance does matter, but following the wardrobe instructions helps. **TERRY BERLAND,** Commercial CD and Author

When actors audition for commercials, they need to be instantly established, so it is beneficial to acquire the appropriate wardrobe basics for your type. If you excel at a skill or sport or audition a lot for specific types of roles (e.g., soldier, doctor, policeman, nun, scientist, nurse, etc.) it would behoove you to have those kinds of clothes. When you have an audition for a role that requires a specific outfit (if it is important), find someone who can loan it to you or maybe you could rent it. If you can't or don't want to get the outfit, suggest the attire with whatever you have. Bottom line; try to dress suitably for the roles you are auditioning for. It shows that you are a professional.

In your car trunk or backpack, keep some basic wardrobe pieces and accessories (e.g., glasses, wigs, facial hair pieces, hair accessories, a few types of shirts and tops, ties, a jacket, etc.) that can quickly change your look for a role. You never know if your representation will give you the wrong wardrobe info, you will be asked to read for a different part at your audition, you might get a last-minute audition and won't have time to go home to change, or your audition is being held at a large casting facility where multiple CDs work and you will be invited to audition for another job while you are there – all would probably necessitate a change of wardrobe. Be prepared. Further audition wardrobe tips are coming up in the "You Are What You Wear" section in this chapter.

Allow time for traffic, parking and unforeseen problems: Auditions make most actors nervous. Being late intensifies the anxiety. It is better to be early.

Actors new to L.A. should make a concerted effort to drive around (without an appointment) and geographically LEARN the city. **KEVIN E. WEST,** President of The Actor's Network

On the way, check the radio for traffic reports. If you are late or lost, call your agent or manager and he/she will inform the CD. Only call the casting facility if you can't contact your representation.

Don't call your agent for directions. One way to get them is to text Google at "46645" with your starting and ending address. They will text you back with directions. **ABBY GIRVIN,** Owner of DDO Agency

IN THE WAITING ROOM

Actors often feel powerless at commercial auditions. It's understandable: sitting in the holding area with a dozen or more actors, waiting up to an hour or being rushed in with little or no preparation, getting confusing direction, and leaving feeling you could have done better. Commercial auditions are not usually conducive to actors' doing their best. But there are several actions that can be taken to help you feel confident, prepared and empowered.

Arrive early: Never be late or even on time because you won't have options if the session is running on schedule. Be early so you can get settled and focused and have time to adjust your hair, makeup and/or wardrobe, and prepare the audition material. When you are early, you have options:

- If the session is running late and there are several actors waiting, then sign in and prepare.

- If the session is running on time and there are just a few actors waiting, then hold off signing in. Take the audition material, leave the room (don't go too far), prepare and then sign in at your appointed time.

- When there are a large number of actors waiting and the session is on time, do sign in.

Ask questions: When you need clarification on the material or what is expected, ask the assistant who is supervising the sign-ins in the waiting area so that you can get the most from your preparation. If you are not sure how to pronounce a word or the product name, ask. If something doesn't make sense, ask. It's better to ask questions before rehearsing than to get corrections from the session director in the audition room and have to adjust your work right before auditioning.

Find Out the "Tone": Every commercial has a style or "tone" that should be factored into the preparation.

> TONE: The general quality or feeling of a production as an indicator of the attitude or view of the writer, director, producer or client.

If this info is not posted or if you have not seen the current TV commercials for the product, ask the lobby assistant, "What is the tone of this commercial?" You might get answers like natural, comedic, quirky, over-the-top, fun/playful, serious, warm, upscale, authoritative, vulnerable, earthy, edgy, over-the-top, understated, etc.

Do your audition preparation: If you haven't obtained your copy in advance, do your preparation now: investigate, motivate, and find your connection and interpretation. If you did receive the copy and worked on it in advance, review your choices and work on your connection. Find a place where you can rehearse in a full voice.

For unscripted commercial auditions, you will not be able to find out what is expected until you arrive at the casting facility. When improvising alone or with another actor(s), so much is unpredictable. Unscripted auditions present their own set of challenges even for the best-trained actors. Most don't know that there is preparation that can be done. Read about the techniques for unscripted auditions that I cover later in this chapter.

Rehearse with your partner: When you are doing scene auditions, either the casting assistant will assign you a partner(s) or you should check the sign-in list and determine the actor(s) with whom you will probably be paired. This is especially valuable when auditioning with children. Rehearse with your partner(s) or, if there is no dialogue, spend time getting comfortable with them. Most actors are willing. If your partner chooses not to practice the script with you, check the list for the next person with whom you could be partnered, and if possible rehearse with him/her. When called into the casting room with your initial partner, if you felt good working with the rehearsal actor, politely ask whether you can audition with that person. Your request could be denied, so don't get too attached to what you two did. If you didn't connect with the actor you rehearsed with, go in with whoever is assigned. In either case you have had an opportunity to investigate and rehearse. Thus you should feel prepared.

Work on several interpretations: Locking in only one way of doing an audition can be problematic. First, it usually creates a fairly shallow interpretation. Second, if the session operator wants a different approach, it can be hard to shake the work you have locked in. Finally, if asked to do the copy or scenario a second or third way, you won't have it. Work on several approaches.

Deal with your nerves: Every audition is a precious opportunity to work, make money, create contacts and fans and move a career forward. When actors fixate on these expectations before auditioning, it normally creates anxiety and pressure. Don't focus on disempowering thoughts and questions, such as

> Did I wear the right outfit? Maybe I should have done something different with my hair. Did I work on the material enough? I hope they don't notice that my skin is broken out. How many people will I be auditioning for? Who are they? Will they direct me before I read? What will they ask me? What should I ask them? Will they think I am physically right for the role? I wonder if the reader is going to be any good? I haven't seen this CD for a few months – maybe she doesn't like my work. How will I do? Will they re-direct my reading? Am I right for the role? What will they think about my audition?

Many of these thoughts flash quickly through almost every actor's mind and especially those who are new. These are the same types of concerns that people usually have interviewing for any job. At callbacks, because the stakes are raised, the concerns get more intense for most. Actors who are unfazed at the initial audition often have callback anxiety. Now, the thoughts are

> They must like me; now the pressure is really on. It's only between

a few others and me; I have to be great. Will my agent (or manager) dump me if I don't book this job? What did I do that made them call me back? I really need the money. My competition must be good. I hope I don't "blow it" now. And so on.

This "noise" is normal. How you deal with your questions, concerns and expectations will determine how much power those thoughts have. You must learn how to alleviate, use or quiet them, or they will take their toll on your work. I know great actors who can't get out of their heads at interviews (and refuse to do anything about it), and their work suffers. I also know less talented ones who shine because they have very little "noise" and are excited to be auditioning.

> *Paranoia is death at auditions. The time you are sure they are insulting you by making you wait as other people go in front of you is the time they could be saving you for when the director gets off the phone and can fully give you his attention. Being paired up with a stiff for a scene partner does not guarantee being erased off a casting recording. Fluffing a line, losing your place, facing an unresponsive room or a coffee stain on your shirt is just a human moment in a very human profession. Don't complicate the situation by being a victim – take the high road, laugh at yourself and move on.* **ALICIA RUSKIN,** Commercial Agent & Partner, KSA Talent Agency

What you think influences how you feel, and how you feel impacts your audition. With time and experience, actors usually figure out how to alleviate the self-imposed stress. In the meantime, work on your audition anxieties whether it is with self-help books, hypnosis, audition classes, coaching, therapy, talking with friends or teachers and/or developing a sense of humor about your disempowering thoughts – the sooner the better.

 SUGGESTION: What you think produces feelings. The feelings are real but the thoughts you created are not real. So be careful what you are saying to yourself.

Stay relaxed and focused: After you have done a <u>thorough</u> preparation and while you wait, <u>don't continually run your lines and review your choices</u>, either out loud or in your head. It's been my experience that when actors do this, they create anxiety and make themselves insecure. Don't let the frustration of having to wait negatively affect your mood, energy or mind-set. Do whatever works to keep you focused, confident and positive, e.g., meditate, sit quietly, read, laugh, walk around by yourself, etc. Don't chat with other actors unless rehearsing or getting comfortable with them.

Don't do a lot of bantering with other actors. If someone tries to engage you in chit-chat, politely tell them that you need to focus but you'll be happy to talk to them when you are both done. If others are discussing the industry negatively (as many actors unfortunately do), find somewhere else to wait. Don't let their negativity "get on you!" Also, reframe the words "nerves" or "nervous" to "excitement" and "energy" – far more empowering.
LAURI JOHNSON, Entertainment Industry Life Coach

When you know that you will be next, review your choices, lines, objectives, motivations, etc. – but only once or twice. Energize and prepare to commit to your choices and instincts and to enjoy the audition. It's your time to <u>be an actor</u>.

IN THE AUDITION

The following audition pointers were formulated from personal audition experience, teaching thousands of students and observing actors who have auditioned at my casting sessions. I truly believe these tips will serve your auditions for commercials as well as TV and film:

- As you walk into the audition, don't think about anything you worked on. Let it all go. Be present to whatever happens.

- Be respectful, positive and professional without losing your personality.

Early in my career, I was lucky enough to work behind the scenes at casting sessions. It was my job to keep the bagels and coffee fresh. I learned so much about auditioning from wandering in and out of those sessions. I learned that the audition begins way before the actor starts his or her read. Usually within two seconds after the actor enters, those running the audition make up their minds whether the actor is right or not (especially with commercials). Some actors try too hard to impress. The most impressive actors were the ones who walked in business-like with little interaction with the people in the room, just a nice smile and a hello. Save your stand-up routine for a comedy club. **LESLIE JORDAN**, Emmy-Award-Winning Actor

Give full attention to the person who is directing you: Don't be distracted by anyone or anything. When you are being given direction, don't be figuring out how to do what they are saying. Just listen and trust that you got it: otherwise, you might miss information.

If clarification is needed, ask questions. You have the right. Questions are only irritating when they are unnecessary. Those running the session won't think less of you because you request clarification. Their answers will help you to do a better audition for them.

If they talk to you or ask questions, don't second-guess what they want to hear. They probably want to get to know you and see your personality. Just talk to them as opposed to trying to impress.

Don't initiate <u>unnecessary</u> banter. It is unprofessional. They are busy and usually stressed. Unless they start a conversation, those running the auditions don't like actors who waste their time chatting.

If the session director or CD is rude, short-tempered or seems ambivalent, <u>do not take it personally</u>. It may be their nature or they may be dealing with problems or previous actors who tested their patience. Stay pleasant, positive and do your work. You are a professional. At those moments, he/she may not be. Remember, when "the powers that be" watch your video audition, they will only see you, not the moody person running the session.

Don't allow yourself to be rushed. Before you start your audition, "get centered."

GETTING CENTERED: Taking a moment to relax, quiet your anxieties and get focused.

- Breathe, take one or two seconds before beginning or find your own way to "get centered" but don't take a self-indulgent period of time to begin. When those running the session are rushed, don't be influenced by their negative energy.

- Do not speed through your audition. When actors are nervous or "in their head," they speed up the dialogue or their improvised scenarios. When actors are connected and focused, they don't rush. On the other hand, don't speak really slowly or take long pauses between the lines.

- Whether you are auditioning for one person or a group, reading into a camera or speaking to an actor or a few actors, auditioning with a bad actor or a great one, in a small room or a large theatre, stay focused and don't allow unexpected incidents to upset you and/or put you "in your head." No matter what happens, go with it and adjust quickly. If you can learn to look at whatever happens as a gift, you can handle anything.

Motivate Out. For improvised and scripted on-camera scenes, when possible, find a way to "motivate out" your actions and/or dialogue at least fifty percent of the time to maximize your facial exposure.

MOTIVATE OUT: *Utilizing environment or behavior to position yourself in the direction of the camera or audience so that your face is seen. It is unlike "cheating out" – which is when an actor plays out in a way that is clearly unmotivated.*

214

Most new actors constantly look at their partner(s), which keeps them in profile. If your partner is playing toward the camera and you are always looking at him or her then you are upstaging yourself.

UPSTAGING YOURSELF: *Giving focus to the other actor by either constantly looking at him or positioning yourself where his or her face is seen and yours isn't.*

Those viewing the audition videos are more compelled to watch the person whose eyes they can see. Professionals understand the value and know how to motivate out. Notice I did not say "cheat out," because that doesn't look natural. Good camera technique enables actors to hold the viewer's attention and look like professionals. Study actors in commercials, plays, sitcoms and soap operas. They all play to the fourth wall.

FOURTH WALL: *An entertainment industry expression used to describe the area where the audience or camera(s) is positioned. In the theatre and on film and TV sets, actors are usually directed to play in the direction of the fourth wall.*

 "Motivating out" at first feels awkward because actors are used to relating to their partners. It takes a good deal of practice to make this an instinctive physicality. "Motivating out" must be integrated into your physicality, or you will need to think about it while auditioning, which distracts from your performance.

Look into camera. When auditioning with a reader and told to do the dialogue looking into the camera, don't look back and forth between the two. It makes you look nervous.

During the read, trust and commit to your instincts. <u>Unless given a specific direction, don't consciously perform anything you rehearsed</u> or that you have learned. Some of the choices that you rehearsed might not feel right in that moment. Don't interrupt your instinctive interpretation trying to perform them. Allow for your read to flow – you will most likely organically do most of what you rehearsed. When you are connected and "out of your head," you are open to instinctive moments that are often better than those you planned.

NOTE It's probably understandable by now why I strongly recommend that actors should wait to start auditioning until they have done at least a year of professional training. Auditioning is challenging. Actors are more proficient at doing my suggested techniques once they have a strong foundation.

Have fun. Getting auditions is what you have trained and worked for – now enjoy the experience.

- When you feel your solo audition was lacking or if you have another interpretation that you would like to do, politely request,

"If you have time, I would like to do it again" or "do another interpretation." It is not a foul to ask. If they refuse, say "thank you" (mean it) and leave. They may have loved what you did and don't need a second version.

Ask to do it again. At the initial call, if you are partnered with an apparent amateur whom you believe was harmful to your audition, you could ask to read again. After you have finished your audition, let the other actor exit and <u>if appropriate</u> politely tell the session director, "I wouldn't mind waiting and working with another actor." Don't speak negatively about the actor. The session operator understands. If there is time and he/she agrees that your partner was bad, he/she might allow you to audition again with a new partner – or not. It's worth asking.

Don't ask "needy" questions, e.g., "When are the callbacks or bookings? Should I wear this outfit if I get a callback? Where will the commercial be shot? Should I keep the script?" The reason most actors ask these kinds of questions is to get an indication of interest. At the initial call, the person running the session has no clue about who is getting a callback or booking. And at the callback, no one knows who will book the job. There will be no decision until the client has weighed in, usually a day or two later, after seeing the finalists on video. Needy inquiries make actors look insecure.

Don't be overly grateful or acknowledging. A simple "thank you" or "it was a pleasure reading for you" is sufficient. Much more might make you look desperate.

Unless they request you leave the audition material, take it. Build a library of sides, copy and scripts that you can use for practice. Often there are rewrites for the callbacks, so if you go back for a second audition, don't memorize the original script unless you know for sure that there have been no rewrites. Just use it as a reference if you can't get the updated material.

Let it go. When you finish the audition, those in charge will say "great" or "thank you," which is your signal to leave. Or they'll give direction and ask you to do the material again. Don't read anything into either scenario. It's not an indication of their interest if they don't ask you to read again. You may have nailed it or they may be in a hurry. When asked to do more readings, many actors interpret this to mean that those doing the directing were not happy with them. It could be they wanted to experiment with different versions or that they liked the actor and wanted to see his/her range. Then there are new actors who believe that if the "powers that be" work with them, it means they will get the job – they are frustrated when they don't. It is difficult to understand all that is involved with the decision-making process. Just do your best, and when you leave, let it go.

AFTER THE AUDITION

After you leave, debrief. Review what you felt you honestly did well and acknowledge yourself for it. This helps build confidence. I believe that when you acknowledge your successes, you can build on them. Next, look at what could use improvement. Notice that I didn't say, "What you did wrong." When actors are self-deprecating or get frustrated, the tendency is to become cautious or work too hard at the next audition. After several of these negative experiences, many actors become hesitant to trust their instincts and thus lose some freedom. It is important when reviewing your work after any audition or performance to be supportive of yourself. Monitor your "after audition" thoughts. It helps determine whether your future auditions will get better or worse.

When assessing "what could be improved," use the following process:

- Identify exactly what needs to be improved. Don't ever say to yourself, "I suck," or anything that resembles that. It's not true. Your training, preparation, audition mind-set, commitment or confidence needs attention.

- If it is a foundation/technique issue, you can work on it with a teacher, coach or actor/friend. If it is not, work on it by yourself. Use commercial copy and work the techniques that need attention. Rehearse for at least ten minutes each day for several days or until you feel secure that the issues are resolved or at least better: then let it go. If you have a camera, video yourself after each of your practice sessions.

Go through this process after every audition. If you do, I believe your auditions will keep getting better.

....

Auditions are a learning experience as well as a work opportunity. A lot is involved in the preparation and auditioning process. There are tools, mind-sets and acting techniques to be understood and applied. Take pleasure in discovering facets of your craft that you can improve. Love to learn and grow. Most creative people enjoy working on their development. Besides making you a better actor, it fortifies the creative process and enhances you as a person.

I have co-created a compact disc program entitled "Getting the Job" that actors can listen to before, on the way to and after auditions. It's designed to give specific coaching for commercial as well as theatrical auditions. I strongly endorse it, even if it is blatant self-promotion.

> *At the start of your acting career, pursuing TV commercials is a*
> *great way to make money, learn your craft and get exposure.*
> **DAVID SWEENEY,** Los Angeles Talent Manager

THERE'S MORE

I have even more tips and techniques to share with you that will better prepare you for commercial auditions and make you truly competitive. I have been a commercial audition technique teacher since 1982, so I have plenty to offer on the subject. Don't be overwhelmed. It might be difficult to digest all the input presented here in one or two readings. It takes study, practice, repetition and experience. Get what you can and refer back to it often. Also, remember that much of this information can be applied to your theatrical auditions.

YOU ARE THE CHARACTER

Actors are trained to play characters. In acting class, the focus is on developing and being true to the character. With theatre, film and TV work, the actor's responsibility is to bring them to life. I believe it is different in commercials. They are very short and the roles depicted are targeted at specific segments of the population. There is little or no time to establish a character. In a few seconds, it has to be clear whom the actors represent. Those for whom the spots are intended must see a semblance of themselves or someone they would like to be in order to identify with and/or be motivated to buy the product. This is why physical types and essences are sometimes more important than talent in commercial casting.

Are you wondering, "If you don't play characters, how does an actor prepare for commercials?" I strongly suggest approaching parts as the <u>roles you are</u>. You play numerous roles in your life, e.g., employee, boss, friend, spouse or significant other, child, parent, neighbor, student or teacher, laborer or professional, etc. Many of the parts that you audition for in commercials are roles you are or have been. Those roles for which you are physically right but haven't experienced are doable with a little work. Approach your auditions using <u>your</u> feelings and reactions. Focus on how <u>you</u>, not a character you create, would behave or react in the given situation. It is easier, faster and you'll have better results when starting with the premise that "<u>you</u> are the character playing a role."

Typecasting: Although you play numerous roles in your life, there are those that suit you better commercially than others. Most of the time, the actors auditioning for a specific role fit a designated physical description; they are all the same age-range, ethnicity, gender, type, and build. Yet those getting the callback and booking have the look (along with the personality, essence and talent) that resonated stronger for the occupation/role being cast. It is a subjective decision of those doing the casting.

To demonstrate how this might work, the next time you are in a group of people whom you don't know, play this game. Pretend you are casting roles in a commercial or film from the people you see. Cast the following characters:

- Members of a wedding party: Who would be the bride or groom, maid/matron of honor, best man, members of the wedding party, various family members, eccentric relatives, photographer, caterer, wedding planner, etc.?

- People in a business office: Who looks like they could be the boss, bookkeeper, human resources person, assistant, executive, computer technician, secretary, "creatives," errand boy or girl, receptionist, etc.?

- Those in a suburban neighborhood: Who looks like members of the family who has lived there the longest, those new to the block, busybodies, problem neighbors, those on the welcoming committee, fast-food-delivery people, mail carrier, gardener, etc? Also, who could be the residents who have all the right products (sold in commercials) and those who don't have them?

You will see that most people physically fit a role or two in each scenario. Play along with a friend and compare how similarly you cast these strangers. Whether you know it or not, you have been conditioned by the media to see distinct physical types of people playing specific kinds of roles. This exercise will give you an insight into casting. Actors want to perform a range of parts, but those who are identifiable types are often more "castable" in commercials.

Identifying Your Roles: Watch TV and analyze magazine ads. Identify the roles that best suit your age, look, personality, body type, and essence. Study yourself on video. Compare your looks with those performers depicted in the media. Be objective about your image and the roles that best fit you – it can be challenging. (In Chapter Seven, there is a questionnaire and a plan that will guide you in determining your type.) For validation, talk to teachers, agents and casting directors and get their suggestions. Once you know the roles you are right for, hone them in your classes. Package your type(s) with the appropriate wardrobe, hairstyle and accessories and then capture it in your pictures.

ASPIRATIONAL LOOKS

Ad agencies do extensive research to target commercials to their product's specific consumers. Every commercial and the characters in them are seriously crafted. Age, ethnicity, gender, body type, and the look of a person's financial status are important considerations in casting: thus the actor's physical appearance is a major factor. The execs and clients contemplate whether the actor's "look" is identifiable or "aspirational" to the targeted market. Physical types are more important to the ad agencies than to the director, who is usually more concerned with the actor's talent and "directability."

I estimate that 60 percent of the reason actors receive callbacks is because they have a "look" that works for the spot. Twenty percent is their talent and/ or the audition they did. The remaining 20 percent, I believe, is about their personalities, confidence and essence. The same factors determine who gets the job but break down a little differently. Since the actors have been physically approved for the callback, their looks have a 40 percent value. Personality, essence, confidence and how actors interact with the director, plus the work they do on the callback are 60 percent of the reason an actor gets cast.

Actors' age, hair color and style, makeup, facial hair, weight, height, physical build, bone structure, wardrobe, skin and teeth help physically define them. Ethnicity is obviously fixed but most physical components can be altered or improved (if necessary) to create a marketable commercial image, e.g.,

- height can be altered with shoes.

- weight and physical proportions can be somewhat altered by gaining or losing weight and/or with wardrobe.

- age and bone structure have some flexibility with makeup, surgery and when actors nurture their appearance and health.

- women (and some men) with deep-set eyes or high foreheads should try <u>light</u> bangs to break up the forehead and better frame their eyes. Prominent foreheads can take attention away from the eyes. Eyes are so powerful on-camera – make sure they have focus.

- hair color or style is easily changed. Being a blonde, redhead or brunette, or having short or long hair facilitates different purposes and characters and does influence casting. Only experiment with a new hair color or style when you are seriously ready to make a change. Then be ready to shoot new pictures.

Commercial Types: There are established physical preferences that usually prevail in commercials. For example, advertising agencies hire actors whose physicality makes a positive statement about the product in most food, drink, candy and beauty product spots (which represent over 60 percent of TV commercials and print work). There must be no suggestion that the products can cause bad teeth, damaged hair, weight gain or blemished skin. These spots usually feature slender actors with good skin, hair and teeth and men with no facial hair. (When shooting a commercial, food can get caught in men's beards when eating and facial hair can be a distraction when men are drinking.) Yet there are many comedic food and drink spots that cast character actors who are heavier. Commercials for other products are not always as rigid about weight, age, teeth, hair and skin issues and facial hair.

Make sure your physicality and facial appearance serve you and the roles for which you audition. Study actors in commercials who are similar to you. Determine if you need to go to a dentist, dermatologist, optician, dietician, hairdresser, or physical trainer or need to shave.

YOU ARE WHAT YOU WEAR

Appropriate wardrobe helps actors to look the part and is beneficial for establishing types. Men and women look different in a tailored suit than when wearing jeans and a tee shirt. Uniforms, dressy evening attire and bathing suits create distinct looks, and you usually feel differently when wearing each. Wardrobe influences how directors, agency execs and clients perceive actors. It is often a subliminal factor when callback and booking choices are made. You and your representation work hard to get auditions, so always be prepared with the appropriate wardrobe to visually create the roles.

Industry Wardrobe Designations: Casting directors use the following terminology to describe the designated audition wardrobe:

- Casual or Home Casual: relaxed or socializing-with-friends-at-home clothes

- Upscale Casual: fashionable, informal, comfortable party clothes

- Outdoors or Camping: jeans, sweaters, denim, wool shirts and jackets

- Formal: very dressy outfits, e.g., tuxedos, cocktail dresses and gowns

- Business or "Spokes": business suit or a nice shirt and tie for men and a tailored dress or a suit for women

  SPOKES: *Short for spokesperson – the man or woman speaking on behalf of or representing a company, product or person.*

- Trendy (usually for men and women under thirty): jeans, "cool" t-shirts, and the latest fads in clothing

- Uniforms: outfits worn by policemen, military officers, doctor, nurses, nuns, pilots, postal workers, etc.

- Work Clothes: clothing associated with an occupation, e.g., waitress, trucker, realtor, construction worker, farmer, mechanic, etc.

- Sports Outfits: attire worn by a baseball player, bowler, equestrian, skater, hiker, etc.

These terms are often used theatrically when describing wardrobe that is character-specific.

Dos and Don'ts: Since commercial auditions are usually on-camera, it is beneficial to know the colors, styles and patterns to wear and to avoid so as to look your best. Most of the time the camera will shoot you from the waist up, so I will focus on that part of your wardrobe.

- Choose jewel tones and rich autumn colors (except orange, yellow and gold). Burgundy, emerald green, moss green, purple, grayish blue, and denim blue, are some of the warm colors that enhance skin tones, frame the face and give it focus. Grays and browns don't enhance most skin tones and hair colors but do not distract.

- Choose shirts with collars and tops with a "V" neck. They are the most flattering on-camera. Turtlenecks might have the clients wondering why you are hiding your neck. Crew- and cowl-neck tops can make your neck look distorted.

- Avoid busy patterns, stripes, bright colors, shiny jewelry and garments with distinguishable logos. They draw attention away from your face.

- Avoid black, dark blue, white, beige and light pastel colors. These colors usually reflect or soak up the light. Thus the camera captures a dimmer-looking face. (This is especially problematic for those with dark skin.) Red records differently on every camera: thus it hardly ever looks like the red of the garment being worn and can appear orange, which is usually not flattering.

- Avoid wearing clothes that show too much skin or cleavage unless the commercial calls for it. Depending on the actor's body, it can be distracting or send the wrong message.

 In order to learn what your best colors, hairstyles, makeup and clothing choices are for auditions, I suggest that each week in your on-camera commercial class you try out different looks, colors and wardrobe. Ask the teacher for feedback.

COMMERCIAL AUDITIONING IS ACTING

There are commercial jobs that are cast solely on an actor's "look," their personality or a performance of their reactions to a person, situation, object or product. That is why many think that booking commercials has little or nothing to do with talent or training. They are right about those specific kinds of jobs. Yet actors who are cast in commercials with dialogue or improvisation are usually talented and trained in addition to having the right look. Here is where trained actors usually have an advantage if they use what they have learned. The freedom, confidence and creative skills learned in improvisation workshops are incredibly beneficial for improv auditions. The techniques acquired in professional commercial, scene study and cold-reading classes are major assets when auditioning for dialogue commercials.

Professionals usually approach theatrical auditions working with a "who," "what," "where," and "why." Yet many don't consider using these acting basics for commercials. If they work in every other medium, why would they not be of value for commercials? – especially now when the tone for most of them is underplayed, natural and realistic.

Work with a "Who": Actors are primarily trained to react to the dialogue and the behavior of others, but at commercial auditions, monologues and sometimes scene copy are done looking at the camera. A camera gives you nothing to react to unless, in your mind, you can make it a person. Most actors never think about talking to a specific person for commercial auditions, but it is much easier to make a connection when they do. You might be thinking, "It's a camera, not a person. I can't connect with an inanimate object." Yet when talking on the phone, you don't see the person but you speak as if they were there. You relate to the person, not a visual presence.

We speak and react differently to the various people in our lives. Think about how you relate to your spouse or significant other, best friend or casual acquaintances, boss, employee, mother or father, neighbor, relatives or people you don't like. Your interactions are distinct with each.

> **TIP** Check this out by setting up a video camera in front of the phone. Look into it while talking, and record twenty to thirty second snippets of your conversations with a few different people. Then rehearse a piece of commercial copy for five or ten minutes, look at the camera and record your reading once. Play back the excerpts from your conversations with friends, family members, strangers and/or business associates and notice the differences in behavior, energy, delivery and tone with each person you spoke to. Then watch the reading of your commercial copy and check to see if you are the same person acting as you were on the phone. Do this exercise every day until you have the same honesty and personal connection doing the copy as you had when conversing. This work will also help you become comfortable talking into the camera.

During commercial copy preparation, read the material several times, then choose a person (a "who"). The "who" you select to use for your audition material affects how you feel, which influences interpretation. Be sure it is a person you know: don't just choose a generic friend, relative or neighbor. Be specific. When you read material, the first person you think you would tell this information to can be a good possibility. Sometimes the tone of the commercial might determine your selection. Choose the specific person from your cast of life characters who can evoke the necessary energetic tone and connection when preparing your audition. When you incorporate the "who," your read can embody the appropriate feeling and is better motivated.

Here are suggestions you can use to select your "who" when preparing copy:

- When it requires a playful, positive read, talk to a "fun" friend.

- If it needs warmth, choose someone you love.

- With copy that needs a strong delivery or when your character is talking about the product, talk to someone for whom you are the authority figure and/or who needs your help.

- When you are the one who needs the product information, choose someone who is an authority figure to you.

These choices can also help you <u>in the audition</u>. When you are directed to

- "Have fun with the read" – choose to talk to your fun friend.
- "Warm it up" – talk to the person you love.
- "Be authoritative or make the read stronger" – talk to the person for whom you are the authority figure.
- "Be more vulnerable or approachable" – talk to an authority figure.

Interpreting direction this way will help to keep your audition honest.

Have An Objective: Choose an intent or purpose to motivate your copy. For example, when you are the person seeking the product information, your objective might be "to get the help you need." When you are the person who is knowingly talking about the product, your objective could be "to help." Some "help" suggestions:

- When the commercial is for a diet product, vitamins, breakfast cereal, medicine, food, etc., your objective might be to help the person be healthier.
- When it is for cosmetics, shampoo, clothing, etc., the objective might be to help your person look better.
- For a car, it might just be to help them get the best car.

Often when copy is about you sharing information or a story about yourself, it would still be beneficial to make your intent (if at all possible) to help the person you are speaking to with your narrative. This choice usually connects you to the people watching and makes you more compelling.

When I do dialogue casting, I see too many actors who give little or no attention to motivating the copy with an objective. They usually focus on the words, the product, being energetic and positive, performing the intent of the ad agency or the tone of the commercial, and working the product. These objectives have value and should be part of the actor's focus. But if they drive the audition, it will be one-dimensional or over-performed and not believable or compelling to watch.

> *It's always important to give your own slant to the commercial; otherwise you will blend in with every other actor. Make your own creative choices that are truthful, not act-y.* **HUGH LEON,** Commercial Agent @ Coast to Coast Agency

Create A Pre-Life:

A challenge with dialogue commercials is how to truthfully start speaking. Most "copy" feels like it starts in the middle. So I suggest using a short pre-life. First, think of your "who" and trust that you have your connection with him/her – you don't have to visualize them. Then hear a four-to-five-word question that he/she would ask, and let your response induce a small, simple, unrehearsed physical reaction that will motivate the dialogue. This pre-life should take two or three seconds (no more).

To practice, take one line of commercial copy. Think about someone and what they would say or ask (in five words or less) to prompt the dialogue, and allow for that to motivate a simple reaction that leads you to say the line(s). To create different interpretations, choose a second and third "who" and hear them ask you something else that would motivate the line, respond, and then talk to them. You should feel the difference. If you video it, you will see it.

Commit To Your Instincts: Trust, never question, your instincts while auditioning. Committing to them helps keep you "out of your head." Don't be concerned with how or what you are doing.

....

Know your objective, choose your "who," motivate the dialogue, trust your instincts, and do a solid preparation – approaching commercial auditions using these acting basics gives actors the connection and freedom to do their best work. Auditioning this way should result in more callbacks and bookings. It also reinforces the craft, which assists actors in becoming better actors.

> *I spent the first five years of my career doing commercials. I once had a TV/film audition and the casting director said, "Wow, you can act. I knew I had seen you in lots of commercials but I had no idea you were such a good actor." I thought that was possibly the dumbest observation I had ever heard. In commercials actors are asked to say it all in 22 seconds! And to say it over and over as those advertising people pick apart the performance to the point of ludicrousness. Commercials are the very best training ground for any actor!* **LESLIE JORDAN,** Emmy-Award-Winning Actor

TO MEMORIZE OR NOT TO MEMORIZE

The majority of actors believe that they must memorize commercial copy in order to do their best at auditions. I disagree. I have seen too many actors who are so sure that they know the material that they refuse to look at their scripts or cue cards when they forget a line and thus hurt their auditions. How many times were you convinced that you had memorized material and hadn't? Cue cards were instituted to assist and take the pressure off.

The main reasons actors think <u>they</u> must memorize the scripts:

1. When "off book" they will do better auditions.
2. When they look at the cue cards, it breaks the flow and puts them in their head.
3. Those watching the tape will think less of them.
4. With scenes or long copy, they will lose their place on the cue card.
5. It is their professional responsibility.

Here is why I truly believe that these reasons are either fallacies, misconceptions or invalid:

1. It's fairly easy to memorize when preparing material at home or in a waiting room. Yet when being recorded inside the casting office, actors often forget some lines – and because they are sure they know them, they will think hard to remember. This puts actors in their heads and often they get frustrated, which interrupts the flow. Taking the moment to quickly glance at the card prevents these problems.
2. When actors focus on memorizing they usually lock in line readings, which impairs instinctive interpretation.
3. When the "powers that be" watch the audition videos, they are accustomed to actors looking at the cards. It is expected and accepted. Decision-makers focus mainly on performances, types, believability and looks. They don't judge actors negatively if they read a few lines as long as the flow and the life are maintained.
4. If you practice using cue cards and scripts as an audition tool on your own or in a class, you will become adept. It takes practice, but it is time well spent to give you the freedom and confidence to avail yourself of them.
5. As for its being a responsibility, I don't totally agree. Do try to memorize your lines but remember that your real responsibility is doing a great audition. Most working actors who do instinctive, freed-up, emotionally connected and authentic auditions will tell you that their readings are helped because they check the script or cue cards whenever there is doubt about lines.

TIP To practice, find short magazine ads or go online and find commercial copy. Buy a very large pad of drawing paper, write out the copy on a page and hang it next to your video camera. (If you don't have a camera, draw a big black dot on a paper and hang it up next to your cue card.) When finished with your copy preparation, look at your camera lens (or big black dot) and start recording yourself doing the rehearsed dialogue. Whenever you need a line, look at your cue card and then look back into the camera (or at the dot). The more you practice this, the better you become at using cards effectively.

Memorization can be valuable if actors don't obsess on it. When preparing material, remember this is a creative time. Focus on doing your actor's work: the "who," "what," "where" and "why" and pre-life work to understand what you are saying and why. While you are doing this audition preparation, you will automatically be memorizing. I do recommend that you memorize the first and last lines because it is important to have eye contact with the camera at the start and finish of the dialogue. Then feel free to look at the lines when needed.

SLATING

SLATE: *At the start of an on-camera audition, the actor identifies himself by saying his/her name (and when requested, his agent's name) and sometimes holds up a piece of paper with his/her name on it.*

The video recording that goes to the director, advertising agency and client will present fifty to several hundred actors per role, per day. The slate is the first time each actor is seen (seemingly) just saying his or her name. Often during those few seconds, the "powers that be" will determine whether they will watch that actor's audition or skip it. There is no second chance to make a first impression. This is especially true for commercial auditions.

The slate seems simplistic, which is why many give it no real thought. This can be a mistake because the slate gives important information about the actor. It depicts his or her confidence, essence and personality. Granted, actor's looks are a strong determining factor, but their presence and how they connect on the slate also has influence. Actors who are visibly nervous, insecure or arrogant present little reason to watch their work. Those who are relaxed, self-assured and likeable, in addition to being the right type, are more inviting and usually their audition will be viewed. Also, a genuine "slate" helps you make a connection, which puts you in a good starting place for your audition.

No-No's: From years of casting and teaching, I have seen most of the ways that actors make bad first impressions with their slates. When actors speak

- too fast or softly, it makes them appear nervous

- too slowly, it often comes off as patronizing or monotone
- too loudly, it suggests they have done more theatre than film work or that they are trying to reach the camera with their voices, which makes them appear inexperienced.

> **TIP** ▶ Although the camera is ten to twenty feet in front of the auditioning actor, it is framing, for most auditions, from the actor's chest or neck to the top of their head – so the image and the audio will appear as if the camera were just three feet away. Therefore, projecting vocally is not a necessity; in fact, it is a distraction and can make actors look amateurish. Those who have done a lot of theatre tend to speak loudly. For them, I suggest that when rehearsing, they stand two feet away from a wall and face it. Talking normally to a surface that close will help condition actors to speak at the best volume for their on-camera auditions.

When actors are

- too perky or "cutesy" or if they have a forced smile on their slate, it appears that they are trying to be "commercial" or working too hard to be likeable, which makes them seem insincere, insecure or badly trained
- moody, sullen or arrogant, it gives the impression that they are going to be a problem
- slick or uptight, they appear unbelievable or unlikeable
- not making eye contact with the camera, they seem afraid, shifty or inexperienced
- working excessively to be interesting, they look amateurish.

Most actors don't knowingly choose to do their slates any of these disempowering ways. It is usually an unconscious act, habit or a manifestation of their nerves. If you have been told or feel you are not authentically introducing yourself on your slate, then you should give it some attention.

Suggestions: Bottom line, a slate is an introduction, not a presentation, announcement or line reading. When auditioning,

- honestly introduce yourself to someone in the room (usually the person running the session) while looking into the camera lens
- be positive and enjoy introducing yourself
- smile, <u>if</u> it feels right
  - If you smile just to smile, it will look insincere. Smile because you are confident and/or having fun: then it is relaxed and engaging.

- be spontaneous
  - Don't lock in one way of introducing yourself. Be aware that each time you say your name the inflection is a little different. If there isn't some difference each time, then you have probably locked into a "line reading." This could become a bad habit.

LINE READING: *When actors are "in their heads" saying dialogue the way they planned in order to emphasize their intent – as opposed to the lines being motivated.*

- if you're nervous, laugh <u>a little</u> before you "slate"
  - It helps to break up the tightness and quickly shifts you into a positive energy.

If your slate needs work

- practice on-camera
  - Look into the lens, think about whom you are introducing yourself to, and slate your name. Maybe add a "Hi," "My name is" or "I'm" before saying your name. Watch the video and ask yourself, was that really me, my personality or essence; did I look confident or insecure?
- think about how you say your name when you introduce yourself to people
  - Be aware of how it feels. Notice that your energy moves forward, your voice is full and when you truly want to meet someone, you speak slowly, you're often smiling, and your voice is usually in a lower register.

MISTAKES ARE GIFTS

If actors were asked how they felt before an audition, most would say that they were nervous. If asked why, they'd probably say they were apprehensive about making a mistake or doing bad work. Most define mistakes as not doing the copy correctly, not following the direction, freezing, mispronouncing words and/or forgetting the lines or what was directed or rehearsed. This self-imposed pressure of worrying about making mistakes is often the very concern that prevents actors from doing their best. I have seen rookies ruin auditions after making simple mistakes and confident professionals book jobs with the way they handle them.

Most actors are unforgiving of themselves after making real or imagined errors during auditions. Many stop after floundering for a few seconds and ask, "Can I do it again?" That is usually not a good move. Besides appearing unprofessional, it can disturb the session director because it looks self-indulgent and often requires them to stop, delete the recording(s) and start again. Or worse, if they choose to tell the person to "pick up where you left off," then the clients will see the actor's frustration on the playback and it could create a negative impression. Also, I have seen that if actors are given the opportunity to start over, it is difficult for most to get back on track.

You never know what to expect at commercial auditions, especially the unscripted ones. Feeling fully prepared is challenging so there is a high probability that there will be mishaps — that is also why actors are anxious. When you can confidently work with <u>everything</u> that happens during the audition, then there are no perceived mistakes, you will probably be a lot less nervous, and you'll do better work.

My suggestions for handling most mistakes and making them work for you:

- During an audition, when that voice in your head finds fault with what you did or are doing, don't consider stopping. Quickly adjust <u>without self-deprecation</u>. If you are talking too fast, slow down. If you are talking too loudly, lower your voice. If you are judging or realize that you are not doing what you rehearsed or were directed to do, quickly modify your approach. Or ignore your critical voice and continue — maybe your instincts have taken the lead, so trust them.

- When you say the wrong words or mispronounce one, laugh, play with it or correct it in character and then continue. Every day when we misspeak or don't do what we planned, as soon as we realize it, we correct ourselves naturally (often with humor) and move on. And that's the same way you can handle mistakes in your auditions. In addition to benefiting your audition, this way of handling mistakes gives those watching an engaging glimpse of your personality.

TIP ▶ Amateurs are thrown by mistakes and professionals get jobs with them.

- As a casting director, I see actors make mistakes most of the time. It's predictable. You are <u>not</u> the only one. It's rare that an actor walks out of an audition knowing he/she did a flawless job. Accepting this will ease the pressure.

- Know that in the split second you are aware you slipped up, you are totally in that moment. You can choose to ignore a mistake. BUT if you choose to work with it, you will get connected to a real feeling, and when it is applied to the next piece of dialogue or action, unique moments and interpretations are created. When you truly experience this occurrence, you will understand why mistakes are gifts.

If you are concerned about making mistakes, practice what you have learned here. Whenever you make a mistake and think about stopping, utilize my tips. And to help build the confidence to better handle audition pressures, take an improvisation workshop. There, actors learn to trust and commit to their instincts, adjust quickly without judgment and turn mistakes into great moments.

Everyone makes mistakes – it is a given in acting as in life. How we handle our mistakes is the real issue. During the training process, the more mistakes you make, the more opportunities there will be to deal with them and make those moments work. The sooner you learn to capitalize on these opportunities, the quicker and easier you will be able to respond to them. Notice that I refer to problematic times as opportunities, not disasters. Once you accept this premise on a visceral level, you will tend to be less afraid or maybe not at all. When you are not afraid to make mistakes, you usually don't make many. When you believe they are gifts, you look forward to them. I do believe in this pun – "Mistakes are gifts: they get you present."

SCRIPTED COMMERCIAL SCENE AUDITIONS

The better your preparation for scripted scene auditions in the minimal time you are given, the better you will do.

PREPARATION:

- Study the script. Do <u>your</u> acting preparation work.

- Find your partner(s) and rehearse.

- Decide what your relationship is with the partner. It can help you to make appropriate creative choices. Often the relationship is defined in the copy, but if not, create one. For example, if the commercial involves a couple, ask yourself: Are you engaged, recently wed, married for a few years or longer, or is this a first, second or twentieth date? If the scenario has two or more girls or guys, decide whether you are best friends, neighbors, siblings, co-workers, strangers, etc., and for how long. Make sure your relationship choices are age- and type- appropriate.

- Determine a contrast. To create dynamics as well as help actors to be distinct, I suggest utilizing a "contrast", especially when the scene is a generic situation and people are talking about the product.

CONTRAST: *I use this word to describe actors playing energetic opposites in scene work. For example, one knows, the other needs help; secure/confused; serious/playful; confident/anxious; positive/skeptical, etc.*

You would normally use "conflict" choices for TV, film and theatre scene work. In commercials there are usually no "conflicts" (except when a competitor is portrayed), which is why I suggest using a contrast. Whatever "contrast" you choose; make sure it is authentically you. Choosing one that you are not able to honestly play will usually hurt your performance. When there is already a natural energetic difference between actors, creating one is not as beneficial as playing the one that actually exists.

CONFLICT: *The opposition between incompatible desires, needs, intentions, impulses, or characters in a literary work that shapes or motivates the action of the plot.*

- Make your choices with or without your partner. Many actors love to work together to investigate and create. Others become overwhelmed or frustrated and/or are inexperienced at making choices. The input of another actor is helpful, but you don't need it to make your relationship and contrast choices.

- Trade parts for a few run-throughs. When you familiarize yourself with the other actor's lines, it helps you to understand why you are saying your dialogue. Plus, you will be prepared if the session director chooses to have you switch parts, which can happen when the scene involves actors of the same gender and age.

- Practice picking up the cues without rushing the dialogue. Unnecessary pauses slow down a scene.

IN THE AUDITION:
- While the session director takes care of the paperwork, get settled and acquainted with the dialogue on the cue card.

- Listen carefully to any additional direction and if necessary, ask questions.

- Ask for a rehearsal in order to work with the cue card, practice the direction and get feedback.

My experience is that actors often "blow it" on the rehearsal and have nothing left for the take. Unless it's something that requires blocking or there is intricate direction, I'd personally rather record the rehearsal and then give them a second take.
MICHAEL DONOVAN, Casting Director, Commercial, Film and Theatre

- When directed to improvise dialogue leading into the script, do it in a full voice.

- Motivate actions and dialogue towards the camera when possible.

- Don't depend on what was rehearsed. Rather often the actor(s) with whom you are auditioning will do something other than what was directed or rehearsed, forget a line or say yours. You must not get locked into choices, be stubborn and insist on doing what was planned or directed, or become frustrated with your partner. If you do, <u>you</u> will usually look bad. Then there are times when you are the culprit who inadvertently makes these errors. In either case, intend to do what was rehearsed and directed. <u>Don't</u> try to make mistakes, improvise or deviate from what was planned or expected – and when either you or your partner(s) makes a mistake or does a variation, trust whatever transpires and make it work. It's crucial, creative and fun to remain flexible.

You are auditioning for yourself. Casting directors can tell the difference between a bad audition and a bad actor. Stay true to the scene and if you get a callback or booked, it will be regardless of your partner(s). **HUGH LEON,** Commercial Agent @ Coast to Coast Agency

- Keep your "life" going while the other person speaks. React with truthful physical behavior and reactions and maybe even some <u>little</u> utterances. This helps you to stay motivated and hold the viewer's focus. If you are paired with an experienced actor, your reactions will give him or her more with which to work.

 WARNING: When actors indicate or perform behavior in an attempt to be interesting, then this technique doesn't work. Reactions must be motivated in order to make a positive contribution to your audition. If they are not authentic, actors look unprofessional.

- Close up the pauses without speeding up the dialogue. It will keep the appropriate energy needed for most scenes.

UNSCRIPTED COMMERCIAL AUDITIONS

Many commercial auditions are unscripted and there are various types. Most actors find unscripted commercial auditions more challenging than those with dialogue. This is probably because the audition is not predictable, there is little or no rehearsal, and many times what is expected won't be explained until you walk in the room to audition. Many actors feel uncertain when asked to do a short personality conversation initiated by a question(s); play out a scenario; react to a person, dialogue or situation; demonstrate skills or physical activities; improvise scenes with an actor(s); or perform any combination of these scenarios. To the novice these auditions might seem like "no-brainers" – just get in front of the camera and talk, perform the scenario or do facial expressions. It's not that simple. The clients look for believability and personality. These auditions necessitate confidence, creativity and an understanding of what is truly required, which comes with training and experience.

Solo Improvisation Auditions

Here I will describe many of the scenarios that you will encounter and offer tips and insights to help you do your best.

Questions: Most times, questions that are asked on-camera at commercial auditions are only a vehicle to show the actor's personality and intelligence. How you answer the question is much more important than any answer. When watching the playback, "the powers that be" sometimes turn off the sound and watch. For auditions requesting answers to questions, I suggest you do the following:

- While looking at the camera, speak to the person asking the question(s) as if he/she was a friend.

- Enjoy the interview.

- Don't struggle to answer. Watching actors think about an answer is not as interesting as seeing their spontaneity. Let the question or topic ignite a free-flowing response that doesn't go on too long. Be aware when the session director signals you to wrap it up.

- Speak at a normal speed. Don't talk fast or be overly energetic.

- With personality questions, don't give one or two word answers. For example, if asked, "What is your favorite color," say what it is and why.

- When asked non-personality questions that require specific information, give them only the data requested – with very little elaboration unless asked to do so.

- Be positive if asked about the product. Don't make statements like, "It's okay, but my favorite is (a competitor) " or "I don't eat (the product) ." If you were the client watching the playback of the person making negative statements regarding your product, would you hire that actor?

- Don't try to do what you think they want or work to be different. They're looking for believable people with personality and intelligence, not actors trying to be interesting.

- Don't try to be a bigger personality than you are in order to be memorable. The real, freed up, confident "you" is the best "you" there is.

- Have a few generic topics to talk about and specific stories to tell but don't over-rehearse how you'll say them or memorize them word-for-word.

Solo Scenarios: Many commercial auditions will be short, unscripted scenarios that you will be asked to improvise.

PREPARING FOR SOLO SCENARIO AUDITIONS:
- Read the scenario that is given to you or posted and/or review the assistant's direction several times. If unclear, ask questions.

- Create several ways to do the scenario being requested. (Don't lock in one way.) Each version should have a beginning, a middle and an end. As you walk around, go through each sequence and verbalize what you would be thinking while doing each one.

IN THE AUDITION:

- Focus on your motivating ideas for the scenario, not what you planned. Allow (don't force) the thoughts or actions that you worked on to occur. You have prepared: trust where your instincts take you.

Reactions: Reaction auditions have no scripted dialogue and require you to react to a person, product, dialogue or an action without speaking (or maybe uttering a few unscripted words). When preparing for these types of auditions, use the same preparation as in the Solo Scenarios.

IN THE AUDITION:

- Allow for a thought that will motivate the first reaction: then let the subsequent thoughts organically create your reactions. Don't perform the reactions because they will probably look indicated.

INDICATE: *As it refers to acting, to pretend to have a feeling or perform a reaction for show. The feeling or reaction is not authentic or truthfully experienced.*

- When done with the scenario, keep an "afterlife" going until they say "cut."

AFTERLIFE: *The thoughts, feelings, words, utterances or simple reactions that the actor utilizes to continue the character life after the scripted scene or scenario (a.k.a. the "button").*

TIP When actors try too hard to be interesting or when they work to be animated or expressive, the session directors will usually tell them to "do less" or to "bring it down." But when reactions are motivated by organic thoughts, they create feelings, which produce simple, believable responses. My advice for reaction auditions: think motivating thoughts and follow your instincts. Do less and feel more.

Skills / Sports / Activities: There are commercial auditions where actors are asked to perform a skill, activity or sport. Often it is one that you listed on your resume as a skill at which you are an expert or have experience. (Sometimes it's one that you might not be good at.) Usually, there is no preparation needed other than going dressed in the appropriate outfit or uniform (if one is needed) or maybe warming up. In the audition, simply focus on what you are doing and have fun. It's that simple. Don't concentrate on doing it so perfectly that the effort shows. There are lots of actors who are good at these skills, activities or sports. The "powers that be" also want someone who embodies the ease and personality of the person who does it.

Improvisation Scene Auditions

Another type of commercial audition requests that actors do a designated but unscripted scenario with another actor(s).

PREPARATION:
In improv scene auditions, the following preparation process is applicable when working with one partner, several actors, or kids.

- Carefully review the posted scenario and/or the directions given by the CD or assistant.

- Determine (if not given) your "who, what, where and why."

- Find your partner(s) and get comfortable with them, especially when working with children or teens.

- Determine what your "contrast" is relative to the other actor's personality, energy or the way they have chosen to play the piece.

- Create several scenarios with a beginning, middle, and end. Make appropriate choices using what you might truthfully say or do in a few key moments. If your partner(s) wants to participate, create together. If they don't or are not creative, make your own choices.

- Know what's "at stake" – your objective.

- Remind yourself before you go into the audition room, "Whatever happens is a gift." You have prepared: now enjoy the experience.

IN THE AUDITION:
- Listen carefully to the direction given by the session director. Don't be concerned on how to do it – just trust that you got the direction, but if you need clarification, ask questions.

- Motivate and commit to the choices that you rehearsed and the directions you were given but allow your instincts to organically propel the audition. (That could sometimes mean that you let go of rehearsed choices.)

- Whenever another actor says or does something you weren't expecting, go with it. To deny or impose your ideas or what was rehearsed is a major mistake. Use the primary rule of improvisation "Yes, and…"

YES, AND: *Primarily utilized when doing improvisation scene work – the acceptance of whatever is said or done by your partner (no matter how ludicrous) and then building on it or justifying it.*

- Give and take. Listen and respond. Don't be the only one talking.

- Never play beneath your intelligence in order to be funny. Play the truth.

- Be positive when speaking about the product.

- Be specific with names, dates, locations, etc. For example, use your partner's name or give him one, and incorporate specifics in the designated location.

- Play out toward the camera as much as can be motivated.

- Be comfortable with being uncomfortable. Auditions, especially improv commercial scene auditions, are unpredictable and daunting. Accept that it is a challenging situation, be confident and have fun with it.

- Play the truth. If an actor won't stop talking, have fun trying to get a word in or play with your frustration. If your partner says something that doesn't make sense, ask what was meant or just make it work. When he/she denies, simply ask, in character and with no attitude, "Why do you keep disagreeing with me?" If they forget to do something that they were directed to do, remind them in character or do it yourself.

- Never judge your partner. It makes you unlikable and gives you nothing to work with.

  If you are partnered with someone in a commercial audition who is NOT skilled in improv (and that likelihood is quite great), YOU need to make whatever they do WORK for YOU. You never want to leave an audition blaming your partner for a lousy experience or for being a crummy improv player. YOU make it work with YOUR improv skills and training. Whatever they do…it should be a gift! **LAURI JOHNSON**, Entertainment Industry Life Coach

- Remember, everything, I mean everything is a gift. Auditioning with talented improvisers is helpful but not the only way to do good work. It's tricky to do your best when working with inexperienced or nervous actors, but very doable as long as you play with everything they do or say.

- If necessary, be prepared to lead the scene but involve and support the other actor(s).

Bottom line, the best preparation for all types of unscripted commercial auditions is a combination of the training you received in your commercial, acting and, most importantly, improvisation classes.

It is best when all these audition techniques are organic – when you own them. Practice in classes and at home before applying these instructions: otherwise you will be "in your head" trying to do them. I truly believe in these techniques and know that they can increase your commercial callbacks and bookings. <u>But</u> CDs and session operators may have their own preferences or have directions from their client that might differ from the instructions presented here. Be flexible enough <u>not to use</u> some or none of my techniques when directed otherwise.

 WARNING: If you have done a professional on-camera class, you should know the techniques that work for you. So, if you are told not to do something that you know works for you, don't do it for that person – but don't stop doing it all together unless several industry professionals give you the same feedback.

WINNING

Doing great auditions, unfortunately, doesn't always get you cast. Actors often get and don't get jobs for reasons that have nothing to do with their talent or audition technique. The "powers that be" have numerous elements to consider when casting. As long as you are a professional and do great auditions, it is a win. It is a win because with every good audition, your skills get stronger and your confidence grows. Plus, the casting director, producer and director will think of you as a professional. Once you have impressed them, there is a good chance they will want to see you for another role in the future or remember you the next time you audition. You may even be called in without being submitted. Many commercial CDs and directors also work on TV shows and films, so you could also indirectly be auditioning for future theatrical work. This is how a career is built.

> *You need to remember that when you're auditioning, you're not just auditioning for THAT job. Say there are 4 people at the table deciding whether or not you will be cast - and let's say that each of those 4 will be working on another 50 jobs in their lifetime - so you really just auditioned for 200 jobs, not just the one.*
> **MICHAEL DONOVAN,** Casting Director, Film, TV, Commercial and Theatre

T.V. & FILM AUDITIONS

Many actors start their careers auditioning for commercials, but that type of work is not why most became actors. Their dream is to act in TV shows, films and theatre. If you have followed The Plan for the first eighteen months or longer, you should have a strong foundation and are now ready to take on the necessary audition tools to start going after theatrical work.

Theatrical auditions demand more preparation, layering and emotional commitment than are required for commercials. Many of my tips and techniques regarding commercial auditions are applicable to theatrical ones. Yet there is other training, and many other specialized tools and pointers that are necessary. Since I am primarily a commercial audition technique teacher, theatrical auditions are not my forte. So I selected Amy Lyndon, a top Hollywood audition and booking coach, to contribute comprehensive information on her specialty. The choice to include the insights and techniques of an authority in this area reinforces my earlier declaration that you should always search out the best person to guide you in every area of your training and marketing. I asked Amy to write about theatrical auditions because I respect her work as a professional actress and as a successful, powerhouse teacher. I am confident that you will benefit from what she offers.

AUDITION AND BOOKING TECHNIQUES – BY AMY LYNDON

Even with extensive acting experience, when I made the bold move to Los Angeles, I was never prepared for what was in store. Auditioning! Cold-reading! The people doing the hiring can't see talent through bumbling auditions no matter how great an actor you are. After years of auditioning and working, I learned what needed to be done and I created "Guideline to Booking" – my method of breaking down scripts and booking jobs. I have taught this technique since 1992, and it has proven time and time again to work.

The most important thing to remember when auditioning for any role is that only one person will get it. That one person could be you. If you are lazy and don't understand the principles of competition and hard work, then don't expect miracles. You can never wing an audition. If you do, you will most certainly end up in the 99 percent of actors who don't book acting work. Here are pointers that should help you be among the one percent who do.

BEFORE AUDITIONS START

Audition preparation begins long before you actually get your first appointment. It begins with how you work your craft and business.

BE A BUSINESS

Think of yourself as a business, a professional one. You can be a small company or a huge corporation. Professionals who run successful businesses

- dedicate all the time needed to run it

    - If you don't work your business for one day, you're limiting exposure and your revenue. Several places in this book Ms. Barry has offered all kinds of valuable information to help you to run your career like a business. Read her information carefully and incorporate what you can.

- keep their offices (or the area designated for the pursuit of a career) in order

- make sure all their marketing tools (pictures, resumes, websites, demo reels, etc.) are accessible and up to date.

> *I spend two to three hours a day at my desk working on my career. I feel very blessed to have this career to work on even though I have all kinds of people (managers, lawyers, producers, publicity people) in my corner. I really love working on my career. I want to be involved. I want to know what is going on. What is happening! I love my job!* **LESLIE JORDAN**, Emmy-Award-Winning Actor

PRACTICE

You are an instrument that needs to be practiced every day. Can you find the exact emotion required by the character and the script when needed? You should practice finding where your emotions are located in your body so that you can easily and quickly tap into them. A good way to practice:

> Pick an emotion and locate where it is in your body. For example, choose "fear." Ask yourself, "When was I afraid?" Think of the event and then be aware of the feeling that comes up. Hang on to the associated reaction and be with it until it becomes deep and strong. Where is it located in your body? When you've located where the strongest fear button is in your body, tap into it, sit with it and know where it is for future use.

There are lots of emotions we experience so there is plenty to work with, and your instrument will have the practice it needs.

> *There are several established acting methods for locating and accessing emotions taught in professional classes where often*

specific scenes are assigned in order to have students work on connecting emotionally. This is one of the reasons it is important to stay with one teacher for an extended period of time. He/she will get to know your strengths and weaknesses and will help you become an emotionally available actor. The longer you stay in class, the more practice you get locating and accessing your feelings. CAROLYNE BARRY

This kind of pre-preparation homework is important so that you are able to push your own buttons when needed. The big difference between a good actor and a brilliant one is depth of feelings. You might get the callback, but you might not get the job if someone comes in and hits that feeling deeper and/or more authentically.

TAKE A PROFESSIONAL AUDITION / COLD-READING CLASS

It doesn't matter how great you are as an actor: no one is going to see it if you don't know how to audition or cold-read. Auditioning is its own skill. Audition/cold-reading workshops need to be a staple. (These classes are either entitled "Cold-reading" or "TV and Film Audition Technique" depending on which the teacher prefers.) Make sure that it's ongoing and/or keep going back as often as you can.

Tips For Selecting a Great Audition Teacher:

- The instructors should be teaching you and not directing you. Really understand this distinction. They need to guide you to the answers, give you an adjustment and let you try again to hit it but not constantly do the work for you. Teachers should give you the tools and insights so that you know how to create strong auditions for yourself.
- Stay away from those who talk too much about themselves.
- Never leave a class feeling discouraged or confused. The instructor must make sure you leave knowing what you did right and what you need to work on to improve for the following week.

    Be careful not to confuse how the teacher deals with you with how you deal with yourself. If the teacher gives you a critique or direction and you hear it as criticism then you are the one making yourself feel bad and discouraged. So many actors tend to convert the teacher's direction into opportunities for self-deprecation. Those who do this are cheating themselves out of the many insights a good teacher has to offer them. CAROLYNE BARRY

- Choose an industry-savvy teacher. He/she will also teach you how to "work the room."

241

WORKING THE ROOM: *(Amy Lyndon's definition) The ability to make adjustments easily and be freed up and confident when interviewed or doing a reading at auditions.*

WATCH LOTS OF TELEVISION AND FILMS

Each TV show has its own style and tone. It's important to understand the differences. You don't want to audition for a gritty, raw, edgy cop show with a slick, sophisticated type of read. Watch every TV program at least one time. If you want to be on television, watch it.

> *When preparing to audition for network TV shows, go online and watch the show. (A great website for this is www.hulu.com) Today, with your computer, you have access to most any show you will be auditioning for which will help with your preparation.*
> **CAROLYNE BARRY**

If you want to work in films, understand the distinctions of each type. There is a range of genres for studio movies, e.g., action, romantic comedy, horror, political intrigue, classical, dramas, family, kids, teens, etc., as well as various eras of historical films. And then understand that festival films are different from studio movies. Watch good and bad films and learn from both. It becomes obvious that each film genre and TV program usually hires specific types of actors.

> *Whether I am auditioning for theatre, sitcoms, episodics, films, or commercials, I always try to feel or find out the "tone" of the piece. Sitcoms go for the laugh – they want it faster and funnier. For theatre auditions it is important to be heard in the last row. For film auditions, I remember that even a lifted eyebrow on screen can say a lot, so I try to bring it down a notch or two. And commercials want you to be able to say or do things in a short time. But always, always, always remain true to yourself. Keep it real.* **LESLIE JORDAN,** Emmy-Award-Winning Actor

> *So many actors tell me they can do drama and comedy: then I have them read a half-hour show script and find they don't know the beats for the 3-camera-comedy medium. I usually have to explain the differences between a funny show like "Desperate Housewives" and a half-hour sitcom like "Two and A Half Men." It's always surprising to see that so many actors think they can do both only to discover they don't know the differences between the two mediums. Do your homework, figure out what your strengths are as a new actor and focus on building your resume on that strength – only for the first year. Building credits with what you're good at will allow you to grow as an actor. Later, with a*

strong resume, you will have the credibility to get a larger range of auditions. **TODD JUSTICE,** Talent Representative @ Marshak/Zachary

DETERMINE YOUR TYPE AND VENUE

To help you determine your type and the right venue for you, compare your appearance and qualities to the actors in various shows and films. Which of these types are you: western, action, comedy, one-hour drama, sitcom, soap, independent film or studio actor? Working actors in each of the mediums have a look. Study them and learn the style of films or TV shows you should be auditioning for: then you won't extend the imagination of the people doing the hiring and you will have a better shot at booking work.

When auditioning for TV shows, know the show, the look, the tone, its genre and the network it is on. For example, the CW network has a specific look for many of their shows: beautiful young people who look like models. If you audition with hair messed up and wearing shabby clothing, don't expect to book anything on that network. If you're a tattooed "down and out" type with long hair, don't expect to work on a courtroom show as a conservative lawyer unless you can totally change your appearance for the audition. That actor, as is, could be hired to be the defendant or the criminal. There are exemptions: e.g., on most episodic shows there is usually a sub-storyline or series regular who is a quirky or humorous character actor who does not fit the type of most of the regulars.

> *While commercial auditions mostly require a very specific type or "occupational" clothing in order to strongly suggest the character, film and television auditions prefer the clothing to be a suggestion of the character. In theatrical auditions, directors and/or casting directors focus mainly on characterization rather than the visual effect of the wardrobe. It is considered "over the top" to dress exactly as the character for most film and TV auditions.*
> **LAURI JOHNSON,** Entertainment Industry Life Coach

RESEARCH AND MARKET TO CASTING DIRECTORS

- Read *The Hollywood Reporter* and *Variety.* Find out who the decision-makers are at the studios and the networks. Learn about the shows that are in production and who is working on them. Read up on the latest news and events. Information is power.

  > *Once a week, Variety lists the productions that are happening and who is casting those shows; use that info to target casting directors you want to get in front of.* **TODD JUSTICE,** Talent Representative @ Marshak/Zachary

- Send your updated pictures and resumes to the CDs casting the shows that you think you'll be best suited for. <u>Hopefully</u> they will keep your promotional material for when they need your type.

This is unrealistic. It's impossible for CDs to keep material on every actor – and the bigger problem is that actors ASSUME you have their pictures and resumes on file. **MICHAEL DONOVAN,** Casting Director, Commercial, Film and Theatre

Even if casting directors don't keep your picture and resume, it can be helpful for them to see your face if only for a moment. After receiving a few of your pictures or postcards over a period of time, when you are submitted for a specific role, you will probably be familiar to them, which might influence them to bring you in to audition when the role is right for you. **CAROLYNE BARRY**

PREPARING FOR THEATRICAL AUDITIONS

Once you or your agent or manager have secured you an audition for an acting role in a project, film, TV program or play, now you can put all your training to work. What follows are my audition preparation techniques and tips that I teach my students.

RESEARCH THE PRODUCERS' AND DIRECTORS' WORK

When you audition for a role in a TV show, it's important to know the work of the show's creators, producers and, often, the directors. The more successful ones are known for specific production genres and/or styles. (In TV, producers and directors have as difficult a job as actors getting work doing anything different from what they have already done.)

When you understand the tone and style of the shows they have created and/or worked on (because you have watched lots of TV and films as suggested earlier), you will know the necessary creative adjustments for your audition preparation.

When you are acquainted with the work of the writer, director, creator and/or producer, and when any of them are present at your audition, you will have something to talk about during your interview. **CAROLYNE BARRY**

I recommend that you also go to Google, click on "Images," then type in the name of the industry pro(s) you will be auditioning for and see their pictures. It is beneficial to know who is who when you meet them. **LAURI JOHNSON,** Entertainment Industry Life Coach

TIP A great way to research any industry pro is on IMDB.com. IMDB is the Internet Movie Database. It's where most every film and TV actor, director, producer, creator and casting director is listed with his or her credits. It is a free information website. If you want extensive information on any industry pro and are willing to pay a membership fee, you can sign up for IMDB Pro.

PREPARE YOUR AUDITION MATERIAL

Spend all the time necessary to prepare you and your audition material.

Make Sure You Know The Character For Which You Are Reading: There are several people involved before you get your audition call. Often information does not get communicated correctly so it is important to double check with your agent to make sure of the character for which you will be auditioning. This way you can be prepared and not be surprised with a character change when you get to the casting office.

> *At the audition, once the CD meets you or after you have read, you might be given a different or second role to read. It could be a larger or smaller role and/or one that is better suited to your type and/or talent. You must do a quick but thorough preparation. Here is where those auditioning classes you have taken really pay off.* **CAROLYNE BARRY**

Get The Audition Material in Advance: When up for a role in a TV show, film or play, you are usually given "sides" to prepare.

> SIDES: *Scenes from the script used for TV, film and theatre auditions – usually one to ten pages, specific to a character.*

Most of the time, sides for theatrical and theatre auditions are either posted on a website, faxed, e-mailed or can be picked up. When actors audition for guest-starring, leading or co-starring roles, a full script is often made available.

> *I get frustrated when actors tell me they were too busy to read their scripts before an audition and only got to work with the sides. Sides do not give you enough information! When a script is available to read, find the time!* **TODD JUSTICE,** Talent Representative @ Marshak/Zachary

> *When auditioning for guest-starring, leading or co-starring roles, reading the full script will help you to understand the character "arc" (if there is one) and the relationship with the other characters, which assists your creative process.* **CAROLYNE BARRY**

ARC: A term referring to a character's emotional progression from the beginning to the end of a scene and/or script.

With the roles that have just a few lines, usually sides will only be available at the casting office, so plan to get to your audition early.

> *If the TV or film script is unavailable, pick up and/or look at ALL the sides for ALL roles. That way you'll have a really good sense of what's going on in the storyline, and where your character fits in. Also with theatre, as a rule, scripts are almost always available – go to the casting office ahead of time to read them.*
>
> **MICHAEL DONOVAN,** Casting Director, Commercial, Film and Theatre

Accept The Material As Is: If you negatively judge your script, then you might as well cancel the audition. You're never going to get inside of it because you're in your head making comments on it. You won't book that way.

> *Decline auditions you can't relate to or for which you dislike the material. When you hate the script, you basically tell yourself you're not going to get the job and it's a waste of everyone's time.*
>
> **TODD JUSTICE,** Talent Representative @ Marshak/Zachary

Accept that you are simply a clean vessel of pure emotion lending yourself to the material to channel the character from the writer's intent. If you want to be more than that, think about directing. Look at the material from the writer's perspective. Then you'll understand why the writer wrote the character the way he/she did.

Respect The Writing: Read the "sides" at least ten times as if it were a novel. Understand the point of view of each character in the script. You'll never understand their story or really be in the scene(s) if you fabricate choices about where the character is coming from instead of doing what is suggested in the script. The writer's intention always comes first. Don't make anything up just to impress. What you read is the truth. If the character says that he/she hates the other person, then he/she hates the other person in that moment unless there's a parenthetical direction suggesting otherwise. Making unmotivated choices is the biggest mistake that actors make. The writer makes the choices for you. At your audition, you want the writer to say, "That actor read it exactly as I wrote it. That's the character!"

> *Theatre is an actor's medium, film is a director's medium and TV is a writer's medium. I always remember in a TV audition to SAY THE WORDS AS WRITTEN. Which is a good rule, period, in general but it really matters in TV auditions. Those writers are paid a fortune and are up nights making sure the rhythm of the words works. If you come in improvising, YOU ARE DEAD IN THE WATER.* **LESLIE JORDAN,** Emmy-Award-Winning Actor

Script ID Tips - When you are reading for a role for a TV show that you are not acquainted with and you are not sure of the style, here is a simple way to help identify the genre so you will know how to prepare for your audition:

- If the script is double-spaced, it is a multi-camera comedy.

- Soap operas are also double-spaced, but the action is in parenthesis and the acts are underlined.

- Single-spaced is either a single-camera comedy or episodic one-hour drama.

Know Your Role: Understand why your role is in the script then you'll know who you are and your place in the story. A lot of actors want so much to be remembered that they overshoot the audition by making their role too important. Unless you are the series lead, guest lead or a major film star, you're simply there to move the story along. Don't try to be more important than the material in an attempt to impress. For example, if you're serving drinks in the scene, then you're just a cocktail waitress. That's it. Keep your work simple and honest.

Find Your Connection To The Character: Understand how you relate to the character on a personal level. If you don't truly know what is going on emotionally with this person, how can you play it? This step can take a while. Allow yourself enough time to find the connection. If you truly relate to who the person is, the scene usually plays itself.

Investigate The Specifics: Most every line of dialogue is a separate thought. The brilliance in a great audition is always in the specifics. In order to find the specifics, take the time to break down your script. If you want to be an interesting actor, investigate every moment and detail with deep understanding. Know what motivates every moment. Every scene is like a song. Listen for the music of each note.

> *Do your "actor work": investigation, interpretation and motivation. This process work will help you find your specifics. Don't focus on trying to be different and/or creating the most interesting choices. If you do, I can almost promise that you will be "in your head" for your read. You are different just because you are you. Your choices will be unique if they come from an honest creative process and they are truly motivated.* **CAROLYNE BARRY**

Respect The Punctuation: Most writers deliberately over-punctuate. It's their indication of how the character speaks. For example, if there's "…" (ellipsis), then the character is reaching for his next thought. If there's an "!" (exclamation mark), then the character is very intense about what he/she is saying. Adhere to punctuation. There you will find clues to your character's emotional state of mind. If you run sentences together, you'll flat-line your audition. Every shred of punctuation separates the thoughts of the character.

> *Punctuation is important, yes — but it shouldn't lock you into a reading. Find a way to understand the author's intent — but then also make it your own.* **MICHAEL DONOVAN,** Casting Director, Commercial, Film and Theatre

> *If everyone prepared the same read, then you're not going to be unique. Don't be so anxious to rush to those periods in a sentence. Find your own beats and make the audition your own.* **TODD JUSTICE,** Talent Representative @ Marshak/Zachary

> *In your acting classes, most teachers will tell you not to pay attention to the punctuation and stage directions. When focusing on developing your craft, there is a lot of value in finding your own expression (and not the writer's) when working a scene. But auditions are not the place to exercise or experiment with craft. It is vital at auditions to motivate the directions (when appropriate) and punctuation and make them your own.* **CAROLYNE BARRY**

Pay Attention To Action Directions: The action directions will tell you what you are doing. When it is appropriate, you can include action in your audition. If the script tells you that the character is making a sandwich but the dialogue is not talking about the sandwich, do not make a sandwich. If you are drinking wine in the scene and some dialogue refers to it, then hold or pretend to hold a glass and to drink. Keep it simple. Remember, you have a small space in which to work. Only pantomime if it is an activity that you do well and when it makes the illusion of the scene stronger. If it is distracting, do not do it.

CAROLYNE BARRY'S ADDITIONAL THEATRICAL AUDITION SUGGESTIONS:

- Allow time to work on your audition material. I have found it most beneficial to do several rehearsals instead of one long one. This way of rehearsing helps to layer the reading.

- Focus mainly on your "process work" (the techniques you learned in your acting and/or cold-reading workshops). They only work if you use them.

- Don't over-rehearse your choices. Pros know that acting as well as auditioning is not about locking in a read, memorizing lines or performing the words.

- The wardrobe for most theatrical auditions is not always specified. Dress as appropriately as possible for the character. Select what you will wear and rehearse in it so that you are comfortable in it at your audition.

- Get coached when it is important. If you feel insecure or have problems with audition material and/or it's a large or challenging role, you might consider getting coached. You can ask an actor/ friend to help, but it has been my experience that often their direction can do more harm then good (unless they have a strong directorial eye and can communicate their direction in a positive way). A good coach, especially one you have studied with, is objective and usually finds additional character choices and/or will flesh out any problems with your read. Most of the better ones are acting teachers and charge anywhere from $50 to $125 an hour. If the session could help you to do better work and give you confidence, it is often worth it.

- I suggest that every professional actor have a video camera. Once you have done your character and script preparation, record yourself, but <u>only</u> if you can be objective about your work. View the recording and see what adjustments (not line readings) would help. Make the adjustments, record once again and view it. <u>Don't record work more than twice</u> or you might focus on the wrong elements. (Don't obsess on what you or your work looks like.)

- Know the location of where the audition is being held. Map out the night before how you are going to get there (unless you have already been there).

WAITING TO AUDITION

In the office before going into the audition is when the actor's "psych out" usually happens. Protect your audition by knowing how to handle yourself in the waiting area.

Stay Focused: Don't look at actors in the outer office. The moment that you catch someone's eye, they might talk to you. Once you engage with another actor, you lose focus on what you need to be doing for your audition. Many actors who are waiting to audition often talk to each other, ask questions, rehearse out loud and talk on their phones. These conversations can be distracting. If you encounter friends who want to chat, tell them that you need to study and that you'll contact them later. Your job is to get the job, not to make friends in the outer office. Keep to yourself, ignore all the noise and make sure your cell phone is turned off. Concentrate on what you're going to do.

Review Your Opening Emotion: Review how the character feels at the beginning of the scene. Be secure about that first feeling because it will help create your audition.

Don't Keep Running the Whole Scene: If you need to run the whole scene over and over, then you didn't do enough homework. Use this time to meditate, recreate and imagine the environment/place and whom you're talking to in the scene, and review your choices.

Never Compare Yourself to the Other Actors Auditioning for Your Role: If you're the one who looks out of place, that could be a great sign. You might be the one who is "the other way to go." Casting directors wouldn't be doing their jobs if they brought in all the same types. They need to present a range of actors to their producers, directors, writers and sometimes the stars.

Don't Cast Someone Else in Your Part: In your mind, don't give your part to other actors in the waiting room because you think they're dressed better or are more right for it. This is a sure fire psyche out. You were asked to audition for a reason. The CD must have seen something in your picture and resume or knows your work. <u>Believe</u> that you have just as great a shot at booking it as anyone there. Psyche yourself up, then go in and get the job.

Wait at the Door of the Audition Room: Find out who is signed up to audition before you. Once that person goes into the casting office, if you can, wait outside the door. This will get you away from the other actors and help you to remain focused.

IN THE AUDITION

Okay, it's time. You've done the preparation; you're focused, psyched up and ready to go. Many new actors make mistakes that can make them look like rookies. Here is a list of things you should <u>not</u> do.

Never Bring Props to Your Audition: This can be viewed as unprofessional unless it's requested or if it is already on you, e.g., a cell phone, keys, nail file, pen, etc. In most acting classes, when actors do their scenes, they populate them with necessary props. Auditioning is not a class.

Never Touch Anything on the Desk: Leave people's personal items alone. They tend to get fussy about their things. Would you like someone to come into your home or office and play with your possessions? Whoever you are reading for doesn't appreciate it either.

Never Throw Anything: If you throw a prop or anything else you could hit someone or break something in the office, which will take you and those for whom you are auditioning out of the scene.

Never Endanger or Scare the CD or Reader: Don't hit, squeeze or shove the person who is reading with you. If you're playing a killer, don't use a knife or a gun or put a stranglehold on the reader. If it looks like you are unstable, they will never hire you. Be the character in the private space across the desk from the CD or reader.

Never Be Concerned with How the CD Reads: Listen from your character's point of view to what the casting director is saying, not how he/she is saying it. Focus on the CD as the other character(s) in your scenes and on your preparation work (the environment, opening emotional moment, and your personalization) to keep you in the scene. If the CD is concentrating on giving a great read, he/she won't be able to pay attention to your audition. If he/she is reading fast, looking down or skipping dialogue, it's probably because he/she wants to get to your lines.

Never Hesitate to Look at the Script Whenever Needed: Don't wait too long and ruin the flow of your audition to fight with yourself to remember. Look at your script when you are unsure of lines!

> *Hold pages in an audition but you should not really need them. They should be there in case you forget a line. You don't get to hold a script when filming, so KNOW YOUR LINES.* DAVID SWEENEY, Los Angeles Talent Manager

Never Show Your Mistakes in the Audition: If you mess up on the first or second line, ask to start over. If you're close to the end, never broadcast your mistakes. Chances are they didn't catch it and they could have thought you were brilliant. But if you make a face or say anything negative about your performance, you tell them that you were not good. Be like a competitive gymnast. When they fall during their routines, they always finish standing strong with their arms held high in the air and stretched out like it was the best performance of their lives.

> *An actor must walk into an audition and own the room. You must be 100 percent confident. I really think confidence is 50 percent of booking the job. You must immediately let people know you mean business. Confidence breeds success. Always look good, speak clearly and don't ever walk in chewing gum.* DAVID SWEENEY

DO Go For It: Committing to your first emotion is 90 percent of your job. When you know how you are feeling and motivate yourself into the scene with it, you won't go off course. Commit to your preparation and go for it! If you don't, someone else will. Which would you prefer, hitting a 10+ read in the room or knocking it out of the ballpark in your car on the way home?

"Go for it," to me, also means letting go of everything you worked on in rehearsal and committing to the instinctive moments that guide your audition. Be "in the moment," not in your head trying to remember all your choices. I truly believe that when you are "in the moment," what you prepared will probably play out – and if it doesn't then you are open to channel inspired choices. **CAROLYNE BARRY**

AFTER THE AUDITION

If you're thinking about the audition for days afterwards and asking for feedback from your representatives, then you didn't do enough preparation. You know when you've hit it.

I don't call casting directors and ask for feedback very often. I feel it negates the actor and makes me look like I doubt my client's abilities. Move on. There are a hundred reasons why you may not get the job. Trust me, if you give a bad read, the agent will hear about it, so assume you did great, left a good impression, and will be seen again by that CD. **TODD JUSTICE,** Talent Representative @ Marshak/Zachary

I give feedback when asked – but it isn't that often that an agent will call to ask. I will VOLUNTEER feedback when it just did not go well at all, or when someone was clearly unprepared – or, on the flip side, when someone was especially good. **MICHAEL DONOVAN,** Casting Director. Film, TV, Commercial and Theatre

You know when you've done your best. You don't need approval or feedback from anyone else about how you did. You know. Be honest with yourself. If you realize you didn't hit it this time, make sure you do the work and preparation to hit it the next time and every time.

AMY LYNDON'S WRAP-UP

Casting directors don't forget actors who do poor auditions. So don't get in the game before you are ready. When you are starting out, you must understand that this is a career, not a job. Your job is to work your career and a career spans a lifetime. Think of yourself as if you are in training for the Hollywood Olympics. Practice every day, become proficient at working the room and the audition techniques, audition as much as possible and become an expert at booking.

....

The empowering tips and techniques that Amy Lyndon has presented here help actors do great theatrical auditions. For more detailed theatre, film and television audition preparation and techniques, I suggest you take professional audition workshops and research the many books written by reputable authors on these subjects. Go online or to the Samuel French bookstore in Los Angeles or New York, the Drama Book Shop in New York, and Amazon.com to find the largest variety of books on the topics that can best serve you. Also, the compact disc program that I co-authored, *Getting the Job*, offers more tools to help you prepare and do your best theatrical (as well as commercial) readings. It also includes sections to play on the way to and from auditions to focus and relax you as well as remind you of the acting basics that should have your focus.

BUILDING YOUR CAREER

At this point you should have a good idea of what to do and expect on your road to becoming a professional actor. If you stay on course with The Plan, after the first two or three years you should have a strong foundation, auditioning skills, representation, pictures, a reel, multiple acting credits, the start of a good resume, networking contacts and a job that works for your life as an actor. You should have accomplished a great deal. This career and the preparation for it is so demanding that the majority of those who started around the time you did have either given up the mission or cut back their efforts. They may have booked a few little jobs but have no real career momentum. Take notice of this but don't let it deter you. Stay on course. You are one of the tens of thousands wanting this career. If it were easy, don't you think many more people would be actors? Being a professional requires talent, an ongoing dedication, often in the face of major frustration – a genuine passion for the craft, determination, courage, confidence, business savvy, and luck to achieve success. If your commitment waivers or takes a hiatus, there are many others who are ready to move past you. (If you have faltered at any point and then become recommitted, get back on The Plan.)

MOVING ON?

The two- or three-year mark is a good time to give serious thought to whether you want to continue. Now you totally understand what is involved: the training, the marketing, the scope of your talent, whether the work is satisfying, and if the lifestyle works for you. The practicality of this pursuit can depend on whether you are married and/or have kids. It can depend on having financial assistance, a supportive family, and/or a job that provides the money as well as the flexibility needed. A talented friend of mine told me that he loved being an actor but hated working as a waiter, so he gave up acting. Many choose to find a new profession at this time if they feel that because of type, money, commitment or talent they may never achieve the success they desire. (Examine this choice with respected professionals before making this decision.) I stopped pursuing my acting career when I realized that my gift was teaching and directing actors and how much more satisfied I was doing that work. There are numerous conscious or unconscious reasons why many decide to pursue a different career. Whatever the reason, it is a choice. Years from now, those who choose another path at this point will probably <u>not</u> look back on this pursuit with regret because they know that they gave it their best shot, learned a lot about themselves and found it to be an empowering experience. If you decide to give up acting, I believe the money, work and effort you put into it will pay off somewhere else. The personal development and business skills you acquired are applicable in most every profession.

> *Ninety percent of those who start in the business move on to another career path. One of the real strengths of a solid academic theatre program is that we teach our student actors how to adapt to change, create self-awareness, and develop discipline and communication skills. Universities strive to create life-long learners who will be able to adapt and lead successful and productive lives.* **DAVID GRAPES,** Professor & Director of the School of Theatre Arts & Dance, University of Northern Colorado

WHAT'S NEXT

If you plan to continue, know that you are not done training, promoting and transforming. The journey continues if you want to grow as an actor and be successful.

> *I represent an actress on a major soap who continued to coach with her teacher for every single scene she shot on the show. She coached for two years! I thought it was a bit excessive, but coaching made her comfortable and it worked – she won the Emmy! You know if you should continue to train and what you need to work on.* **DAVID SWEENEY,** Los Angeles Talent Manager

Unfortunately, at the two- or three-year mark, even the most dedicated working actors may start to pull back their efforts. Like with any other profession, you <u>must</u>

- continue to develop your craft
- keep adding business contacts
- relentlessly endeavor (personally and through representation) to book theatre, TV and film acting work
- build your resume by doing graduate films, Internet spots, "Webisodes" and no-money jobs
- promote and market you and your work to industry professionals
- participate in networking organizations
- periodically update promotional materials: pictures, resumes, reels, websites, etc.
- create projects for yourself that advance your craft and career

- make judicious, savvy business choices
- work with people who will keep taking your career to the next level
- stay on point and don't give up.

Being a working actor is very, very competitive. There are tens of thousands of actors at all levels wanting to audition and book acting work. You will have hundreds if not thousands who want the same roles as you. It is a mistake to rest on your laurels or believe that it will get easier. You must continue your efforts. It's like being a professional athlete. You never stop improving and competing.

NURTURE CONFIDENCE

In Chapter Three, I wrote about the importance of confidence when you first start this journey. It becomes even more important as you deal with the many challenges and obstacles in your career. This business can undermine your belief in yourself and your talent and take a personal toll, one incident at a time, over months or years, unless you intervene early or better yet constantly nurture your confidence.

> *Roy London, a great acting teacher, once said, "Sometimes the actor has to work on the acting and sometimes the actor has to work on the ACTOR!" Emotional issues, such as fear of rejection, being too sensitive, thinking you're not good enough – these MUST be handled to be successful in this industry. If you need help, seek out a good therapist or a life coach in the industry who works primarily with actors. Eliminate these barriers or obstacles to your progress. Remember that while you're having these problems and not tending to them, someone else has already tended to theirs and they are moving quickly ahead of you towards success.* **LAURI JOHNSON,** Entertainment Industry Life Coach

Every job you book builds confidence, but you can't let the jobs you don't get undermine it. Protect and nurture your confidence. Without it, being successful is impossible for most. I strongly suggest that you deal with negative thoughts immediately so they don't fester and take a permanent toll. Whenever you are intensely frustrated, worried, angry or depressed and can't shake it within a reasonable amount of time, get the support you need. Whether it's therapy, life coaching, family, networking groups, teachers, your church, representation or great friends, communicate with those who are supportive and can help. When you're truly confident, you are positive much of the time. When you are positive, you're happy, do better work and enjoy most of this voyage. Being confident, unless you have psychological or physiological issues, is a choice you make one occurrence at a time. For suggestions on building confidence, review the information in Chapter Three in the "Confidence" section. Be vigilant and do what you need to do to nurture yours. It pays off in so many valuable ways.

OWN YOUR SUCCESSES

I encourage you to celebrate all your "wins." Enjoy when you do great work in your classes, auditions and jobs. Take pleasure from every callback and job you book or come close to booking. Whenever you have "wins" for anything, take a few personal moments to acknowledge your accomplishments and yourself. You will belittle your accomplishments with statements like: "If only I had done this or that, I would have been better or achieved more." There is a difference between learning from what you do and don't do and criticizing yourself for what you could have done. If you don't own your successes, you have nothing to build on. Choose to honor yourself.

> *You wanted to become an actor in the first place because it was fun. Don't let "The Business" make you lose sight of the joy we as artists possess in creating and sharing with humanity what it is to be human. If it's not fun, why do it?* **ANTHONY MEINDL,** Los Angeles Acting Teacher

CHOOSE WHOM TO LISTEN TO

Along the way, you will meet lots of people with opinions about what you should do and not do for your career. Listen but don't assume that every actor, teacher, casting director, agent, manager, director and/or producer has the right information and direction. There are lots of people with a great number of opinions. Each one has his or her own point of view of what it takes to be successful. Listening to too many people will get you an array of conflicting opinions. You could become frustrated and confused or waste time and money following advice that is inaccurate and/or might not be right for you. Rely on a few industry pros with proven track records (that you've researched) and whose input feels right. It should feel right not because it validates what you want, but because it makes sense, has worked for others you admire, and is coming from people you respect. You are responsible for those you select to advise you. Carefully choose to whom you listen, and <u>you</u> decide what is best for you.

> *There are too many so-called professionals who don't have a clue about this business and do not hesitate to give their opinions to unsuspecting actors.* **HUGH LEON,** Commercial Agent @ Coast to Coast Agency

Your training and career choices are not carved in stone. You can change your mind and make new choices when necessary. If a teacher, your representation, and/or career choices are working, don't abandon them because someone tells you to do something different. If a choice you made isn't working, then check with industry pros, research alternatives and make a new choice. Being a member of a networking organization(s) and having a large number of industry contacts are very beneficial when researching new craft or business choices. Evaluate the options, make your decisions and take charge of your career.

By the second year you should know "what's what" – what works for you and what doesn't and what is realistic and what is wishful thinking. Listen to yourself.

BE COMFORTABLE WITH BEING UNCOMFORTABLE

Don't expect to feel secure if you want to grow as an artist. Successful actors never play it safe and always challenge themselves. Accept that "the only constant in life is change" – this is one of my favorite Zen sayings.

In your development, it is beneficial to take on techniques and/or roles that are a stretch, whether in workshops, readings, plays, graduate films or projects with your friends. These are the primary places you should challenge yourself in an effort to grow because they are usually safe environments in which to experiment. This doesn't mean making outrageous character choices. It is about making creative and appropriate choices that serve a challenging role, not ones you make just to challenge yourself. When auditioning for your first round of real acting jobs, it is usually not a great idea to experiment. You want to do your best work and get the job.

TIP Normally, attempting anything new the first few times does not feel as good as what you have been used to doing. When working on new training techniques or approaches, don't expect to feel comfortable at the start. Being comfortable in your craft is not always the best indication of growth.

Auditioning is not usually comfortable. Every time you go in, you are putting yourself on the line to be judged. When starting, the self-pressure to prove yourself and get every job creates anxiety and discomfort. Working on the set of your first few professional jobs can also make you apprehensive. As your career continues to progress, there will be changes. Moving up the show business ladder keeps taking you out of comfort zones. Bigger roles, doing higher profile jobs and working with top industry professionals are all exciting, but these moves will take you into new arenas, which are initially uncomfortable. After you have been at this career for a while, you will either become more relaxed with the process or comfortable with being uncomfortable.

TURN DISAPPOINTMENTS INTO GIFTS

As with any business, there are disappointments and frustrating times. How you handle these times and learn from them factors into your ability to create a successful career.

You CHOOSE this profession. That means you choose everything that comes with it. Never become a victim of it. The truth is, it will work out, maybe not the way you think, maybe exactly the way you think...it's all part of your journey. **LAURI JOHNSON,** Entertainment Industry Life Coach

I want to share with you something that happened to me years ago when I was a dancer in summer stock. It was a hurtful event from which I learned a major life and business lesson. I was a really good dancer and was selected to do the lead in most of the production numbers. When the choreographer was staging the ballet for *Brigadoon,* I was asked to sit out that dance. Although I was a good performer, I did not have enough ballet training. I was embarrassed and depressed. I sulked off to a corner and started to cry. An actor who was starring in the current show sat down next to me and listened to my plight. He said, "Don't beat yourself up today for what you can be tomorrow." He went on to explain, "Instead of sitting around feeling bad and sorry for yourself, get out there and learn the ballet number. It is a better use of your time and talent." I'm glad I listened. I stood in back while the other dancers were working and learned the routine. I could see how impressed the choreographer was with how I was handling the situation. During the run of the show one of the dancers became sick and I went on for one performance. I was so proud of myself, not because I did a great job (I was okay but not as good as the others), but because I used the two weeks of rehearsal as an opportunity to become a better dancer. From then on I have used almost every opportunity when I didn't get what I wanted or wasn't as good as I knew I was capable of being to work harder rather than dwell on feeling inadequate or depressed. Whenever you are frustrated or upset with yourself, I encourage you to remember, "Don't beat yourself up today for what you can be tomorrow."

Advice to actors when going through rough periods: keep acting. Keep at it. It is what keeps us more alive than others. **LESLIE JORDAN,** Emmy-Award-Winning Actor

ACTORS ARE ARTISTIC WARRIORS

For some actors, success comes early: for others it might take several years, and for most it will not happen. The reasons can be type, age, appearance, talent development, essence, personality, connections, luck, commitment, choices or, probably, a combination of these factors. With some who succeed, there seems to be no rhyme or reason. Then there are those who seem to have everything going for them and don't make it. There is no foolproof way to predict success. It is not logical. This can be a source of frustration when using the successes of other actors as a road map. If actors have a strong vision of what should happen in their careers and it doesn't work out, they can become despondent and consider quitting. It is crucial to have a plan and work at it. Yet you must be flexible, be willing to try new approaches, and have faith in yourself and your work or there is no chance that you will succeed. These things don't guarantee success, but having them – in combination with your talent, training and everything else I have covered in this book – gives you a much better chance.

You have chosen acting as your career. Your occupation is dedicated to creating characters that entertain, motivate and/or emotionally connect with and move audiences. The creative work you do can change people's lives. It is not about you, but what you do. Be proud of this profession and enjoy the journey. This is an artistic, stimulating, exciting and challenging life. Actors are a unique breed. They are inspired and courageous artistic warriors who pursue their dreams and work to create and compete in a business that provides no security. When actors begin their voyage, they are the main source of their own emotional support. They face and work through doubts, fears and insecurities. Professionals do this because they love to act and are hungry to work. You are choosing a career that many people only dream of having. All actors should acknowledge their bravery and acts of courage and celebrate their creativity.

It is my intention that with the information in this book you will HIT THE GROUND RUNNING. Have a successful and joyous voyage in the pursuit of your acting career.

CONTRIBUTING WRITERS

RAY BENGSTON, Photographer/Actor/Filmmaker/Videographer/Teacher/ Casting Director: Ray is a successful photographer/videographer in Los Angeles. His clients include the Screen Actors Guild (since 1990), AFTRA, Equity, Warner Brothers and the Disney Channel. Numerous agents, managers, acting coaches and casting directors have sent him thousands of actors to shoot headshots. For the last two years, he has directed and edited public service commercials and training films for the city of San Antonio, Texas, as well as completed the filming on a documentary about Viola Spolin and the Spolin Players. He has produced, directed, shot and edited behind-the-scenes videos for commercial clients, and also *Wheel of Fortune.* Ray is co-owner of the award-winning Divisek Casting and has been involved in casting for more than twenty-three years.

TERRY BERLAND, Commercial, Film, TV and Voice-Over Casting Director: Terry has more than twenty-five years of experience casting TV commercials, voice-overs, animation programs, industrials and short films. She has won many major casting awards, including a Clio, Terry comes from a New York advertising agency background and has served as Head of Casting at BBDO/NY Worldwide. She has been an adjunct faculty member of the Lee Strasberg Institute and the American Musical and Dramatic Academy of New York. Terry has been invited to cities all over the United States to work with talent on their commercial technique and to educate them on the world of advertising. She is the co-author of the top-selling book, *Breaking Into Commercials.*

MICHAEL DONOVAN, Casting Director: Michael is the 2005, 2006 and 2007 recipient of the Casting Society of America's Artios Award for Outstanding Casting. He has cast over 150 plays, 45 films, 9 television series and more than 1,000 commercials. In addition to being the resident casting director for the Pasadena Playhouse and the International City Theatre in Long Beach, Michael has also cast shows for the Hollywood Bowl, Arkansas Rep, Cleveland Playhouse, Arizona Theatre Company, the Alliance Theatre (Atlanta), the Laguna Playhouse, the Falcon Theatre and the Colony Theatre. His TV credits include the Emmy-nominated *The Flight That Fought Back.* He has also cast numerous independent film festival winners. Since 1990, Michael has been in demand as a teacher at the Professional Musical

Theatre at UCLA, the American Film Institute, the American Academy of Dramatic Arts, and at the Stella Adler Academy.

ABBY GIRVIN, Director and Co-Owner of DDO Artists Agency: Shortly after graduating from Purdue University, Abby began her agent career at a small high-fashion agency in Washington, D.C. In 1996, she moved to Los Angeles and landed a job at DDO Artists Agency – today Abby is the director and one of the owners. DDO is a full-service talent agency respected for their highly successful Commercial, Dance, Choreography, Print, Theatre, and Hosting Divisions. DDO with offices in New York, Las Vegas and Nashville. The agency provides representation across the country to performers in commercials, TV, film, music videos, live stage and Broadway.

DAVID GRAPES, Professor at the University of Northern Colorado: During his 30-year career in the theatre, David has produced more than 800 major productions and has directed 150-plus productions. He is an award-winning director, actor and playwright and has provided administrative, financial, and artistic leadership for a variety of theatrical institutions: regional theatres, nationally recognized university theatre departments, summer stock companies, civic theatres and numerous professional, not-for-profit regional theatres. Also, he served for six years as the Producing Artistic Director of Tennessee Repertory Theatre's education/outreach department and was the recipient of eight Tennie Awards for Best Direction. At UNC, David is a full tenured professor serving as the Director of the School of Theatre Arts and Dance and is also the Executive Producer for UNC's summer stock company.

LAURI JOHNSON, Life and Entertainment Industry Career Coach and Professional Actress: Lauri has done coaching/consulting work in both the corporate and creative worlds for over 30 years. She has conducted private and group workshops with thousands of individuals seeking breakthroughs in their personal and professional lives. Lauri is an accomplished actress with a busy career in Los Angeles that spans several mediums of the entertainment industry. She has done starring, co-starring, featured and recurring roles in numerous TV shows, films, theatre, commercials and voice work.

LESLIE JORDAN, Emmy-Award-Winning Actor and Author: Leslie has starred in films, television shows, commercials and theatre productions in hundreds of roles. He has had recurring roles on *Ugly Betty, Boston Legal, Hidden Palms, Reba* and *Will and Grace.* In 2006, he won the Emmy for Outstanding Guest Actor in a Comedy Series for his role of "Beverly Leslie" on *Will and Grace.* On stage, Leslie has won the Ovation Award, The Garland Award and the Los Angeles Drama Critics Circle Award for his role in Southern Baptist Sissies. Leslie has written several successful plays, film scripts, and a book, *My Trip Down the Pink Carpet* published by Simon and Schuster (released in 2008), as well as an autobiographical, one-man show.

TODD JUSTICE, Los Angeles Talent Representative, Marshak/Zachary: Todd entered the Agent Training Program at ICM in 1998, working diligently beside the VP of Talent with major movie star clients. In 2001, the Henderson/Hogan/McCabe Agency hired him. In four months, he made partner and the company was renamed McCabe/Justice. In August 2006, Todd made the leap to head the theatrical department of VENTURE I.A.B. and in 2008 he was recruited to be a talent representative at the prominent Marshak/Zachary Management company.

HUGH LEON, Los Angeles Talent Agent, Coast to Coast Agency: Hugh is head of the adult commercial and celebrity sports departments at Coast to Coast Talent Group in Los Angeles. He represents adult actors as well as celebrities and high profile athletes. The agency also represents youth and adult actors both commercially and theatrically as well as voice-over talent and models. The Los Angeles Talent Manager's Association bestowed Hugh with the Seymour Heller Award for Commercial Agent of the Year in 2007. Hugh has also been featured in numerous television program interviews and is quoted in countless national industry publications. He travels around the country speaking to aspiring actors about show business as well as scouting talent for potential representation.

AMY LYNDON, Los Angeles Audition Technique Teacher and Booking Coach, Actress and Multi-Award Winning Filmmaker: Amy studied at the Neighborhood Playhouse (NYC) and at the London Academy of Perform-ing Arts. After earning her BFA from Syracuse University, she moved to Los Angeles to begin her acting career. Ms. Lyndon has guest-starred in over 25 TV shows, booked over 40 films and has worked as a voice-over/commercial artist on numerous national campaigns. Additionally, Amy is a multi-award winning director/writer/producer in films and theatre. She owned and operated Gold-Levin Talent Management for 9 years. Since 1990, Amy has been a top booking coach in Los Angeles. She created the successful Lyndon Technique, A 15 Guideline Map to Booking that has helped thousands of her students learn how to book acting jobs.

ANTHONY MEINDL, Los Angeles Acting Teacher, Producer and Director: Anthony is the founder and artistic director of the award-winning Meta Theatre Company, where he has taught thousands of students at all levels of the art. He has directed and produced four critically acclaimed and suc-cessful productions at his theatre and received back-to-back Best Director awards. He is founder of the Director's Workshop, an adjunct to the studio, where film and TV directors work with his member-actors. Anthony has numerous theatre acting credits in several Off-Broadway and Los Angeles plays as well as at prestigious regional theatres. In Los Angeles, he won The Ovation Award and LA Weekly Award nominations for his roles at the West Coast Ensemble and the Musical Theatre Guild at the Pasadena Playhouse. Anthony has numerous TV, film and commercial acting credits.

ALICIA RUSKIN, Los Angeles Commercial Agent and Partner, Kazarian/ Spencer/Ruskin & Associates: As a theatre major Alicia attended Brandeis

University, The Sorbonne in Paris and the London Academy of Music and Dramatic Arts. During this time she performed at the Kennedy Center and on tour with the USO in Germany and Italy. After graduating with her MFA, Alicia moved to New York, where she worked on local stages and toured in musical theatre productions throughout the United States. After leaving acting, Alicia started on the reception desk at Kazarian/Spencer & Associates and was promoted to agent 18 months later. Today, she is head of the commercial division and a partner in the agency. Alicia is a member of the Television Academy, a published poet, and an active supporter of local theatre.

DAVID SWEENEY, Talent Manager/Film Producer: David started his career as the co-producer of the Sundance hit: *Wigstock*: The Movie, which received national distribution. Then he shifted his focus to talent management, where he has developed several successful careers, including those of Emma Roberts (*Nancy Drew*), Constance Zimmer (*Entourage*), Erinn Hayes (*Worst Week*), and Emmy-winning soap star Natalia Livingston (*General Hospital*). David has recently returned to producing, serving as an Executive Producer of *The Winning Season*, which premiered in 2009. He has several films in development and continues to manage the aforementioned talent as well as several new, promising young actors.

BERNARD TELSEY, Theatre, Film and TV Casting Director: Mr. Telsey co-founded New York City's MCC Theater and in 1988 founded Telsey + Company Casting. His Broadway casting credits include *Godspell, Equus, In the Heights, De la Guarda, The Drowsy Chaperone, Hedwig and the Angry Inch, Wicked, Hairspray,* and *Rent.* His company has also done the casting for many award-winning Off-Broadway shows and for numerous prominent theatre companies all over the United States. Bernard has also cast actors for the big screen, including *Sex and the City: The Movie, Across the Universe, Dan in Real Life, Rent, Pieces of April, Finding Forrester* and *Rachel Getting Married.* He is a member (and New York VP) of the Casting Society of America.

KEVIN E. WEST, Actor and President/Founder of The Actors' Network: Kevin has been a working actor in Hollywood since 1990. He has co-starred and starred in several films, has been a guest on dozens of television shows and portrayed "Tim Reese" on ABC's *General Hospital* in 1991, and has starred in numerous commercials. On May 1, 1991 Kevin founded The Actors' Network, a professional business networking organization (www.actors-network.com). It has become the preeminent actor's organization in Hollywood and has been featured on *Entertainment Tonight*, CNBC, and in a front-page story in *Back Stage West.*

THE ACTOR'S GLOSSARY

ABILITY: The quality of being able to do something. A natural or acquired skill.

ACROSS THE BOARD: Agents representing clients in all the mediums that the agency handles, e.g., commercial, theatrical, print and voice work.

ACTOR IS THE PRODUCT: As an actor, you the person, your work, your talent, and your appearance are what you are "selling" to the decision-makers.

AEA: The Actors' Equity Association. The union that governs actors performing in professional theatre productions.

AFTER-LIFE: The thoughts, feelings, utterances and/or simple reactions that the actor utilizes to continue the character life after the scripted scene or scenario (a.k.a. the "button").

AFTRA: The American Federation of Television and Radio Artists. The union that governs videotape productions, TV broadcasters and most of radio performers.

AGMA: American Guild of Musical Artists. The guild that represents opera singers, ballet and other dancers, opera directors, backstage production personnel at opera and dance companies, figure skaters and concert musicians.

AGVA: The American Guild of Variety Artists. The union that represents performers in variety entertainment, including circuses, Las Vegas showrooms and cabarets, comedy showcases, dance revues, magic shows, theme park shows and arenas.

ARC: Referring to a character's emotional progression from the beginning to the end of a scene and/or script.

ASPIRATIONAL: A term used in commercial casting describing actors with the appearance or qualities that the TV audience aspires to be or have.

AUDIT: As it relates to acting classes, means to be a non-participating observer. Actors watch and are not allowed to ask question or give comments.

AVAIL: When the production company requests, usually through an agent, that an actor keep the date(s) of a commercial shoot open/available as he/she is one of the finalists for the job. This is not a booking. It is also not a legal obligation, just a courtesy on the part of the production company and the actor.

BAR CODE CARD: A card with a bar code that contains the actor's picture(s), resume and size information. Actors simply swipe their card at auditions and everything is printed out. Use of these is prevalent at commercial auditions.

BOOK/BOOKED: Designates that an actor(s) has been hired for a specific job.

BOOKING OUT: The act of an actor notifying his/her agent that they will be unavailable or out of town for a specific period of time.

BOOKING RATIO: The percentage of jobs for which an actor has been hired as it relates to the number of auditions he/she has gone out for.

BUTTON: A simple physical action or a few spoken words that continue the character life at the end of an audition (a.k.a. the after-life).

BUY-OUT: The fixed (sometimes negotiated) sum the producer pays the actor to own his or her performance for an unlimited amount of time, usually in a non-union (or sometimes union) commercial, project or show.

CALLBACK: After the initial audition, the decision-makers select which actors they are interested in and invite them to return for a second (and sometimes a third) audition. There can be a few actors called back or many. The producer, director, writer and maybe even the stars of the TV or film project are usually present for the callback. In commercials it is usual for the ad agency execs and/or the director and maybe the product client to be present.

CASTING BREAKDOWN: A casting director posts, on-line, the descriptions of the roles in a project they are casting for the agents, managers and/or actors to see. The roles are delineated by gender, age and physical type.

CLIENT: The representative(s) from the company whose product is being advertised in a commercial (e.g., Johnson & Johnson).

CLOUT: The power to direct, shape or otherwise influence. It is determined by the success of the agent or manager's talent list and their relationships with a large number of top CDs as well as producers and directors,

COLD-READING: Describes the scripted auditions actors do for TV and film productions. Usually, actors are given hours or days to prepare a script. With a few lines of dialogue or if another role is suggested at the audition, then the actor may only have minutes to prepare.

COMMERCIAL LOOK: Describes a physical appearance that is desired for most of the TV commercials: usually an attractive but average, middle-American, wholesome "look."

COMMERCIAL CONFLICTS: The products for which actors have shot commercials and that either the advertising agency is holding or are currently running on TV, the Internet or in movie theaters.

CONFLICT: The opposition between incompatible desires, needs, intentions, impulses, or characters in a literary work that shapes or motivates the action of the plot.

CONNECTION/CONNECTING: When the actor, without thinking about dialogue, choices or direction, is immersed in and/or linked to the core, authentic energy, feelings and emotions of the character he/she is portraying. This is the opposite of being "in your head."

CONTRAST: I use this word to describe actors playing energetic opposites in scene work. For example, one knows, the other needs help; secure/confused; serious/playful; confident/anxious; positive/skeptical, etc.

COPY: The scripted dialogue in the TV commercial that is being used for the audition.

CRAFT: A profession requiring skill and training or experience or specialized knowledge. The knowledge and development of the investigation and techniques that are essential to creating authentic, multi-dimensional characters and performances and the ability to apply them

CREATIVES: The advertising agency executives who create, write and oversee the production of commercials.

CUE CARD: A large sheet of paper or cardboard on which audition copy is written so that actors can refer to it when needed. It is usually positioned in the casting room near the camera.

DEMO REEL: A short compilation of an actor's best work on a DVD, typically 3-5 minutes in length.

EMOTIONAL FOUNDATION TRAINING: Acting instruction that focuses on motivating the dialogue, character and action primarily with instincts and feelings.

ESSENCE: The intrinsic or indispensable properties that serve to characterize or identify something or someone.

FOURTH WALL: An entertainment industry expression used to describe the area where the audience or camera(s) is positioned. In the theatre and on film and TV sets, actors are directed mostly to play in the direction of the fourth wall.

GETTING CENTERED: Taking a moment to relax, quiet anxieties and get focused.

GIFT/GIFTED: A talent, endowment or aptitude to do something: an artistically and instinctively endowed actor.

HEADSHOT (a.k.a. 8x10): A photograph that actors submit to be considered for work.

> **TIGHT HEADSHOT:** A photo framing the actor from the lower neck to the top of the head.

> **LOOSE HEADSHOT:** A photo framing the actor from the chest to the top of the head.

> **¾ SHOT:** A photo framing the actor from the knees to the top of the head.

HIP POCKET: Small and mid-sized agencies and some managers may choose to "hip pocket" new clients instead of signing them. This means that they will submit these actors for auditions for a period of time and see how they do before making them a client

HOST: The person who presents and/or interviews guests or contestants on radio and TV programs and game shows or pitches products on "infomercials" (thirty-minute TV sales programs).

IMDB: The Internet Movie Database Website; lists almost every film and TV credit for most every actor, director, writer and producer.

INDICATE: As it refers to acting: to pretend to have a feeling or perform a reaction for effect. The feeling or reaction is not authentic or truthfully experienced.

INDUSTRY PROS/INDUSTRY PROFESSIONALS: Agents, managers, casting directors, directors, producers and writers; the individuals who represent, hire, create for and oversee actors.

INDUSTRY SHOWCASES: Productions of scenes that are directed, rehearsed and then mounted in a theatre setting, specifically for an industry audience.

INTERN: An actor who works, usually part-time, for a limited time as a low-level assistant for agents, managers and/or casting directors to gain practical experience. An internship pays very little or (most often) no money.

IN YOUR HEAD: As it relates to acting: being totally conscious of how and what you are doing while you are in a scene, scenario or monologue. This is the opposite of being "connected."

I-9: The form that is filled out and filed with the government to verify employment eligibility.

LINE READING: When an actor is "in their head" saying dialogue technically – the way they planned in order to emphasize their intent – as opposed to the lines being motivated.

LITHOGRAPHS: High quality picture reproductions but not actual photographic prints. They tend to be less expensive, and of somewhat lesser quality in terms of definition and clarity.

MARKETING: The action or business of promoting or selling a person, service or product.

MOTIVATE OUT: Utilizing environment or behavior to position yourself in the direction of the camera so that your face is seen.

MOTIVATION/MOTIVATING DIALOGUE: The instinctive choices one makes to organically drive the character and dialogue.

OBJECTIVES: What an actor is attempting to "get," achieve or do in the scene, e.g., to convince, trust, hurt, love, or help.

OPEN CALLS: Auditions, listed in trade papers or on websites, inviting appropriate actors to show up during a specific time of the day to audition without an appointment.

OUT OF YOUR HEAD: Being so focused and involved in the scene that the thoughts and feelings an actor is having are totally instinctive and relative only to what is being performed. Actors are not thinking about how or what they are doing. It's as if the performance is coming through them, not from them.

PERSONAL SPACE: The imaginary space in the audition room that separates actors from the people they're auditioning for.

PHYSICAL TYPE: A phrase used to categorize actors based on stereotypical appearance.

POWERS THAT BE: Those making creative, auditioning and hiring decisions; usually refers to casting directors, directors, writers, advertising executives, clients, producers, studio executives and/or investors.

PRACTICE AUDITIONS: Auditions for low-profile films, theatre and projects where actors can practice and gain confidence and that won't give them exposure to the mainstream industry pros.

PRE-LIFE: The thoughts, feelings and/or action that the actor thinks, feels or does that precedes and motivates the scripted dialogue or the directed or created physical action.

PRE-READ: The initial audition that takes place with the theatrical casting director. At this time, the casting director determines if an actor is right for a callback with the producers and/or director.

PRESENT: Being mentally and emotionally focused and aware, not distracted by others comments or actions or your own thoughts.

PRINT ADS: Photographic advertisements appearing in magazines and on billboards and websites.

PROFILES: In on-camera commercial auditions, an actor will be asked to show the left and right sides of his/her face and body to the camera.

PROOF PRINTS: Low quality 4 x 6 inch prints of the pictures from a photo session – used to narrow down and choose the final pictures that will be used for headshots and posting on the casting websites.

PROOF SHEET: A one-page sheet of 24-36 miniature photos from the photo shoot.

READER: An actor brought in to read opposite the auditioning actors, instead of the casting director or assistant.

REPRESENTATION: As it pertains to the entertainment industry: the people who speak, negotiate and/or act on behalf of an actor.

RIGHT–TO–WORK STATE: A state in which they have a law that prohibits required union membership of workers

ROLE LABELS:

Films

> **STAR:** Largest part(s) in film. The film is either about this character or he/she is essential to the main character or the story.

> **CO-STARRING:** Usually the second biggest role in the film. This character is involved with the star or is the antagonist and is integral to either the main or the secondary plot(s) of the story.

> **SUPPORTING:** These are roles that have one or several solid scenes (at least two pages of dialogue), usually with the star(s) or antagonist(s). They can be but are not always essential to the main story.

> **FEATURED:** Characters with a minimum of one line or a significant piece of business. They can have more to do or say, but, bottom line, it is a small role that supports the story line but is not vital to it.

Episodic TV and Sitcom

> **SERIES STAR:** This role is the pivotal character in a series (there can be more than one series star). The stories revolve primarily around this person(s).

SERIES REGULAR: These are secondary roles, e.g., the spouse, boss, co-worker, neighbor, or a relative of the series star(s).

RECURRING REGULAR: These are peripheral roles (with character names) who appear in thirty to sixty percent of the episodes in a season, depending on the show.

GUEST STAR: These characters traditionally have a major impact on the plot of an episode(s). They have a character name and several scenes.

CO-STAR: This role has a character name, several lines or (sometimes) a few, short scenes with the series star(s) or one of the regulars. Their participation usually assists the story line but doesn't fuel it.

FEATURED: The "featured" roles do not usually have a character name. They can either have physical business with no dialogue or have one line or a few lines, and can appear in one or several scenes.

Soap Operas

CONTRACT ACTOR: This is an established lead character whose role will run for several months or years.

SUPPORTING: These characters support the story line for the contract principals. Their roles can play out over a few episodes or up to six months.

RECURRING: These roles have a character name and traditionally appear in a minimum of three shows. Some have been known to recur for years and may even have a limited contract.

PRINCIPAL: This role traditionally shoots for a day or two and has more than five lines. He/she may or may not have a character name.

UNDER-5: Just like the name indicates, this role has five lines or less and does not usually have a character name, just a role description, e.g., nurse, detective, teacher.

CAMEO: This is a role in which a well-known actor or actress or a celebrity plays himself or herself or a one-time character.

Theatre

LEAD: The largest role in the production. The story is either about this character or he/she plays the major role.

FEATURED: Actors filling a secondary role have a "featured" credit (which is a different use of this description than in film, TV and soaps). They have character names, appear in multiple scenes and have strong focal moments in a theatrical production.

MULTIPLE: An actor who plays numerous small roles in a play or musical. Some of the characters they portray will have names and others may not.

ENSEMBLE: Actors who appear as background players or as part of group scenes. They sometimes have a few lines. In musicals, "ensemble" usually refers to singers and dancers.

UNDERSTUDY/SWING: Actors will understudy the lead, a featured actor and/or multiple small roles. The swing actor fills in when needed for members of the ensemble.

SAFE PEOPLE: Little-known casting directors, producers and directors who cast low-profile, minor acting jobs and who have no real effect on a career, for whom actors can do confidence-building auditions.

SCALE: The minimum amounts of money SAG, AFTRA and AEA actors can be paid for a daily, weekly or contract job.

SCREEN ACTORS GUILD (SAG): The union that governs the salaries, residuals and working conditions of the majority of film and TV actors.

SIDES: Scenes from the script used for TV, film and theatre auditions – usually one to ten pages, specific to a character.

SIGN-IN: Union auditions have a specific SAG form on which each actor fills in his/her name, agency name, social security number, call time, initials, and the time that the audition was completed. When utilizing this sheet the actor is "signing in" or "signing out."

SKILLS: Talents or abilities to do anything, especially those that might help you get an acting job that requires competently doing that skill. These skills are listed in a designated position on a resume.

SLATE: At the start of an on-camera audition, the actor identifies himself by saying his/her name (and when requested, his agents' name) and sometimes holds up a piece of paper with his/her name on it.

SPEED REEL WEBSITES: Sites that upload one-minute reels (and can edit actors' reels to sixty seconds) and post them for instant access by industry pros.

SPOKESPERSON: The man or women speaking on behalf of or representing a company, product or person.

STAGE DIRECTION: The descriptions in a script that explain what the characters are physically doing before, during or after the dialogue.

STORYBOARD: The primary scene-by-scene visual description, with dialogue, that outlines the commercial and is usually posted at auditions.

SUBMISSIONS: 8 x10 headshots, postcards or any actor-marketing tool that is sent to any industry pro's office for the purpose of procuring auditions. Also refers to online pictures and resumes that are uploaded.

SUBMIT YOURSELF: The act of actors getting their pictures and resumes to casting directors, directors or producers to be considered for work or to agencies and managers for representation.

TAFT HARTLEY STATUS: Once an actor works a union job, they have 30 days during which he/she can do non-union and union work, enjoying all the benefits before having to join SAG. After 30 days, if an actor intends to book more SAG work, membership is mandatory.

TALENT: A marked innate, exceptional ability for artistic accomplishment. A natural acting endowment or ability of a superior quality.

TOOLS: The equipment or elements needed to manufacture or create things.

TONE: The general quality or feeling of a production as an indicator of the attitude or view of the writer, director or producer.

TRADE PAPERS: *Variety* and *The Hollywood Reporter* are the two main show business papers distributed daily in various major entertainment cities. *Backstage East* and *Backstage West* are the main weekly actor publications.

TYPE: Refers to an actor's physical image and identifying qualities that suggest the kinds of characters and roles for which he/she can be cast.

UNION PRODUCTION: Any production that is a signatory of the union and operates under the Screen Actors Guild (SAG), the American Federation of Television and Radio Artists (AFTRA), or Actors' Equity Association (AEA) union guidelines.

UPSTAGE YOURSELF: To give focus to the other actor(s) in a scene by constantly looking at them or positioning yourself where your face is not seen.

VOICE-OVER (VO): Refers to the work of those doing the voices in commercials, films, TV, recordings, and books on DVD. They narrate the story, pitch or promo the product, are the background voices in programs and films and give voice to animated or inanimate characters.

VOUCHER: A document that is given to an extra when he or she is featured. It is a credit that is registered with SAG, qualifying actors for membership when three are acquired.

Wardrobe Designations:

CASUAL OR HOME CASUAL: Relaxed and/or "socializing with friends at home" type of clothes.

UPSCALE CASUAL: Fashionable, simple party clothes.

BUSINESS/SPOKES: Business suit and/or a nice shirt and tie for men; tailored dress and/or suits for women.

TRENDY: Jeans, "cool" t-shirts and often the latest fads (usually for actors under thirty).

UNIFORMS: Outfits worn by policemen, military, nurses, postal workers, etc.

WORK CLOTHES: Clothing associated with an occupation, e.g., waitress, trucker, tour guide, motorcyclist, etc.

SPORTS OUTFITS: Attire worn by a baseball player, bowler, equestrian, skater, hiker, etc.

WEBISODES: A range of shows/programs of various lengths created for and run solely on websites.

WORKING THE ROOM: The ability to make adjustments easily and be freed up and confident when interviewed or doing a reading at auditions.

YES, AND: Primarily utilized when doing improvisation scene work – the acceptance of whatever is said or done by your partner (no matter how ludicrous) and then building on it or justifying.

ZED CARD: Several model/fashion-type pictures (tight headshots and full body shots) are arranged on two sides of a piece of small card stock. It is the model's business card.

INDEX